WORLD ECONOMIC DATA

WORLD ECONOMIC DATA

A COMPENDIUM OF CURRENT ECONOMIC INFORMATION FOR ALL COUNTRIES OF THE WORLD

Cecelia A. Albert
Editor

Foreword by
James E. Davis

ABC-CLIO

Santa Barbara, California
Oxford, England

ISBN 0-87436-485-X
ISSN 0891-4125

10 9 8 7 6 5 4 3 2 1

ABC-Clio, Inc.
2040 Alameda Padre Serra, Box 4397
Santa Barbara, California 93103

Clio Press Ltd.
55 St. Thomas Street
Oxford, OX1 1JG, England

This book is printed on acid free paper ∞.
Manufactured in the United States of America.

Contents

Foreword

Quantitative statistical techniques are employed extensively by social scientists today, especially economists. Moreover, various kinds of quantitative data are prevalent in the daily lives of most Americans. As citizens in a democratic, market-oriented society, we frequently make decisions. We may not always be aware that many of these decisions are based on inferences drawn from quantitative data--results of polls and consumer surveys, manufacturers' claims for products, government reports, published scientific research, and data published about other countries. In order to retain the power to make informed decisions, and to remain knowledgeable about the world around us, we must have access to relevant data and possess the skills necessary to evaluate the data we receive. Sound decision making and an understanding of our economic system and other economic systems will enhance our effectiveness as participating citizens of our society and the world.

Today there is more than a passing interest in understanding both our own economy and the economies of the world. At least twenty-seven states have mandated precollegiate economics instruction of some kind, and there are indications that more states are, or will be, following suit. This is just one sign of a strong resurgence of the study of economics in the school curriculum, particularly in secondary schools.

The National Commission on Excellence in Education report, *A Nation at Risk: The Imperative for Educational Reform* (Washington, D. C.: National Commission on Excellence in Education, 1983), cites a public survey recommending that both college-bound and non-college-bound students take two years of economics or business at the secondary level. The report further recommends that students gain an understanding of the fundamentals of our economy and that curriculum materials be upgraded for the purposes of economic study. Upgrading implies more rigorous presentation, timeliness of information, currency of data, and attention to critical analysis. Other national reports underscore the *Nation at Risk* recommendations. A report from the College Board, entitled *Academic Preparation for College: What Students Need to Know and Be Able to Do* (N.Y.: College Examination Board, 1983), states, "If people are to perform effectively as citizens in a democratic society, they need knowledge about central institutions and values in their own society and in other major societies around the world."

Why should we study other as well as our own economies? Television, travel, and newspaper headlines provide millions of Americans with a constant flow of information that thirty years ago would have been unimaginable. Subarus, Toyotas, Sonys, Ataris, bauxite, bananas, coffee--these and other products and resources remind us that, even at the local level, we are closely linked with the rest of the world. Jet airplane routes, oil pipelines, giant ships, advanced systems of instantaneous global communication--these networks have all but eliminated the possibility of isolation from the rest of the world. The death of a Leader in the Middle East becomes grave cause for concern, not only about peace, but also about the worldwide flow of oil resources.

Increasing economic interdependence is a powerful force that cannot be halted and must be taken into account in economic education. Writing in 1980 about key economic issues for the coming decade, the Committee for Economic Development (CED) stated,

> Recent events have highlighted the extent to which inflation and recession can spread across national borders and the rapidity with which supply shocks related to energy and food, for example, can exert cumulative effects throughout the world economic system. Economic policies in a wide variety of fields formerly regarded as purely domestic can be expected to exert an increasingly significant influence on economic developments in other countries and on their industrial policies.
>
> (Schiff, Frank W., *Looking Ahead: Identifying Key Economic Issues for Business and Society in the 1980s*. Washington, D.C.: Committee for Economic Development, 1980.)

As interdependence and rapid change become facts of life, the emerging complex global society will require a high level of competence if we are to deal adequately and intelligently with changing situations. In terms of economics, we must develop an increasing awareness that the U.S. economy in only part of a much larger interdependent world economy. We must recognize that competitive forces operate on an international basis, that resources--especially nonrenewable resources--are distributed throughout the world, and the economic policy decisions in one country significantly impact other countries. As a society, we need to develop a pluralistic outlook, competence in dealing with diversity, and the ability to analyze economic events and information from a global perspective. The logical place to acquire and begin to develop these skills is in the classroom.

In American society we have thought it noble to respect diversity. Unfortunately, our educational system has not always been guided by this belief. Much attention has been focused on the "American Way." Given a Global society, the teaching of a single set of values is imprisoning. Diversity, adaptation, understanding, compromise, peacemaking--these are essential characteristics for all persons living in the current global age.

Hard information--data--is vital and useful to our understanding of ourselves and others. How large is the U.S. federal government budget and how does that budget compare with the government budget of India? Of France? What is the primary export of South Africa? What is the major import of Great Britain? How do imports and exports impact a country's GNP and GDP? Where are the world's oil resources located? Who exports and imports these resources and what effect do these transactions have on the economies of their countries? What is the rate of inflation in Argentina? In Cuba? How does inflation in these and other countries affect U.S. citizens? These and other questions often require an extensive, time-consuming search.

World Economic Data: A Compendium of Current Economic Information for All Countries of the World is an important and timely resource whose purpose is to provide librarians, teachers, students, and interested readers selected economic data for all counties of the world--information pertinent to the understanding and analysis of current national and international economic issues. As the shift to global economic interdependence takes place, our need for accurate, up-to-date data from which to make reasoned decisions also increases. *World Economic Data* provides valuable, concrete information to further the understanding of our own economic system and policies and the systems and policies of the world. It is a first step to increasing our effectiveness as policy and decisionmakers, and furthering our goal to become enlightened world citizens.

JAMES E. DAVIS
Vice President, Research. Development, Administration, Graphic Learning Corporation and President, Foundation for Development of Learning Technologies

Introduction

Written for librarians, teachers, students, and those seeking information on a variety of factors affecting the economy, *World Economic Data* provides extensive, current economic data for 170 countries throughout the world. Compiled from documents not readily available to the general reader, this book will assist in the study and analysis of U.S. and worldwide economic principles. The convenient, uniform format used for reporting the data provides for easy comparison between countries and fosters greater understanding of the various factors within countries.

As economics and economic policymaking play increasingly significant roles in both national and international affairs, an understanding of the fundamentals of economics and their impact on policymaking also grow in importance. This publication was compiled to aid the investigation of economic systems and to make available data necessary to the formulation of reasoned judgments about economic questions, both on the individual (micro) and societal (macro) level.

SCOPE AND ARRANGEMENT

The data and information contained in this work (with the exception of the glossary) are taken from ABC-CLIO's KALEIDOSCOPE: CURRENT WORLD DATA database. The contents are divided into two major parts--Part I: Country Data and Part II: U.S. Economic Indicators--followed by a table of world currency rates, a glossary of terms used in the work, and a bibliography of primary sources of information. Countries are arranged alphabetically under their familiar names followed by their official names in English. Categories of information provided include budget, expenditures by function, economic aid extended and received, external public debt, GNP and GDP, consumer price changes, imports and exports, trading partners, tourist figures, balance of payments, labor profile, agricultural and industrial products, natural resources, electric power generation, generating capacity, nuclear power plants and output, and crude oil and natural gas production.

U.S. Economic Indicators

Covering a broad spectrum of some of the most useful economic factors relating to the U.S. economy and economic system, this section provides readers a basic understanding of the U.S. economy and the means to compare this system with those of other countries. This section explains terms and concepts such as banking practices and institutions, stocks and bonds, competition, profit and loss, business cycles and their periods of inflation, deflation, employment, and unemployment, and forms of business ownership. This section also outlines the role of the Federal Reserve System and discusses the financial institutions that intermediate between savers and borrowers. Charts, graphs, and tables provide information such as yearly unemployment rates, U.S. energy use by source and by sector, yearly CPI (consumer price index) for commodity groups, U.S. yearly average money supply, and an explanation of how to read the stock page. Because of the growing importance of economics within the secondary school curriculum, this section should prove to be of special significance to librarians and teachers. Use of the data will facilitate the process of economic analysis, encourage critical analyses, and promote more educated economic projections.

World Currency Rates

A comprehensive table listing the world currency rates for countries of the world follows the section on U.S. Economic Indicators. In addition to listing each country's name, currency unit, and a recent exchange rate for U.S. dollars, this section illustrates how to convert other currencies into U.S. dollars and vice versa. All figures were taken from the September 1986 NOMINAL NEW YORK CLOSING QUOTATIONS published by the Chase Manhattan Bank.

Glossary

The glossary included in this work is intended as a guide to those terms considered relevant to the use of this publication and not as a comprehensive source of concepts related to the science of economics in general. Sources consulted in the compilation of the glossary include the KALEIDOSCOPE database; international relations, public policy, and political analysis texts; and other economic dictionaries.

GATHERING AND INTERPRETATION OF DATA

As in all compilations of international statistics, there are problems to be addressed in the gathering and interpretation of data; namely, the reliability, consistency, and comparability of information. For example, not all categories of data are available for all countries, particularly Third World, Eastern bloc, and non-International Monetary Fund (IMF)-member countries. Some very small, newly independent countries do not have a history of data reporting. Terminology may vary among countries (i.e., one country may use "net materials produced" versus "GNP"), and different categories of data may not be available for the same year. Thus, readers may find a GNP for 1986 but a GDP for 1984 for the same country. In those cases where percentages do not equal one hundred, this could be the result of several factors, including the rounding off of figures and category overlap, i.e., part of the "Transportation and communication" percentage may also be included in the "Other communication" category. The variations in data collection techniques, years of data availability, and methods of reporting result in differences in dates and information available for each country and the fact that not all categories of information are available for all countries. What the reader will find in this publication is true for any compilation of international statistics--the data can be no better than the sources from which they are derived.

In examining reputable sources of published data, one frequently finds discrepancies between publications for the same data. This may result from several factors: (1) selection criteria for the same categories varies considerably between sources; (2) some publications use estimated figures, while others cite actual figures; (3) data reported in 1982 may be revised in 1983 to reflect more accurate information; and so on.

Whenever discrepancies exist among sources for the same time periods, the editors have favored the use of data from United Nations, World Bank, and IMF sources. In all cases, editors used reliability and objectivity as guidelines in researching and providing data. A bibliography of major sources consulted is provided in the back of the book.

CURRENCY

The time lag between collection of data and their availability varies, depending upon the methods of data gathering and frequency of reporting, i.e., updates may be monthly, bimonthly, yearly, or variable. Censuses may be held only once every five, ten, twenty, or more years. Discontinuities in the publication of collected data resulting from internal political strife within countries is also a factor in the currency of data.

While data may be reported for varying years within the same country, the editors have sought to use the most reliable, accurate, complete, and current information available in published form.

USE IN THE CLASSROOM

The format, organization, and content of this work make it particularly appropriate for classroom use. Used in conjunction with economics instruction and investigation, it provides an opportunity for students to develop and utilize critical thinking skills, become familiar with basic tools of analysis, e.g., charts, graphs, and statistics, compare and contrast various economic data between countries of the world, examine the characteristics of the U.S. economic systems, etc. For example, students can discuss the objectives of the U.S. monetary policy and how the Federal Reserve System can assist in achieving these objectives or compare inflation rates among countries, discussing their impact on domestic economies and world trade. Numerous cross-country comparisons are possible, facilitated by the standardized presentation and detailed illustrative material. Students can utilize this work as a springboard to further study and investigation of the principles of economics and of the U.S. and international economic systems.

FUTURE PUBLICATION PLANS

As always in a work of this nature and scope, changes will have taken place between the time the information was collected, analyzed, edited, and published, and the time the work reaches the shelves. Future editions of this work are planned as necessary to maintain currency. ABC-CLIO remains committed to providing and maintaining high-quality reference sources and welcomes recommendations furthering this commitment.

Part One: Country Data

AFGHANISTAN
Democratic Republic of Afghanistan

Budget
Revenues
1980: $117,300,000
Expenditures
1982: $664,031,621
1980: $117,300,000

Economic Aid Extended
None

Economic Aid Received
Total: $3,624,000,000 (1946-83)
USA only: $525,000,000

Gross National Product (GNP)
$2,800,000,000 (1979)
GNP per capita: $163

Gross Domestic Product by Sector (1982)

Agriculture, forestry, and fishing	9.10%
Manufacturing	13.80%
Construction	3.20%
Commerce	9.10%
Transportation and communication	3.50%
Other	1.60%

International Liquidity
Reserves (minus gold): $303,420,000 (1985)
Gold reserves: 965,000 fine troy ounces

Imports
Petroleum products, vehicles and spare parts, textile goods, sugar, wheat

Total Imports
1984: $940,000,000
1983: $959,010,000
1982: $880,000,000

Exports
Natural gas, dried fruit, carpets and rugs, fresh fruit

Total Exports
1984: $680,000,000
1983: $571,720,000
1982: $670,000,000

Trading Partners
Imports (1984)

USSR	47.20%
Japan	12.90%
Singapore	3.40%
West Germany	2.60%
Hong Kong	2.40%

Exports (1984)

USSR	62.40%
West Germany	5.20%
United Kingdom	4.30%
Netherlands	2.90%
USA	0.20%

Tourists
Total: 6,623
Revenue: $1,000,000 (1980)
Country of origin

Pakistan	37.08%
India	15.00%
West Germany	3.09%

Labor Profile (1979)

Agriculture, forestry, and fishing	60.05%
Manufacturing	11.01%
Transportation and communication	1.07%
Trade	3.05%
Services	19.03%
Construction	1.03%
Other	2.06%

Agricultural Products
Wheat, cotton, fruit and nuts, karakul pelts, wool, mutton

Industrial Products
Textiles, soap, furniture, shoes, carpets, fertilizers, cement

Natural Resources
Natural gas, crude oil, coal, copper, talc, sulphur, gems

Electric Power Generation
1,300,000,000 kwh
kwh per capita: 96

Generating Capacity
465,000 kw (1984)

Nuclear Power Plants and Output
None (1986)

Crude Oil Production
None (1986)

Natural Gas Production
876,949 terajoules; 787,500,000 cubic feet (1983)

ALBANIA
People's Socialist Republic of Albania

Budget
Revenues
1983: $1,314,000,000
Expenditures
1983: $1,307,000,000

Gross National Product (GNP)
$2,150,000,000 (1979)
GNP per capita: $830

Total Imports
$137,000,000

Total Exports
$151,000,000

Trading Partners
Imports

Greece	24%
Italy	19%
West Germany	17%
Netherlands	4%
France	4%

Exports

Italy	8%
Greece	8%
France	8%
Austria	6%
Netherlands	5%

Tourists
Total: 6,000

Labor Profile (1978)

Agriculture	22.00%
Manufacturing	38.00%
Construction	9.00%
Commerce	7.00%
Transportation	6.00%
Education	8.10%
Health services	6.00%
Administration	2.40%

Agricultural Products
Wheat, corn, potatoes, sugar beets, cotton, tobacco

Industrial Products
Textiles, timber, construction materials, fuel, semiprocessed minerals

Natural Resources
Oil, coal, copper, iron, nickel

Electric Power Generation
4,635,000 kwh
kwh per capita: 600

Generating Capacity
1,390,000 kw

Crude Oil Production
2,600,000 metric tons; 19,058,000 barrels (1977)

Natural Gas Production
None

ALGERIA
Democratic and Popular Republic of Algeria

Budget
Revenues
1984: $20,000,000,000
1982: $16,000,000,000
Expenditures
1984: $20,000,000,000
1982: $16,000,000,000
Deficit
None (1984)

WORLD ECONOMIC DATA

Economic Aid Extended
None

Economic Aid Received
Total: $2,121,000,000 (1954-83)
USA only: $2,700,000 (1977)

External Public Debt
$12,942,500,000 (1983)
Service payments: 32.20% of exports of goods and services

Gross Domestic Product (GDP)
$51,900,000,000
GDP per capita: $2,430 (1984)

Gross Domestic Product by Sector (1979)

Agriculture, forestry, and fishing	6%
Mining	28%
Manufacturing	12%
Utilities	1%
Construction	13%
Transportation and communication	5%
Commerce	13%
Other	21%

International Liquidity
Reserves (minus gold): $1,464,000,000 (1984)
Gold reserves: 5,580,000 fine troy ounces

Consumer Price Change (Inflation)
1984: 7.40%
1983: 10.30%
1982: 11.50%

Imports
Food, capital goods, consumer goods

Total Imports
1984: $10,286,000,000
1983: $10,393,000,000
1982: $10,754,000,000

Exports
Petroleum products, wine

Total Exports
1984: $10,600,000,000
1983: $12,297,000,000
1982: $13,131,000,000

Trading Partners

Imports (1984)

France	29.10%
West Germany	9.40%
Italy	8.30%
Japan	5.80%
USA	5.50%

Exports (1984)

USA	28.80%
France	22.00%
Italy	13.60%
West Germany	7.60%
Netherlands	7.40%

Tourists
Total: 278,302 (1982)
Country of origin (1982)

France	43.20%
Tunisia	29.00%
Italy	5.60%

Balance of Payments
1984: -$626,000,000
1983: +$177,000,000
1982: +$641,000,000

Labor Profile (1983)

Agriculture, forestry, and fishing	27.00%
Mining and manufacturing	13.30%
Transportation, communication, and trade	4.40%
Civil service	22.30%
Construction	17.10%
Services and other	15.90%

Agricultural Products
Wheat, barley, oats, wine, grapes, citrus fruits, olives, figs, dates, tobacco, esparto grass

Industrial Products
Petroleum, gas, petrochemicals, fertilizers, iron and steel

Natural Resources
Oil, natural gas, iron ore, phosphates, lead, zinc, mercury

Electric Power Generation
12,546,000,000 kwh (1984)
kwh per capita: 587

Generating Capacity
3,113,000 kw

Nuclear Power Plants and Output
None

Crude Oil Production
28,296,000 metric tons; 207,409,680 barrels (1984)

Natural Gas Production
881,832,000 terajoules; 79,188,513,600 cubic feet (1983)

ANDORRA

Budget
Revenues
1983: $23,737,715
1979: $48,615,151
Expenditures
1983: $23,506,606
1979: $48,615,151

Economic Aid Extended
None

External Public Debt
None (1985)

Imports
Fuel, clothing, perfumes, television sets, radios

Total Imports
1977: $208,062,976

Exports
Cattle, timber, wool, furniture

Total Exports
1977: $5,928,473

Tourists
Total: 10,000,000 (1982)
Country of origin
Spain 67.20%
France 32.80%

Agricultural Products
Wool, oats, barley, tobacco

Industrial Products
Tourism, free port for consumer goods, tobacco industry

Natural Resources
Water power, iron ore, lead, alum

Electric Power Generation
140,000,000 kwh
kwh per capita: 3,121

Generating Capacity
35,000 kw

Nuclear Power Plants and Output
None (1986)

Crude Oil Production
None (1986)

Natural Gas Production
None (1986)

ANGOLA
People's Republic of Angola

Budget
Revenues
1981: $3,974,000,000
Expenditures
1981: $3,974,000,000

External Public Debt
$2,500,000,000

Gross National Product (GNP)
$3,320,000,000 (1980)
GNP per capita: $470

Gross Domestic Product (GDP)
$4,020,000,000
GDP per capita: $550

Imports
Raw materials and partly finished goods

Total Imports
1983: $1,500,000,000

Exports
Coffee, crude oil, diamonds, iron ore

Total Exports
1983: $1,600,000,000

Trading Partners
Imports

Portugal	16.90%
USA	11.30%
France	10.80%
Brazil	9.90%
Spain	8.30%

Exports

USA	42.40%
Bahamas	18.90%
United Kingdom	8.60%
Spain	7.80%
Netherlands	7.00%

Balance of Payments
$209,000,000

Labor Profile (1981)

Agriculture	64.00%
Industry	14.01%
Services	22.01%

Agricultural Products
Coffee, cotton, sisal, corn

Industrial Products
Chemicals, tobacco, food

Natural Resources
Diamonds, iron ore, petroleum

Electric Power Generation
1,650,000,000 kwh
kwh per capita: 212

Generating Capacity
630,000 kw

Nuclear Power Plants and Output
None

Crude Oil Production
10,900,000 metric tons; 75,400,000 barrels

ARGENTINA

Argentine Republic

Budget
Revenues
$15,800,000,000
Expenditures
$22,200,000,000

External Public Debt
$24,490,000,000
Service payments: 24% of exports of goods and services

Gross National Product (GNP)
$58,200,000,000
GNP per capita: $1,995

Gross Domestic Product (GDP)
$31,030,000,000
GDP per capita: $1,070

Gross Domestic Product by Sector

Agriculture, forestry, and fishing	11.60%
Extractive industries	2.80%
Manufacturing	27.70%
Utilities	2.10%
Construction	5.00%
Commerce	17.60%
Transportation and communication	6.00%
Other	16.90%

Consumer Price Change (Inflation)
1984: 626.70%

Imports
Machinery and electrical equipment, crude oil, vehicles, chemicals

Total Imports
1983: $4,500,000,000

Exports
Meats, grains, wool

Total Exports
1983: $7,840,000,000

Trading Partners

Imports

USA	18.40%
Brazil	18.00%
West Germany	11.00%
Bolivia	8.20%
Japan	7.60%

Exports

USSR	15.30%
USA	9.90%
Netherlands	9.50%
Brazil	5.50%
Italy	5.99%

Tourists

Total: 1,000,000 (1981)

Balance of Payments

$2,495,000,000

Labor Profile

Agriculture, forestry, and fishing	16.00%
Mining	0.04%
Manufacturing	19.06%
Utilities	19.00%
Construction	7.08%
Commerce	14.00%
Transportation and communication	6.05%
Social services	16.70%

Agricultural Products

Grains, oilseeds, livestock products

Industrial Products

Food processing, motor vehicles, consumer durables, textiles

Natural Resources

Fertile plains (pampas), minerals, lead, zinc, tin, copper, iron

Electric Power Generation

39,500,000,000 kwh
kwh per capita: 1,312

Generating Capacity

13,660,000 kw

Nuclear Power Plants and Output

935 mwe nuclear generating capacity on line now; the Comision Nacional de Energia Atomica has 2 plants in operation (in Lima), 1 under construction, 3 on order, and 1 in the planning stage

Crude Oil Production

24,650,000 metric tons; 180,670,000 barrels

Natural Gas Production

497,724 terajoules; 446,900,000,000 cubic feet

AUSTRALIA

Commonwealth of Australia

Budget

Revenues

1984: $43,843,000,000

Expenditures

1984: $50,387,000,000

Economic Aid Received

None

Gross National Product (GNP)

$139,120,000,000 (1983)
GNP per capita: $8,900

Gross Domestic Product by Sector (1980)

Agriculture, forestry, and fishing	5.70%
Mining	6.40%
Manufacturing	20.50%
Utilities	2.90%
Construction	6.50%
Transportation and communication	6.90%
Commerce	14.00%
Other	36.70%

Consumer Price Change (Inflation)

1984: 5.30%

Imports

Industrial and electrical machinery, transportation equipment, chemicals, crude materials

Total Imports

1984: $22,100,000,000

Exports
Metal ores, textile fibers, beef, cereal grains, coal

Total Exports
1984: $22,400,000,000

Trading Partners
Imports (1983/84)

USA	21.60%
Japan	22.30%
United Kingdom	7.20%
West Germany	5.80%
Saudi Arabia	2.80%

Exports (1983/84)

Japan	26.50%
USA	10.90%
New Zealand	5.60%
United Kingdom	4.60%
Singapore	3.80%
South Korea	3.80%

Tourists
Total: 943,000 (1983)

Balance of Payments
1984: $7,953,000,000

Labor Profile (1984)

Agriculture, forestry, and fishing	6.20%
Manufacturing	17.00%
Transportation and communication	7.50%
Trade	20.00%
Civil service, defense, and community service	23.00%
Mining	1.50%
Public utilities	2.00%
Construction	6.50%

Agricultural Products
Wool, cereals, sugarcane, fruits, sheep, cattle, dairy products

Industrial Products
Automobiles and engines, iron and steel, electrical and electronic equipment, aircraft, ships, chemicals and drugs, clothing

Natural Resources
Iron, bauxite, zinc, lead, coal, titanium, timber, crude oil and gas

Electric Power Generation
105,758,000,000 kwh (1982)
kwh per capita: 7,000

Nuclear Power Plants and Output
One nuclear plant in the planning stage; uranium production in 1980 totaled 780 short tons

Crude Oil Production
19,380,000 metric tons; 142,055,000 barrels (1983)

Natural Gas Production
443,268 terajoules; 39,800,000 cubic feet (1983)

AUSTRIA

Republic of Austria

Budget
Revenues
1984: $19,030,000,000
1983: $17,220,000,000
Expenditures
1984: $24,310,000,000
1983: $21,120,000,000

Gross National Product (GNP)
$58,000,000,000 (1984)
GNP per capita: $7,733

Gross Domestic Product (GDP)
$58,363,600,000 (1984)
GDP per capita: $7,781

Gross Domestic Product by Sector

Agriculture and forestry	3.60%
Mining	0.40%
Manufacturing	26.70%
Utilities	3.20%
Construction	7.30%
Commerce	16.80%
Transportation and communication	5.60%
Other	36.30%

Consumer Price Change (Inflation)
1984: 4.00%
1983: 12.00%
1982: 3.10%

Imports
Machinery, vehicles, chemicals, iron and steel, metal goods, raw materials, fuels, foodstuffs

Total Imports
1984: $19,629,000,000
1983: $19,367,000,000
1982: $19,502,000,000

Exports
Iron and steel products, timber, paper, textiles, electrotechnical machines, chemical products

Total Exports
1984: $15,739,000,000
1983: $15,428,000,000
1982: $15,642,000,000

Trading Partners

Imports (1984)

West Germany	39.70%
Italy	8.70%
USSR	5.00%
Switzerland	4.50%
France	3.70%

Exports (1984)

West Germany	29.70%
Italy	9.40%
Switzerland	7.00%
USSR	4.50%
United Kingdom	4.40%

Tourists
Total: 14,481,531 (1983)
Revenue: $5,119,760 (1982)

Balance of Payments
1984: -$646,000,000
1983: +$177,000,000
1982: -$641,000,000

Labor Profile (1983)

Agriculture, forestry, and fishing	9.50%
Manufacturing	28.30%
Construction	9.10%
Trade	13.10%
Transportation and communication	6.30%
Services	31.50%
Other	2.20%

Agricultural Products
Livestock, forest products, grains, sugar beets, potatoes

Industrial Products
Iron and steel, chemicals, capital equipment, consumer goods

Natural Resources
Iron ore, petroleum, timber, magnesite, aluminum, coal, copper

Electric Power Generation
43,750,000,000 kwh
kwh per capita: 5,800

Generating Capacity
14,610,000 kwh (1984)

Nuclear Power Plants and Output
One nuclear plant is under construction (Tullnerfeld at Zwentendorf) and another is planned (at Stein/ St. Pantaleon); nuclear generating capacity 700 mwe

Crude Oil Production
1,212,000 tons; 8,883,960 barrels (1984)

Natural Gas Production
47,316 terajoules; 4,248,977 cubic feet

BAHAMAS

Commonwealth of the Bahamas

Budget
Revenues
1981: $433,200,000
Expenditures
1981: $352,200,000
Deficit
0.62% of GDP

Gross Domestic Product (GDP)
$1,073,000,000 (1979)
GDP per capita: $4,474

Gross Domestic Product by Sector (1978)

Agriculture, forestry, and fishing	4.32%
Extractive industries	12.00%
Manufacturing	12.00%

Utilities	12.00%
Construction	2.26%
Commerce	25.55%
Transportation and communication	11.68%
Other	44.08%

International Liquidity
Reserves (minus gold): $113,500,000

Consumer Price Change (Inflation)
1982: 6.00%

Imports
Crude oil, foodstuffs, manufactured goods

Total Imports
1981: $5,310,000,000

Exports
Petroleum and petroleum products, chemicals

Total Exports
1981: $1,770,000,000

Trading Partners
Imports (1980)

Iran	28.20%
Nigeria	20.40%
USA	7.90%
Gabon	7.00%
Angola	5.40%

Exports (1980)

USA	26.90%
West Germany	6.90%
Netherlands	3.20%
United Kingdom	2.60%
Italy	2.00%

Tourists
Revenue: $641,100,000 (1980)

Balance of Payments
1982: -$19,200,000
1981: -$26,000,000

Labor Profile

Agriculture	9.00%
Industry, tourism and commerce	91.00%

Agricultural Products
Fruits, vegetables

Industrial Products
Fishing, petroleum, pharmaceuticals

Natural Resources
Salt, aragonite, timber

Electric Power Generation
830,000,000 kwh (1982)
kwh per capita: 3,500

Generating Capacity
320,000 kw (1982)

Crude Oil Production
None

Natural Gas Production
None

BAHRAIN
State of Bahrain

Budget
Revenues
1983: $1,175,275,000
1982: $1,319,170,000
Expenditures
1983: $1,418,015,000
1982: $1,255,305,000
Deficit
1.60% of exports of goods and services (1982)

Expenditures by Function (1983)

General public services	22.60%
Defense	11.60%
Education	10.10%
Health	6.50%
Social security and welfare	2.20%
Housing and community amenities	7.80%
Other community and social services	3.20%
Economic services	31.40%
Agriculture, forestry, fishing and hunting	1.10%

Roads	6.00%
Other transportation and communication	3.00%
Other	4.80%

Economic Aid Extended

None

External Public Debt

$172,200,000

Service payments: 0.30% of exports of goods and services

Gross Domestic Product (GDP)

$4,000,000,000 (1982)

GDP per capita: $10,000

International Liquidity

Reserves (minus gold): $1,498,200,000 (1984)

Gold reserves: 150,000 fine troy ounces

Consumer Price Change (Inflation)

1984: 0.30%

1983: 3.00%

1982: 8.90%

Imports

Machinery and transportation equipment, consumer goods, food and live animals, chemicals

Total Imports

1984: $3,531,000,000

1983: $3,342,000,000

1982: $3,614,000,000

Exports

Petroleum products, nonferrous metals, textile yarn and fabrics, fish

Total Exports

1984: $3,139,000,000

1983: $3,200,000,000

1982: $3,791,000,000

Trading Partners

Imports (1984)

Saudi Arabia	44.80%
Japan	10.30%
United Kingdom	7.00%
Italy	6.00%
USA	5.50%

Exports (1984)

United Arab Emirates	17.30%
Japan	12.50%
Singapore	7.30%
Saudi Arabia	4.40%
India	4.30%

Tourists

Total: 203,141 (1982)

Balance of Payments

1984: -$ 10,600,000

1983: +$243,100,000

1982: +$664,400,000

Labor Profile (1982)

Agriculture	2.50%
Mining	0.30%
Manufacturing	11.60%
Transportation and communication	7.80%
Trade	13.20%
Services	2.90%
Construction	20.10%
Other	9.40%

Agricultural Products

Eggs, vegetables, fruit

Industrial Products

Oil, aluminum

Natural Resources

Oil, fish

Electric Power Generation

5,952,000,000 kwh

kwh per capita: 14,480

Generating Capacity

1,408,000 kw (1984)

Nuclear Power Plants and Output

None

Crude Oil Production

2,100,000 metric tons; 15,393,000 barrels (1984)

Natural Gas Production

125,856 terajoules; 11,301,869 cubic feet (1983)

BANGLADESH

People's Republic of Bangladesh

Budget

Revenues

1983: $1,358,720

1982: $1,292,409

Expenditures

1983: $965,000

1982: $926,182

Deficit

0.60% of exports of goods and services (1983)

Expenditures by Function (1979)

Defense	8.60%
Education	10.70%
Health	8.60%
Social security and welfare	2.20%
Economic services	32.00%
Agriculture, forestry, fishing and hunting	10.00%
Other transportation and communication	4.10%

Economic Aid Extended

None

External Public Debt

$4,184,500,000 (1983)

Service payments: 8.90% of exports of goods and services

Gross National Product (GNP)

$11,600,000,000 (1983)

GNP per capita: $121

Gross Domestic Product (GDP)

$12,159,230,770 (1984)

GDP per capita: $125

Gross Domestic Product by Sector (1983)

Agriculture, forestry, and fishing	45.70%
Mining	0.01%
Manufacturing	9.50%
Utilities	0.40%
Construction	4.60%
Commerce	8.60%
Transportation and communication	8.50%
Other	22.50%

International Liquidity

Reserves (minus gold): $132,520,000 (1984)

Gold reserves: 61,000 fine troy ounces

Consumer Price Change (Inflation)

1984: 15.10%

1983: 12.30%

1982: 14.50%

Imports

Foodgrains, fuels, raw cotton, yarn, manufactured goods

Total Imports

1984: $2,481,515,000

1983: $1,919,000,000

1982: $1,899,000,000

Exports

Jute, tea, fish, paper

Total Exports

1984: $909,230,769

1983: $713,480,000

1982: $710,375,000

Trading Partners

Imports (1984)

USA	11.60%
Japan	10.50%
Singapore	9.10%
Canada	4.70%
Australia	4.30%

Exports(1984)

USA	13.90%
Iran	7.60%
United Kingdom	7.20%
Italy	6.90%
Japan	6.60%

Tourists

Total: 100,000

Balance of Payments

1984: $426,700,000

1983: $ 78,900,000

1982: $655,800,000

Labor Profile (1974)

Agriculture, forestry, and fishing	77.10%
Manufacturing	4.60%

Transportation and communication	1.60%
Trade	3.80%
Civil service	10.20%
Services	0.30%
Construction	1.60%
Other	0.80%

Agricultural Products
Jute, rice, tea, sugarcane, chilies, tobacco

Industrial Products
Jute goods, textiles, leather goods

Natural Resources
Land, extensive natural gas deposits, possible petroleum reserves

Electric Power Generation
3,860,000,000 kwh
kwh per capita: 39

Generating Capacity
1,025,000 kw (1984)

Nuclear Power Plants and Output
None

Crude Oil Production
None (1985)

Natural Gas Production
71,592 terajoules; 6,428,964 cubic feet (1984)

BARBADOS

Budget
Revenues
1983: $242,000,000
1982: $285,350,000
Expenditures
1983: $247,300,000
1982: $304,000,000
Deficit
1.90% of exports of goods and services (1982)

Expenditures by Function (1983)

General public services	16.40%
Defense	2.80%
Education	18.55%
Health	10.53%
Social security and welfare	17.45%
Housing and community amenities	4.72%
Other community and social services	1.47%
Economic services	19.34%
Agriculture, forestry, fishing and hunting	8.77%
Roads	5.03%
Other transportation and communication	2.50%
Other	8.80%

Economic Aid Extended
None

Economic Aid Received
Total: $94,000,000 (1970-82)
USA only: None

External Public Debt
$277,600,000 (1983)
Service payments: 4.00% of exports of goods and services

Gross National Product (GNP)
$993,000,000 (1982)
GNP per capita: $3,819

Gross Domestic Product (GDP)
$1,002,000,000 (1982)
GDP per capita: $3,854

Gross Domestic Product by Sector (1984)

Agriculture, forestry, and fishing	6.12%
Mining	1.26%
Manufacturing	11.46%
Utilities	2.95%
Construction	5.64%
Commerce	26.87%
Transportation and communication	7.42%
Other	38.21%

International Liquidity
Reserves (minus gold): $139,590,000 (1985)
Gold reserves: 61,000 fine troy ounces

Consumer Price Change (Inflation)
1984: 4.60%
1983: 5.30%
1982: 10.30%

Imports
Foodstuffs, fuels, manufactured goods

Total Imports
1984: $606,000,000
1983: $573,000,000
1982: $508,000,000

Exports
Sugar, molasses, rum

Total Exports
1984: $392,180,000
1983: $323,010,000
1982: $258,755,000

Trading Partners

Imports (1984)

USA	45.66%
Trinidad and Tobago	8.37%
United Kingdom	7.46%
Canada	5.78%
Netherlands Antilles	5.63%

Exports (1984)

USA	52.54%
Trinidad and Tobago	9.23%
United Kingdom	7.18%
Guyana	4.10%
Windward Islands	2.95%

Tourists
Total: 328,325 (1983)
Revenue: $251,000,000 (1982)

Balance of Payments
1984: +$19,100,000
1983: -$42,000,000
1982: -$35,600,000

Labor Profile (1983)

Agriculture, forestry, and fishing	8.05%
Manufacturing	13.30%
Transportation and communication	5.64%
Trade	22.46%
Civil service	36.78%
Services	3.66%
Construction	8.15%
Other	1.96%

Agricultural Products
Sugar

Industrial Products
Light industrial products for local and nearby island markets, processed sugar, rum, molasses, electric parts

Natural Resources
Limestone and coral quarries

Electric Power Generation
399,000,000 kwh
kwh per capita: 1,345

Generating Capacity
146,000 kw (1984)

Nuclear Power Plants and Output
None (1986)

Crude Oil Production
60,000 metric tons; 440,000 barrels (1983)

Natural Gas Production
432 terajoules; 387,936 cubic feet (1983)

BELGIUM
Kingdom of Belgium

Budget

Revenues
1984: $21,381,000,000
1983: $24,500,000,000

Expenditures
1984: $30,000,000,000
1983: $35,700,000,000

Deficit
12.00% of exports of goods and services (1984)

Expenditures by Function

General public services	5.50%
Defense	5.20%
Education	13.60%
Health	1.60%

Social security and welfare	41.00%
Housing and community amenities	1.70%
Other community and social services	7.80%
Economic services	16.20%
Agriculture, forestry, fishing and hunting	7.30%
Roads	3.70%
Other transportation and communication	5.00%
Other	1.40%

Economic Aid Extended
$3,300,000,000

Economic Aid Received
None (1985)

External Public Debt
None (1985)

Gross National Product (GNP)
$71,000,000,000 (1984)
GNP per capita: $7,197

Gross Domestic Product (GDP)
$71,635,000,000 (1984)
GDP per capita: $7,250

Gross Domestic Product by Sector (1983)

Agriculture, forestry, and fishing	23.80%
Mining	0.50%
Manufacturing	24.40%
Utilities	3.60%
Construction	5.70%
Transportation and communication	7.70%
Commerce	9.90%
Other	4.60%

International Liquidity
Reserves (minus gold): $4,564,000,000 (1984)
Gold reserves: 34,180,000 fine troy ounces

Consumer Price Change (Inflation)
1984: 6.30%
1983: 7.70%
1982: 8.70%

Imports
Mineral ores, machinery and equipment, chemicals, petroleum products, grains

Total Imports
1984: $55,455,000,000
1983: $55,313,000,000
1982: $58,227,000,000

Exports
Metal products, transportation equipment, textiles, glassware, ceramics, live animals

Total Exports
1984: $51,891,000,000
1983: $51,937,000,000
1982: $52,354,000,000

Trading Partners

Imports (1984)

West Germany	19.80%
France	18.20%
Netherlands	14.10%
United Kingdom	9.80%
USA	6.10%

Exports (1984)

West Germany	19.80%
Netherlands	18.20%
France	14.40%
United Kingdom	8.60%
USA	6.40%

Tourists
Total: 8,359,370
Revenue: $1,500,000,000 (1981)

Balance of Payments
1984: +$ 193,000,000
1983: -$ 431,000,000
1982: -$2,616,000,000

Labor Profile (1982)

Agriculture, forestry, and fishing	2.50%
Manufacturing	21.00%
Transportation and communication	6.50%
Civil service	27.90%
Services	6.00%
Construction	5.60%
Other	16.00%

Agricultural Products
Livestock, poultry, grain, sugar beets, flax, tobacco, potatoes, vegetables, fruits

Industrial Products
Fabricated metal, iron and steel, coal, textiles, chemicals

Natural Resources
Coal and small amounts of iron, lead, zinc, copper, manganese and phosphates

Electric Power Generation
54,198,000 kwh
kwh per capita: 5,490

Generating Capacity (1984)
14,941,000 kw

Nuclear Power Plants and Output
Six in operation; 2 under construction; 3,473 total mwe (1984)

Crude Oil Production
None (1985)

Natural Gas Production
576 terajoules; 51,725 cubic feet (1984)

BELIZE

Budget

Revenues
1984/85: $49,000,000
1983/84: $50,000,000
1982/83: $50,000,000

Expenditures
1984/85: $90,000,000
1983/84: $64,000,000
1982/83: $93,000,000

Deficit
8.00% of exports of goods and services (1983)

Economic Aid Extended
None

Economic Aid Received
Total: $135,000,000 (1970-83)
USA only: $25,000,000

Gross Domestic Product (GDP)
$176,000,000 (1983)
GDP per capita: $1,143

Gross Domestic Product by Sector (1983)

Agriculture, forestry, and fishing	19.00%
Mining	0.20%
Manufacturing	11.60%
Utilities	1.70%
Construction	4.50%
Commerce	14.70%
Transportation and communication	11.10%
Other	37.20%

Imports
Vehicles, building materials, petroleum, food, textiles, machinery

Total Imports
1984: $96,440,000
1983: $90,185,000
1982: $87,990,000

Exports
Sugar, molasses, citrus fruits, bananas, forestry products

Total Exports
1984: $94,435,000
1983: $77,730,000
1982: $90,985,000

Trading Partners

Imports

USA	47.20%
United Kingdom	13.60%
Netherlands Antilles	10.40%
Mexico	5.60%
Netherlands	4.00%

Exports

USA	45.70%
United Kingdom	20.20%
Trinidad and Tobago	9.60%
France	4.70%
Canada	2.60%

Labor Profile (1970)

Agriculture, forestry, and fishing	31.90%
Manufacturing	21.60%

Commerce 5.40%
Transportation and
communication 0.90%
Services 20.00%
Other 20.20%

Agricultural Products
Fishing and cattle farming are being developed

Industrial Products
None

Natural Resources
Agricultural products, potential oil deposits

Electric Power Generation
57,000,000 kwh
kwh per capita: 360

Generating Capacity
23,000 kw

Crude Oil Production
None (1985)

Natural Gas Production
None (1985)

BENIN
People's Republic of Benin

Budget
Revenues
1982: $168,200,000
1981: $156,485,294
Expenditures
1982: $187,000,000
1981: $175,966,911
Deficit
2.60% of exports of goods and services (1982)

Expenditures by Function (1979)
General public services 13.00%
Defense 8.80%
Education 20.50%
Health 5.50%
Social security and
welfare 8.80%
Housing and community
amenities 2.30%
Other community and
social services 0.50%
Economic services 21.00%
Agriculture, forestry,
fishing and hunting 7.80%
Roads 6.90%
Other transportation and
communication 0.04%
Other 9.00%

Economic Aid Extended
None

Economic Aid Received
Total: $135,000,000 (1970-83)
USA only: $25,000,000

External Public Debt
$614,800,000 (1983)
Service payments: 2.60% of exports of goods and services (1978)

Gross National Product (GNP)
$1,100,000,000 (1982)
GNP per capita: $310

Gross Domestic Product (GDP)
$923,261,391 (1983)
GDP per capita: $248

Gross Domestic Product by Sector (1978)
Agriculture, forestry, and
fishing 42.50%
Mining 0.20%
Manufacturing 5.40%
Utilities 0.90%
Construction 3.30%
Transportation and
communication 7.50%
Commerce 20.90%
Other 19.40%

International Liquidity
Reserves (minus gold): $2,500,000 (1984)
Gold reserves: 11,000 fine troy ounces

Imports
Textiles, machinery, tobacco, petroleum products

Total Imports
1982: $590,300,000
1981: $662,400,000
1980: $269,911,504

Exports
Cotton, cacao, palm oil

Total Exports
1982: $304,300,000
1981: $368,400,000
1980: $ 58,716,814

Trading Partners
Imports (1984)

France	22.80%
Austria	8.80%
Brazil	7.70%
India	6.30%
Netherlands	5.90%

Exports (1984)

Spain	32.10%
West Germany	20.50%
France	15.80%
Portugal	6.30%
Netherlands	4.00%

Tourists
Total: 41,000 (1980)

Balance of Payments
1978: -$96,400,000
1977: -$47,000,000
1976: -$69,000,000

Labor Profile (1979)

Agriculture, forestry, and fishing	70%
Manufacturing and civil service	30%

Agricultural Products
Corn, cotton, coffee, rice, beans, manioc, palm products, yams, peanuts

Industrial Products
Palm oil products, textiles, furniture, nails

Natural Resources
Crude oil, iron ore, limestone

Electric Power Generation
27,000,000 kwh
kwh per capita: 7

Generating Capacity
21,000 kw (1984)

Nuclear Power Plants and Output
None

Crude Oil Production
None (1985)

Natural Gas Production
None (1985)

BERMUDA

Budget
Revenues
1982/83: $158,980,000
Expenditures
1982/83: $154,290,000

Economic Aid Received
USA only: $34,000,000 (1970-81)

Gross Domestic Product (GDP)
$598,000,000 (1980)
GDP per capita: $16,150 (1983)

Consumer Price Change (Inflation)
1980: 14.80%

Imports
Food, fuel, machinery

Total Imports
1982: $466,400,000

Exports
Mainly re-exports of drugs and bunker fuel

Total Exports
1982: $84,500,000

Trading Partners
Imports (1982)

USA	36.80%
South Korea	13.00%
Netherlands Antilles	10.40%
Canada	10.20%
United Kingdom	6.80%

Exports (1982)

Colombia	26.60%
USA	13.30%
United Kingdom	9.80%
Sweden	6.10%
West Germany	5.10%

Tourists
Total: 544,466 (1982)

Labor Profile (1980)

Agriculture, forestry, and fishing	13.10%
Manufacturing	30.10%
Construction	8.70%
Utilities	1.20%
Commerce	32.40%
Transportation and communication	8.10%
Services	31.80%

Agricultural Products
Semitropical produce, dairy products, flowers

Industrial Products
Concrete structures, paints, perfumes, furniture

Natural Resources
Limestone

Electric Power Generation
350,000,000 kwh (1984)
kwh per capita: 6,035

Generating Capacity
110,000 kw (1984)

Nuclear Power Plants and Output
None

Crude Oil Production
None

Natural Gas Production
None

BHUTAN

Kingdom of Bhutan

Budget
Revenues
1984: $53,600,000
1983: $48,500,000
Expenditures
1984: $63,900,000
1983: $50,900,000
Deficit
1.60% of exports of goods and services (1983)

Economic Aid Extended
None

Economic Aid Received
Total: $180,000,000

Gross Domestic Product (GDP)
$150,000,000 (1983)
GDP per capita: $110

Imports
Kerosene, sugar, textiles

Total Imports
1983: $58,500,000
1982: $50,800,000

Exports
Rice, limestone, gypsum, handicrafts

Total Exports
1983: $16,700,000
1982: $20,900,000

Tourists
Total: 2,000 (1982)

Labor Profile (1982)

Agriculture, forestry, and fishing	94.31%
Manufacturing	0.90%
Trade	1.38%
Civil service	3.38%
Other	0.03%

Agricultural Products
Rice, corn, wheat, barley

Industrial Products
Handicrafts

Natural Resources
Timber, river water for power generation

Electric Power Generation
9,000,000 kwh
kwh per capita: 6

Generating Capacity
15,700 kw (1984)

Nuclear Power Plants and Output
None (1986)

Crude Oil Production
None (1986)

Natural Gas Production
None (1986)

BOLIVIA
Republic of Bolivia

Budget
Revenues
1983: $284,000,000
Expenditures
1983: $965,000,000

Economic Aid Received
Total: $1,000,000,000 (1942-75)
USA only: $63,000,000 (1983)

External Public Debt
$6,000,000,000 (1984)

Gross National Product (GNP)
$4,900,000,000 (1983)
GNP per capita: $833

Gross Domestic Product (GDP)
$3,030,000,000 (1983)
GDP per capita: $497

Gross Domestic Product by Sector (1983)

Agriculture, forestry, and fishing	22.50%
Mining	6.60%
Manufacturing	16.00%
Utilities	1.00%
Construction	1.80%
Commerce	24.00%
Transportation and communication	8.60%
Other	19.20%
Communication	10.00%
Other	23.10%

Consumer Price Change (Inflation)
1984: 791%

Imports
Chemicals, transportation equipment, capital goods, pharmaceuticals, foodstuffs

Total Imports
1984: $332,000,000

Exports
Tin, petroleum, other minerals, natural gas, sugar, cotton, coffee

Total Exports
1984: $724,000,000

Trading Partners
Imports (1984)

USA	22.50%
Brazil	21.70%
South Korea	17.60%
Argentina	13.60%
West Germany	4.00%

Exports (1985)

Argentina	44.40%
USA	23.70%
West Germany	6.40%
United Kingdom	4.10%
France	3.90%

Tourists
Total: 155,412

Balance of Payments
1984: -$178,000,000
1983: -$149,800,000

Labor Profile

Agriculture	46%
Industry	10%
Extractive industries	4%

Services and utilities 20%
Other 20%

Agricultural Products
Potatoes, corn, sugarcane, cassava, cotton, barley, rice, wheat, coffee, bananas

Industrial Products
Textiles, cottage industries, processed food, beverages

Natural Resources
Petroleum, natural gas, tin, lead, zinc, copper, tungsten, gold, sulphur, silver, iron ore

Electric Power Generation
1,900,000,000 kwh (1984)
kwh per capita: 315

Generating Capacity
490,000 kw (1984)

Nuclear Power Plants and Output
None

Crude Oil Production
960,000 metric tons; 7,040,000 barrels (1984)

Natural Gas Production
868,080 terajoules; 82,100,000,000 cubic feet (1983)

BOTSWANA
Republic of Botswana

Budget
Revenues
1984: $420,000,000
1983: $287,000,000
Expenditures
1984: $460,000,000
1983: $372,500,000
Deficit
5.30% of exports of goods and services (1984)

Expenditures by Function
General public services 18.20%
Defense 6.40%
Education 17.70%
Health 4.80%
Social security and welfare 1.80%
Housing and community amenities 9.10%
Other community and social services 1.30%
Economic services 32.40%
Agriculture, forestry, fishing and hunting 8.60%
Roads 9.60%
Other transportation and communication 7.20%
Other 8.30%

Economic Aid Extended
None

External Public Debt
$230,300,000 (1983)
Service payments: 2.90% of exports of goods and services

Gross National Product (GNP)
$593,964,000 (1979)
GNP per capita: $752

Gross Domestic Product (GDP)
$752,000,000 (1984)
GDP per capita: $716

Gross Domestic Product by Sector (1982)
Agriculture, forestry, and fishing 7.40%
Manufacturing 8.20%
Mining 2.90%
Utilities 3.00%
Construction 4.30%
Commerce 9.60%
Transportation and communication 3.00%
Other 35.80%

International Liquidity
Reserves (minus gold): $474,290,000 (1984)
Gold reserves: 10,000 fine troy ounces (1983)

Consumer Price Change (Inflation)
1984: 10.50%
1983: 13.30%
1982: 13.40%

Imports
Machinery, transportation equipment, manufactured goods

Total Imports
1984: $531,200,000
1983: $660,480,000
1982: $628,860,000

Exports
Meat products, diamonds, hides and skins

Total Exports
1984: $553,472,000
1983: $599,420,000
1982: $438,980,000

Trading Partners
Imports (1983)

Customs Union of Southern Africa	82.30%
Other Africa	8.30%
Other Europe	5.20%
United Kingdom	1.20%
USA	1.10%

Exports (1983)

Other Europe	70.30%
Other Africa	9.20%
Customs Union of Southern Africa	8.30%
USA	7.50%
United Kingdom	4.40%

Tourists
Total: 97,260
Revenue: $5,120,000 (1984)

Balance of Payments
1984: +$59,100,000
1983: +$ 4,800,000
1982: -$63,600,000

Labor Profile (1983)

Agriculture	4.50%
Manufacturing	9.90%
Mining	7.20%
Transportation and communication	3.90%
Trade	15.30%
Civil service	42.20%
Services	6.00%
Construction	9.50%
Other	1.50%

Agricultural Products
Livestock, sorghum, corn, millet, cowpeas, beans

Industrial Products
Diamonds, copper, nickel, frozen beef

Natural Resources
Diamonds, copper, nickel, salt, soda ash, potash, coal

Electric Power Generation
651,000,000 kwh
kwh per capita: 627

Generating Capacity
105,000 kw (1984)

Nuclear Power Plants and Output
None

Crude Oil Production
None (1985)

Natural Gas Production
None (1985)

BRAZIL
Federative Republic of Brazil

Budget
Revenues
1984: $10,610,000,000
Expenditures
1984: $10,580,000,000

External Public Debt
$58,815,600,000
Service payments: 31.90% of exports of goods and services

Gross National Product (GNP)
$211,000,000,000 (1983)
GNP per capita: $1,607

Gross Domestic Product (GDP)
$121,500,000,000 (1984)
GDP per capita: $917

Gross Domestic Product by Sector (1982)

Agriculture, forestry, and fishing	10.50%
Mining	0.70%
Manufacturing	24.40%
Utilities	1.60%
Construction	4.90%
Commerce	15.10%
Transportation and communication	5.20%
Other	37.50%

Consumer Price Change (Inflation)
1984: 1,937.60%

Imports
Capital goods, intermediate goods, petroleum, consumer goods

Total Imports
1984: $13,900,000,000

Exports
Coffee, iron ore, soy meal and soybeans, electric and nonelectric machinery, cocoa beans, transportation equipment

Total Exports
1984: $27,000,000,000

Trading Partners

Imports (1984)

USA	16.40%
Iraq	14.50%
Saudi Arabia	15.20%
Nigeria	6.60%
West Germany	4.50%

Exports (1984)

USA	28.50%
Japan	5.50%
Netherlands	5.70%
West Germany	4.80%
Italy	4.10%

Tourists
Total: 1,146,881 (1982)

Balance of Payments
1983: -$6,800,000,000

Labor Profile (1981)

Agriculture, forestry, and fishing	29.00%
Manufacturing	16.00%
Construction	7.00%
Trade	9.00%
Transportation and communication	5.00%
Social and other services	23.00%
Other	11.00%

Agricultural Products
Coffee, corn, rice, sugar, cocoa, livestock

Industrial Products
Steel, chemicals, petrochemicals, machinery, consumer goods, motor vehicles, aircraft

Natural Resources
Iron ore, manganese, bauxite, nickel, other industrial metal ores

Electric Power Generation
160,000,000,000 kwh (1984)
kwh per capita: 1,191

Generating Capacity
41,300,000 kw (1984)

Nuclear Power Plants and Output
One plant in operation, 1 nuclear plant under construction; 626 mwe nuclear generating capacity on line now

Crude Oil Production
23,190 metric tons; 117,000,000 barrels (1984)

Natural Gas Production
78,840 terajoules; 70,700,000,000 cubic feet (1984)

BRITAIN

See United Kingdom

BRUNEI
Sultanate of Brunei

Budget
Revenues
1984: $3,497,000,000
1979: $ 883,000,000
Expenditures
1984: $1,970,000,000
1979: $ 500,000,000
Deficit
None (1984)

Economic Aid Extended
None (1986)

Gross Domestic Product (GDP)
$3,833,809,524 (1984)
GDP per capita: $17,987

Gross Domestic Product by Sector (1984)

Agriculture, forestry, and fishing	1.09%
Mining	60.56%
Manufacturing	9.97%
Utilities	0.20%
Construction	3.33%
Commerce	11.21%
Transportation and communication	2.60%
Other	11.04%

Consumer Price Change (Inflation)
1984: 143.10%
1983: 138.80%
1982: 137.20%

Imports
Machinery and transportation equipment, manufactured goods, foodstuffs, beverages, tobacco

Total Imports
1984: $ 634,000,000
1983: $ 701,000,000
1981: $2,700,000,000

Exports
Crude petroleum, natural gas, rubber

Total Exports
1984: $ 3,244,285,000
1983: $ 3,260,000,000
1981: $18,600,000,000

Trading Partners
Imports (1984)

Thailand	39.68%
United Kingdom	22.11%
Japan	9.70%
USA	4.66%
Malaysia	4.42%

Exports (1984)

Japan	72.91%
Thailand	7.29%
Singapore	6.55%
South Korea	5.00%
Philippines	1.85%

Tourists
Total: 7,513 (1984)

Labor Profile (1981)

Agriculture, forestry, and fishing	0.00%
Manufacturing	0.00%
Transportation and communication	5.53%
Construction	15.51%
Other	78.96%

Agricultural Products
Rubber, rice, pepper

Industrial Products
Crude petroleum, natural gas, rubber

Natural Resources
Crude petroleum, natural gas, rubber

Electric Power Generation
470,000,000 kwh (1985)
kwh per capita: 2,026

Generating Capacity
153,000 kw (1985)

Nuclear Power Plants and Output
None (1986)

Crude Oil Production
7,735,334 metric tons; 56,700,000 barrels (1984)

Natural Gas Production
370,000 terajoules; 323,544,000,000 cubic feet (1984)

BULGARIA
People's Republic of Bulgaria

Budget
Revenues
1982: $17,560,000,000
Expenditures
1982: $17,390,000,000

Gross National Product (GNP)
$35,400,000,000 (1983)
GNP per capita: $3,977

Gross Domestic Product by Sector (1983)

Agriculture, forestry, and fishing	16.80%
Mining, manufacturing, and utilities	56.00%
Construction	9.60%
Commerce	6.50%
Transportation and communication	7.90%
Other	2.70%

Imports
Machinery and transportation equipment, fuels, raw materials, metals, agricultural raw materials

Total Imports
1983: $11,900,000,000

Exports
Machinery and transportation equipment, fuels, minerals and raw materials, agricultural products

Total Exports
1983: $11,900,000,000

Trading Partners
Imports (1983)

USSR	58.00%
East Germany	5.70%
West Germany	3.90%
Czechoslovakia	4.10%
Poland	4.00%

Exports (1983)

USSR	56.00%
East Germany	5.40%
Czechoslovakia	4.00%
Poland	3.00%
Romania	2.00%

Tourists
Total: 5,771,163 (1983)
Country of origin

Turkey	47.00%
Yugoslavia	9.10%
Czechoslovakia	7.00%
Poland	6.00%
USSR	5.70%

Labor Profile (1975)

Agriculture and forestry	23.00%
Industry	32.00%
Construction	8.10%
Commerce	8.10%
Transportation and communication	7.20%
Finance	0.50%
Education and culture	7.00%
Public health, welfare, and sports	4.00%
Administration	1.60%
Science and scientific institutes	1.60%
Housing and community services	2.30%
Other	4.60%

Agricultural Products
Grain, tobacco, fruits, vegetables

Industrial Products
Processed agricultural products, machinery

Natural Resources
Metals, minerals, timber

Electric Power Generation
41,040,000 kwh
kwh per capita: 4,582

Nuclear Power Plants and Output
None

Crude Oil Production
300,000 metric tons; 2,200,000 barrels (1981)

BURKINA FASO

Budget

Revenues

1982: $152,000,000

Expenditures

1982: $150,000,000

Economic Aid Received

Total: $214,700,000 (1979)

USA only: $23,000,000

Gross National Product (GNP)

$1,100,000,000 (1982)

GNP per capita: $169

Gross National Product by Sector (1979)

Agriculture, forestry, and fishing	37.20%
Mining	0.10%
Manufacturing	11.30%
Utilities	0.80%
Construction	3.30%
Commerce	15.50%
Transportation and communication	6.30%
Other	25.60%

Consumer Price Change (Inflation)

1982: 11.30%

Imports

Textiles, foodstuffs, consumer goods, transportation equipment, machinery, fuels

Total Imports

1982: $275,000,000

Exports

Livestock, peanuts, shea nut products, cotton

Total Exports

1982: $120,000,000

Trading Partners

Imports (1982)

France	31.50%
Ivory Coast	12.20%
USA	6.50%
Netherlands	4.20%
West Germany	3.70%

Exports (1982)

Ivory Coast	21.10%
France	14.40%
West Germany	7.20%
Japan	6.60%

Tourists

Total: 116,600 (1981)

Balance of Payments

1978: -$242,600,000

Labor Profile (1981)

Agriculture	83%
Industry	12%
Commerce, services and government	5%

Agricultural Products

Sorghum, millet, cowpeas, rice, corn, yams, cassava, sweet potatoes, sisal, sesame

Industrial Products

Processed fats and oils, cotton ginning, sisal twining, textiles, soap, beverages

Natural Resources

Manganese, limestone, bauxite, gold, copper, tin, graphite

Electric Power Generation

123,000,000 kwh (1983)

kwh per capita: 20

Nuclear Power Plants and Output

None

Natural Gas Production

70,584 terajoules; 274,570,000,000 cubic feet (1979)

Crude Oil Production

1,200,000 metric tons; 8,790,000 barrels (1979)

BURMA

Socialist Republic of the Union of Burma

Budget

Revenues
1982: $ 954,487,179
1981: $1,000,410,999
Expenditures
1982: $1,012,564,103
1981: $ 965,205,479
Deficit
7.00% of exports of goods and services (1982)

External Public Debt

$2,226,100,000 (1983)
Service payments: 33.80% of exports of goods and services

Gross Domestic Product (GDP)

$6,064,634,146 (1983)
GDP per capita: $165

Gross Domestic Product by Sector

Agriculture, forestry, and fishing	48.30%
Mining	1.20%
Manufacturing	9.40%
Utilities	0.50%
Construction	1.80%
Commerce	23.80%
Transportation and communication	3.90%
Other	11.00%

Consumer Price Change (Inflation)

1984: 10.50%
1983: 9.40%
1982: 12.50%

Imports

Machinery, transportation equipment, textiles, raw materials, manufactured goods

Total Imports

1984: $210,689,655
1983: $238,414,600
1982: $370,384,615

Exports

Rice, teak, jute, rubber

Total Exports

1984: $238,149,000
1983: $370,658,537
1982: $370,384,615

Trading Partners

Imports (1984)

Japan	35.80%
West Germany	12.60%
Singapore	9.50%
China	6.10%
United Kingdom	4.30%

Exports (1984)

Singapore	14.80%
Thailand	7.30%
Japan	7.10%
Malaysia	6.60%
Hong Kong	6.10%

Balance of Payments

1984: -$234,200,000
1983: -$344,100,000
1982: -$498,700,000

Labor Profile

Agriculture, forestry, and fishing	63.40%
Manufacturing	8.20%
Construction	1.50%
Trade	9.70%
Transportation and communication	3.30%
Civil service	3.80%
Services	2.20%
Other	8.10%

Agricultural Products

Rice, jute, sesamum, groundnuts, tobacco, cotton, pulses, sugarcane

Industrial Products

Textiles, wood and wood products, petroleum refining

Natural Resources:

Oil, timber, tungsten, nickel, copper, precious stones

Electric Power Generation

1,700,000,000 kwh
kwh per capita: 47

Generating Capacity
818,000 kw (1984)

Nuclear Power Plants and Output
None

Crude Oil Production
1,567,121 metric tons; 11,487,000 barrels (1984)

Natural Gas Production
329,532,000 terajoules; 29,592,000,000 cubic feet (1984)

BURUNDI
Republic of Burundi

Budget
Revenues
1983: $109,500,000
Expenditures
1983: $126,600,000

Economic Aid Received
$94,200,000 (1979)
USA only: $1,884,000

External Public Debt
$407,400,000 (1981)

Gross Domestic Product (GDP)
$879,200,000 (1983)
GDP per capita: $208

Gross Domestic Product by Sector (1982)

Agriculture, forestry, and and fishing	51.70%
Mining	0.50%
Manufacturing	7.80%
Construction	5.30%
Commerce	7.00%
Transportation and communication	2.10%
Other	24.90%

Consumer Price Change (Inflation)
1984: 18.40%

Total Imports
1984: $154,600,000

Total Exports
1984: $94,600,000

Trading Partners
Imports (1983)

Belgium	15.40%
France	10.30%
West Germany	8.70%
Japan	6.40%
Italy	3.90%

Exports (1983)

West Germany	49.50%
Belgium	4.60%
Italy	3.40%
USA	2.10%

Tourists
Total: 31,800 (1978)

Labor Profile

Agriculture, forestry, and fishing	96.80%
Other	6.50%

Agricultural Products
Coffee, cotton, tea

Industrial Products
Light manufactured goods, beer

Natural Resources
Nickel, timber

Electric Power Generation
4,000,000 kwh (1983)
kwh per capita: 1

Generating Capacity
27,000 kw (1984)

Nuclear Power Plants and Output
None

Crude Oil Production
None

Natural Gas Production
None

CAMBODIA

See Kampuchea

CAMEROON

United Republic of Cameroon

Budget

Revenues
1984: $1,777,000,000
1983: $1,468,273,381

Expenditures
1984: $1,696,000,000
1983: $1,311,055,000

Deficit
1.50% of exports of goods and services (1984)

Expenditures by Function (1983)

General public services	24.90%
Defense	9.60%
Education	13.20%
Health	3.70%
Social security and welfare	3.90%
Housing and community amenities	4.40%
Other community and social services	1.30%
Economic services	25.90%
Agriculture, forestry, fishing and hunting	8.30%
Roads	8.50%
Other transportation and communication	8.00%
Other	12.60%

Economic Aid Extended
None

External Public Debt
$1,882,900,000 (1983)
Service payments: 13.70% of exports of goods and services

Gross Domestic Product (GDP)
$6,436,000,000 (1984)
GDP per capita: $706

Gross Domestic Product by Sector (1982)

Agriculture, forestry, and fishing	23.20%
Mining	15.30%
Manufacturing	11.10%
Utilities	1.10%
Construction	5.60%
Transportation and communication	4.90%
Commerce	11.80%
Other	27.00%

International Liquidity
Reserves (minus gold): $53,850,000 (1984)
Gold reserves: 30,000 fine troy ounces

Consumer Price Change (Inflation)
1984: -11.40%
1983: -16.60%
1982: -13.30%

Imports
Manufactured consumer goods, capital goods, food, beverages, tobacco, fuel

Total Imports
1984: $1,112,000,000
1983: $1,224,000,000
1982: $1,211,000,000

Exports
Cocoa and coffee, timber, aluminum, cotton

Total Exports
1984: $ 886,000,000
1983: $ 976,000,000
1982: $1,064,000,000

Trading Partners

Imports (1984)

France	47.30%
West Germany	6.20%
USA	5.50%
Japan	5.20%
Italy	4.50%

Exports (1984)

USA	27.00%
France	22.40%
Netherlands	14.00%
United Kingdom	7.70%
West Germany	6.60%

Tourists
Total: 116,152

Balance of Payments
1984: -$165,200,000
1983: -$413,900,000
1982: -$397,000,000

Labor Profile (1976)

Agriculture, forestry, and fishing	77.20%
Manufacturing	4.70%
Transportation and communication	1.40%
Trade	4.10%
Civil service	7.80%
Services	0.20%
Construction	1.70%
Other	2.90%

Agricultural Products
Coffee, cocoa, tropical agriculture

Industrial Products
Small manufacturing, consumer goods, aluminum

Natural Resources
Timber, some oil, bauxite

Electric Power Generation
1,793,000,000 kwh
kwh per capita: 188

Generating Capacity
569,000 kw (1984)

Nuclear Power Plants and Output
None

Crude Oil Production
6,468,000 metric tons; 47,410,440 barrels (1984)

Natural Gas Production
None (1985)

CANADA

Budget
Revenues
1984: $63,416,666,000
1983: $61,903,225,000
Expenditures
1984: $84,462,000,000
1983: $81,112,903,000
Deficit
7.00% of exports of goods and services (1984)

Economic Aid Extended
$14,200,000,000

Economic Aid Received
Total: $1,800,000,000
USA only: $1,800,000,000

Gross National Product (GNP)
$318,800,000,000 (1984)
GNP per capita: $12,551

Gross Domestic Product (GDP)
$330,363,636,400 (1984)
GDP per capita: $13,006

Gross Domestic Product by Sector (1983)

Agriculture, forestry, and fishing	3.30%
Mining	5.60%
Manufacturing	15.90%
Utilities	3.70%
Construction	4.60%
Transportation and communication	9.30%
Commerce	7.20%
Other	50.50%

International Liquidity
Reserves (minus gold): $2,136,000 (1984)
Gold reserves: 20,140,000 fine troy ounces

Consumer Price Change (Inflation)
1984: 4.8%
1983: 5.0%
1982: 7.5%

Total Imports
1984: $75,979,000

Total Exports
1984: $88,632,575

Trading Partners

Imports (1984)

USA	69.70%
Japan	5.80%
United Kingdom	2.40%
West Germany	2.20%
Mexico	1.30%

Exports (1984)

USA	73.60%
Japan	4.70%
United Kingdom	2.00%
USSR	1.70%
China	1.10%

Tourists

Total: 34,256,000
Revenue: $2,608,000,000

Country of origin

USA	94.70%

Balance of Payments

1984: -$1,098,000
1983: +$1,893,000
1982: +$1,365,000

Labor Profile (1983)

Agriculture, forestry, and fishing	4.00%
Manufacturing	15.50%
Transportation and communication	6.10%
Trade	15.20%
Civil service	6.40%
Services	27.90%
Construction	4.60%
Other	20.30%

Agricultural Products

Wheat, livestock and meat, feedgrains, oilseeds, dairy products, tobacco, fruits, vegetables

Industrial Products

Motor vehicles and spare parts, fish and forest products, petroleum and natural gas, processed and unprocessed minerals

Natural Resources

Metals and minerals, fish, forests, wildlife

Electric Power Generation

419,118,000,000 kwh
kwh per capita: 16,670

Generating Capacity

92,725,000 kw

Nuclear Power Plants and Output

Sixteen nuclear plants are in operation, 7 are under construction; 9,521 mwe (1984)

Crude Oil Production

70,596,000 metric tons, 517,468,680 barrels (1984)

Natural Gas Production

2,964,228 terajoules; 2,661,876,744 cubic feet (1984)

CAPE VERDE

Republic of Cape Verde

Budget

Revenues
$17,100,000
Expenditures
$22,100,000

Gross National Product (GNP)

$142,000,000 (1980)
GNP per capita: $473

Consumer Price Change (Inflation)

1978: 44.00%

Total Imports

1981: $74,700,000

Total Exports

1981: $3,800,000

Trading Partners

Imports (1981)

France	11.20%
Netherlands	5.80%
West Germany	5.00%
Spain	4.20%
Angola	3.90%

Exports (1981)

Portugal	86.80%

Agricultural Products

Bananas, corn, sugarcane, coffee

Industrial Products
Fish and fish products, salt, siliceous rock

Natural Resources
Salt, siliceous rock

Electric Power Generation
10,000,000 kwh (1983)
kwh per capita: 35

Generating Capacity
8,000 kw (1983)

CENTRAL AFRICAN REPUBLIC

Budget
Revenues
1983: $ 95,300,000
1982: $101,980,000
Expenditures
1983: $113,700,000
1982: $129,890,000
Deficit
3.00% of exports of goods and services (1983)

Expenditures by Function (1981)

General public services	22.90%
Defense	9.60%
Education	17.60%
Health	4.80%
Social security and welfare	6.00%
Housing and community amenities	0.18%
Other community and social services	1.20%
Economic services	19.50%
Agriculture, forestry, fishing and hunting	10.60%
Roads	5.60%
Other transportation and communication	0.28%
Other	7.71%

Economic Aid Extended
None

Economic Aid Received
Total: $3,000,000 (1954-83)
USA only: None

External Public Debt
$215,000,000 (1983)
Service payments: 11.30% of exports of goods and services

Gross Domestic Product
$616,000,000 (1983)
GDP per capita: $244

Gross Domestic Product by Sector (1971)

Agriculture, forestry, and fishing	32.20%
Mining	5.60%
Manufacturing and utilities	9.50%
Construction	3.20%
Commerce	13.30%
Transportation and communication	3.90%
Other	32.20%

International Liquidity
Reserves (minus gold): $52,680,000 (1984)
Gold reserves: 11,000 fine troy ounces

Consumer Price Change (Inflation)
1984: 12.40%
1983: 13.30%
1982: 13.20%

Imports
Machinery and equipment, petroleum products, textiles

Total Imports
1982: $136,500,000
1981: $ 74,296,000
1980: $108,373,333

Exports
Diamonds, cotton, timber, coffee

Total Exports
1982: $113,600,000
1981: $ 68,738,676
1980: $ 57,893,938

Trading Partners
Imports (1984)

France	47.25%
Zaire	12.08%
Japan	5.49%
West Germany	4.39%
Italy	3.02%

Exports (1984)

France	57.89%
Japan	5.26%
West Germany	5.21%
USA	3.50%
Switzerland	3.45%

Tourists

Total: 86,000
Revenue: $15,000,000 (1980)

Balance of Payments

1984: -$34,800,000
1983: -$54,200,000
1982: -$ 4,300,000

Labor Profile (1971)

Agriculture, forestry, and fishing	81.19%
Manufacturing	8.88%
Transportation, communication, and trade	5.47%
Civil service	1.36%
Other	3.10%

Agricultural Products

Cotton, coffee, peanuts, food crops, livestock

Industrial Products

Timber, textiles, soap, cigarettes, processed food

Natural Resources

Diamonds, uranium, timber

Electric Power Generation

80,000,000 kwh
kwh per capita: 30

Generating Capacity

46,000 kw (1984)

Nuclear Power Plants and Output

None (1986)

Crude Oil Production

None (1986)

Natural Gas Production

None (1986)

CEYLON

See Sri Lanka

CHAD

Republic of Chad

Budget

Revenues
1983: $20,000,000
Expenditures
1983: $162,000,000

Economic Aid Received

$93,000,000

External Public Debt

$255,000,000 (1981)
Service payments: 3.60% of exports of goods and services

Gross Domestic Product

$500,000,000 (1980)
GDP per capita: $100

Gross Domestic Product by Sector (1977)

Agriculture, forestry, and fishing	41.40%
Mining	0.30%
Manufacturing	16.30%
Utilities	0.60%
Construction	1.10%
Commerce	30.10%
Transportation and communication	2.40%
Other	8.00%

Consumer Price Change (Inflation)

1983: 9.10%

Imports

Food, motor vehicles and spare parts, petroleum products, machinery and parts, construction materials

Total Imports

1983: $84,000,000

Exports

Cotton, livestock and its products

Total Exports

1983: $45,800,000

Trading Partners

Imports (1984)

France	24.10%
USA	10.60%
Cameroon	8.00%
Italy	3.70%
Netherlands	3.30%

Exports (1984)

Portugal	16.90%
West Germany	12.40%
Spain	7.90%
France	7.40%
Cameroon	4.90%

Tourists
Total: 3,000 (1967-68)
Revenue: $7,000,000 (1977)

Labor Profile (1977)

Agriculture	84.50%
Fishing	1.90%
Industry	5.40%
Transportation and other services	8.10%

Agricultural Products
Cotton, gum arabic, sorghum, peanuts, rice, livestock

Industrial Products
Livestock and its products, beer, bicycle and radio assembly, textiles, cigarettes

Natural Resources
Petroleum, uranium (unexploited), natron, kaolin

Electric Power Generation
43,000,000 kwh (1984)
kwh per capita: 8

Generating Capacity
25,000 kw

Nuclear Power Plants and Output
None

Crude Oil Production
None

Natural Gas Production
None

CHILE
Republic of Chile

Budget
Revenues
1983: $5,300,000
Expenditures
1983: $5,700,000,000

Economic Aid Received
USA only: $3,000,000 (1983)

External Public Debt
$17,200,000,000 (1983)

Gross National Product
$16,260,000,000 (1983)
GNP per capita: $1,355

Gross Domestic Product
$17,800,000,000 (1983)
GDP per capita: $1,483

Gross Domestic Product by Sector (1982)

Agriculture, forestry, and fishing	6.00%
Mining	6.00%
Manufacturing	20.70%
Utilities	3.00%
Construction	5.00%
Commerce	18.20%
Transportation and communication	4.90%
Other	3.70%

Consumer Price Change (Inflation)
1984: 33.20%

Imports
Food fuel, capital goods

Total Imports
1984: $2,700,000,000

Exports
Copper, cellulose, iron ore

Total Exports
1984: $3,650,000,000

Trading Partners

Imports (1984)

USA	23.30%
Japan	9.90%
Brazil	9.20%
Venezuela	7.80%
West Germany	6.80%

Exports (1984)

USA	26.00%
Japan	11.10%
West Germany	10.00%
Brazil	6.20%
United Kingdom	5.30%

Tourists

Total: 275,000 (1983)

Balance of Payments

1984: -$2,100,000,000

Labor Profile (1983)

Agriculture, forestry, and fishing	16.00%
Mining and quarrying	1.80%
Manufacturing	12.70%
Construction	2.90%
Utilities	0.80%
Commerce	17.00%
Transportation and communication	6.00%
Services	39.60%
Other	3.20%

Agricultural Products

Wheat, rice, oats, barley, fruits, potatoes, corn, beans, wine

Industrial Products

Light industry, refining

Natural Resources

Copper, timber, iron ore, nitrates

Electric Power Generation

12,500,000,000 kwh (1984)
kwh per capita: 1,072

Generating Capacity

3,250,000 kw

Nuclear Power Plants and Output

One nuclear plant in the planning stage

Crude Oil Production

840,000 metric tons; 5,280,000 barrels (1979)

Natural Gas Production

27,300 terajoules; 24,300,000,000 cubic feet (1980)

CHINA

People's Republic of China

Budget

Revenues
$63,080,000,000
Expenditures
$65,280,000,000

External Public Debt

$4,700,000,000

Gross National Product

$309,000,000,000
GNP per capita: $300

Gross Domestic Product

$313,800,000,000 (1983)
GDP per capita: $308

Gross Domestic Product by Sector

Agriculture	45.00%
Industry	42.00%
Commerce	4.60%
Transportation	4.00%
Construction	4.00%

Consumer Price Change (Inflation)

2.90%

Imports

Grain, chemical fertilizer, steel, industrial raw materials, machinery and equipment

Total Imports

1984: $20,200,000,000

Exports

Manufactured goods, agricultural products, oil, minerals

Total Exports

1984: $20,800,000,000

Trading Partners

Imports

Japan	30.80%
USA	14.60%
Hong Kong	10.90%
West Germany	5.10%
Canada	4.10%

Exports

Hong Kong	26.60%
Japan	20.90%
USA	9.30%
Jordan	5.00%
Singapore	4.80%

Tourists
Total: 9,500,000

Balance of Payments
1980: -$1,383,000,000

Labor Profile

Agriculture	71.60%
Industry	13.30%
Commerce	4.10%
Other	9.60%

Agricultural Products
Rice, wheat, corn, millet, cotton, sweet potatoes

Industrial Products
Iron and steel, coal, machine building, textiles, light industrial products, armaments

Natural Resources
Coal, iron, petroleum, mercury, tin, tungsten, antimony, manganese, molybdenum, magnetite, aluminum, lead, zinc, uranium, hydroelectric power

Electric Power Generation
345,000,000,000 kwh (1983)
kwh per capita: 325

Generating Capacity
73,000,000 kw

Nuclear Power Plants and Output
Two plants in the planning stage

Crude Oil Production
114,500,000 metric tons; 839,300,000 barrels

Natural Gas Production
477,888 terajoules; 429,900,000,000 cubic feet

CHINA (TAIWAN)

Republic of China

Budget

Revenues
1984: $8,078,625,000
1983: $8,457,000,000

Expenditures
1984: $8,078,625,000
1983: $8,457,000,000

Deficit
None (1983)

Economic Aid Received
Total: $4,875,000,000 (1946-82)
USA only: $4,600,000,000

External Public Debt
$5,169,000,000 (1979)
Service payments: 4.00% of exports of goods and services

Gross National Product (GNP)
$56,600,000,000 (1984)
GNP per capita: $2,985 (1984)

Gross Domestic Product (GDP)
$43,781,450,000 (1983)
GDP per capita: $2,337

Consumer Price Change (Inflation)
1983: 1.90%
1982: 17.40%

Imports
Crude oil, logs, metals and scrap

Total Imports
1984: $21,600,000,000
1983: $20,300,000,000
1981: $21,200,000,000

Exports
Clothing, plastic articles, electrical equipment

Total Exports
1984: $30,400,000,000
1983: $25,500,000,000
1981: $22,600,000,000

Trading Partners
Imports (1983)

Japan	66.30%
USA	22.70%
Saudi Arabia	9.40%
Kuwait	5.60%
Australia	3.40%

Exports (1983)

USA	45.30%
Japan	9.90%
Hong Kong	6.50%
West Germany	3.40%
Saudi Arabia	3.10%

Tourists
Total: 1,457,404 (1983)

Balance of Payments
1983: $4,452,000,000
1982: $2,248,000,000
1981: $ 519,000,000

Labor Profile (1983)

Agriculture, forestry, and fishing	17.80%
Manufacturing	31.50%
Transportation and communication	4.80%
Trade	16.80%
Civil service	14.50%
Services	2.40%
Construction	7.20%
Other	5.00%

Agricultural Products
Rice, sweet potatoes, sugarcane, bananas, pineapples, citrus fruits

Industrial Products
Textiles, clothing, chemicals, plywood, electronics, sugar milling, food processing, cement, shipbuilding.

Natural Resources
Fish

Electric Power Generation
45,500,000,000 kwh (1984)
kwh per capita: 2,390

Generating Capacity
13,071,000 kw (1984)

Nuclear Power Plants and Output
Five plants; total output: 4,011 mwe (1984)

COLOMBIA
Republic of Colombia

Budget
Revenues
1982: $3,900,000,000
Expenditures
1982: $5,300,000,000

Economic Aid Received
Total: $1,800,000,000 (1946-75)
USA only: $4,000,000 (1983)

External Public Debt
$10,500,000,000 (1983)

Gross National Product
$48,000,000,000 (1984)
GNP per capita: $1,660

Gross Domestic Product
$33,100,000,000 (1984)
GDP per capita: $1,002

Gross Domestic Product by Sector (1983)

Agriculture, forestry, and fishing	18.70%
Mining	3.00%
Manufacturing	2.10%
Construction	5.10%
Commerce	13.40%
Transportation and communication	8.00%
Other	29.00%

Consumer Price Change (Inflation)
1984: 30.60%

Imports
Capital goods, crude and refined products, durable consumer goods, nondurable consumer goods

Total Imports
1984: $4,050,000,000

Exports
Coffee, fuel oil, textiles and garments, bananas, chemicals, frozen beef

Total Exports
1984: $3,500,000,000

Trading Partners

Imports (1984)

USA	35.10%
Japan	9.70%
West Germany	8.40%
Venezuela	6.70%
Brazil	4.10%

Exports (1984)

USA	34.10%
West Germany	15.10%
Venezuela	5.90%
Japan	4.20%
Netherlands	3.80%

Tourists
Total: 1,200,000 (1981)

Balance of Payments
1984: $1,219,000,000

Labor Profile (1980)

Agriculture	28.00%
Mining	.0.70%
Manufacturing	13.30%
Utilities	0.40%
Construction	3.00%
Trade	15.00%
Transportation and communication	4.00%
Finance and business services	3.00%
Community and personal services	24.00%
Other	8.60%

Agricultural Products
Coffee, bananas, rice, corn, sugarcane, plantains, cotton, tobacco, flowers

Industrial Products
Textiles, processed food, clothing and footwear, beverages, chemicals, metal products, cement

Natural Resources
Petroleum, natural gas, coal, iron ore, nickel, gold, copper, emeralds

Electric Power Generation
26,000,000,000 kwh (1984)
kwh per capita: 920

Generating Capacity
8,350,000 kw (1985)

Nuclear Power Plants and Output
One nuclear plant is in the planning stage (1981)

Crude Oil Production
63,420,000 barrels; 8,650,000 metric tons (1982)

Natural Gas Production
None

COMOROS

Federal Islamic Republic of the Comoros

Budget

Revenues
1982: $ 6,000,000
1980: $10,200,000

Expenditures
1982: $30,000,000
1980: $23,000,000

Economic Aid Extended
None

Economic Aid Received
Total: $185,000,000 (1970-78)
USA only: None

External Public Debt
$182,800,000

Gross National Product
$90,000,000 (1982)
GNP per capita: $230

Gross Domestic Product
$1,800,000,000 (1984)
GDP per capita: $1,332

Imports
Foodstuffs, cement, fuels, chemicals, textiles

Total Imports
1983: $607,600,000
1981: $ 33,000,000
1980: $ 45,350,553

Exports
Perfume oils, vanilla, copra, cloves

Total Exports
1981: $17,000,000
1980: $ 200,000

Trading Partners

Imports (1977)

France	49.30%
Madagascar	23.60%
Kenya and Tanzania	11.20%
Pakistan	9.90%
People's Republic of China	5.80%

Exports (1977)

France	68.70%
USA	22.40%
Madagascar	5.30%
West Germany	3.60%

Tourists
Total: 2,000 (1984)

Labor Profile (1984)

Agriculture, forestry, and fishing	87%
Civil service	3%
Other	10%

Agricultural Products
Vanilla, copra, perfume plants, tropical fruits, rice and maize

Industrial Products
Distilled perfume products

Natural Resources
Tropical fruits

Electric Power Generation
268,000,000 kwh
kwh per capita: 153

Generating Capacity
175,000 kw (1984)

Nuclear Power Plants and Output
None (1986)

Crude Oil Production
None (1986)

Natural Gas Production
None (1986)

CONGO
People's Republic of the Congo

Budget

Revenues
1983: $717,000,000
1982: $634,000,000

Expenditures
1983: $477,000,000
1982: $634,000,000

Economic Aid Extended
None

External Public Debt
$1,486,800,000 (1983)
Service payments: 20.50% of exports of goods and services

Gross National Product (GNP)
$1,600,000,000 (1981)
GNP per capita: $1,065

Gross Domestic Product (GDP)
$1,100,000,000 (1984)
GDP per capita: $1,332

Gross Domestic Product by Sector (1981)

Agriculture, forestry, and fishing	7.80%
Mining	39.00%
Manufacturing	6.30%
Utilities	60.00%
Construction	4.60%

Commerce	11.00%
Transportation and communication	8.00%
Other	22.00%

International Liquidity
Reserves (minus gold): $4,110,000 (1984)
Gold reserves: 11,000 fine troy ounces

Consumer Price Change (Inflation)
1984: 12.70%
1983: 7.80%
1982: 12.80%

Imports
Machinery, iron and steel, road vehicles, paper and pulp, pharmaceuticals

Total Imports
1984: $599,520,384
1983: $610,119,047
1982: $348,432,056

Exports
Crude oil, diamonds, wood, timber, potassium, raw sugar, coffee

Total Exports
1984: $974,292,565
1983: $970,684,525
1982: $768,048,781

Trading Partners

Imports (1984)

France	47.60%
Spain	5.00%
West Germany	4.80%
Gabon	4.70%
Netherlands	3.40%

Exports (1984)

USA	73.70%
France	8.50%
Belgium	3.60%
Netherlands	1.90%
Spain	2.10%

Tourists
Total: 36,000 (1980)

Balance of Payments
1983: $400,000,000
1982: $330,800,000
1981: $459,800,000

Labor Profile (1970)

Agriculture	41.80%
Manufacturing	21.50%
Services	33.70%
Other	3.00%

Agricultural Products
Sugarcane, cassava, peanuts, maize, rice, bananas, cocoa, coffee, palm kernals

Industrial Products
Processed palm oil, cane sugar refining, beer, soap, tobacco

Natural Resources
High grade potash, high grade iron ore, crude oil, small amounts of gold and lead

Electric Power Generation
268,000,000 kwh
kwh per capita: 153

Generating Capacity
175,000 kw (1984)

Nuclear Power Plants and Output
None (1985)

Crude Oil Production
4,404,000 metric tons; 32,281,320 barrels (1984)

Natural Gas Production
None (1984)

COSTA RICA
Republic of Costa Rica

Budget
Revenues
1983: $321,000,000
Expenditures
1983: $544,000,000

External Public Debt
$5,400,000,000 (1982)

Gross National Product
$2,070,000,000 (1982)

Gross Domestic Product(GDP)
$3,300,000,000 (1983)
GDP per capita: $1,308

Gross Domestic Product by Sector (1983)

Agriculture, forestry, and fishing	20.80%
Mining and manufacturing	21.70%
Utilities	3.80%
Commerce	20.20%
Construction	3.20%
Transportation and communication	4.10%
Other	26.00%

Consumer Price Change (Inflation)
1984: 41.30%

Imports
Transportation equipment, machinery, paper products, petroleum, electrical machinery

Total Imports
1984: $914,000,000

Exports
Industrial products, bananas, coffee, meat, sugar

Total Exports
1984: $902,600,000

Trading Partners

Imports (1985)

USA	37.14%
Venezuela	9.80%
Japan	8.72%
Guatemala	5.10%
West Germany	5.00%

Exports (1985)

USA	41.33%
West Germany	9.10%
Guatemala	5.88%
El Salvador	4.60%
Honduras	4.03%

Tourists
Total: 326,242
Revenue: $130,613,348 (1983)

Balance of Payments
1984: -$342,500,000

Labor Profile (1985)

Agriculture	38.00%
Manufacturing	12.00%
Services	22.99%
Commerce	18.19%
Other	8.82%

Agricultural Products
Coffee, bananas, livestock, cacao, sugar, basic grains, forestry

Industrial Products
Processed foods, pharmaceuticals, beverages, wood products, textiles

Natural Resources
Forests, bauxite, sulphur, hydroelectric power

Electric Power Generation
2,700,000,000 (1984)
kwh per capita: 1,040

Generating Capacity
820,000 kw (1985)

Nuclear Power Plants and Output
None

Crude Oil Production
None

Natural Gas Production
None

CUBA
Republic of Cuba

Budget
Revenues
1982: $11,800,000,000

Economic Aid Extended
None

Economic Aid Received
Total: $16,700,000,000 (1960-78)
USA only: None

Gross National Product
$14,900,000,000 (1982)
GNP per capita: $1,534

Gross Domestic Product by Sector (1983)

Agriculture, forestry, and fishing	10.40%
Mining, manufacturing, and utilities	32.20%
Construction	8.40%
Transportation and communication	7.40%
Commerce	41.00%
Other	0.60%

Imports
Capital equipment, raw materials, foodstuffs

Total Imports
1983: $7,200,000,000
1982: $6,600,000,000
1980: $6,400,000,000

Exports
Sugar and its byproducts, nickel oxide and sulphide, tobacco, fish, rum, fruits

Total Exports
1983: $6,400,000,000
1982: $5,900,000,000
1980: $5,600,000,000

Trading Partners

Imports (1982)

USSR	67.30%
East Germany	3.70%
Czechoslovakia	3.30%
Bulgaria	3.10%
Japan	2.50%

Exports (1982)

USSR	67.30%
East Germany	3.30%
Bulgaria	3.20%
Czechoslovakia	2.30%
Spain	1.80%

Tourists
Total: 100,000 (1983)

Labor Profile (1982)

Agriculture, forestry, and fishing	21.90%
Manufacturing	20.70%
Transportation and communication	7.00%
Trade	11.20%
Civil service	5.30%
Services	2.90%
Other	31.00%

Agricultural Products
Sugar, tobacco, coffee, rice, beans, meat, vegetables, tropical fruits

Industrial Products
Refined sugar, refined metals, refined oil, cement, electric power, food processing, light consumer and industrial products

Natural Resources
Metals (primarily nickel)

Electric Power Generation
10,420,000 kwh (1984)
kwh per capita: 1,043

Generating Capacity
3,360,000 kw (1984)

Nuclear Power Plants and Output
None in operation; 1 under construction (1984)

Crude Oil Production
744,000 metric tons; 5,453,520 barrels (1983)

Natural Gas Production
3,240 terajoules; 2,909,500 cubic feet (1983)

CYPRUS
Republic of Cyprus

Budget

Revenues
1984: $222,266,666
1983: $491,300,000

Expenditures
1984: $272,666,667
1983: $645,400,000

Deficit
16.30% of GDP (1984)

Expenditures by Function (1983)

General public services	17.14%
Defense	5.42%
Education	11.42%
Health	6.85%
Social security and welfare	18.00%
Housing and community amenities	4.00%
Other community and social services	8.57%
Economic services	22.28%
Agriculture, forestry, fishing and hunting	13.71%
Roads	4.00%
Other transportation and communication	22.85%
Other	13.42%

Economic Aid Extended
None (1986)

External Public Debt
$649,700,000 (1983)
Service payments: 10.60% of exports of goods and services

Gross National Product
$849,032,258 (1984)
GNP per capita: $1,286

Gross Domestic Product
$601,935,000 (1984)
GDP per capita: $910

Gross Domestic Product by Sector (1984)

Agriculture, forestry, and fishing	9.19%
Mining	0.58%
Manufacturing	16.38%
Utilities	2.00%
Construction	10.42%
Commerce	16.53%
Transportation and communication	9.11%
Other	35.70%

International Liquidity
Reserves (minus gold): $556,400,000 (1986)
Gold reserves: 495,000 fine troy ounces

Consumer Price Change (Inflation)
1985: 5.00%
1984: 6.00%
1983: 6.00%

Imports
Petroleum, manufactured goods, machinery, food, chemicals

Total Imports
1985: $321,666,666
1984: $478,666,666
1983: $371,666,666

Exports
Potatoes, citrus fruits, wheat, barley, carobs, sheep, goats, pigs

Total Exports
1985: $162,400,000
1984: $224,666,666
1983: $145,000,000

Trading Partners

Imports (1984)

France	12.35%
United Kingdom	12.28%
Italy	9.71%
Japan	9.00%
Greece	7.35%

Exports (1984)

United Kingdom	17.03%
Lebanon	14.45%
Libya	9.98%
Saudi Arabia	7.40%
USA	3.44%

Tourists
Total: 736,972
Revenue: $141,333,333 (1984)

Balance of Payments
1984: -$204,400,000
1983: -$187,400,000
1982: -$156,200,000

Labor Profile (1983)

Agriculture, forestry, and fishing	20.83%
Manufacturing	20.50%
Construction	9.82%
Other	48.85%

Agricultural Products
Potatoes, grapes, citrus fruits, wheat, barley, carobs, sheep, goats, pigs

Industrial Products
Food and beverage processing, nonmetallic mineral goods

Natural Resources
Copper, pyrites, asbestos, umber, gypsum, chromite, marble, salt

Electric Power Generation
1,415,000,000 kwh (1984)
kwh per capita: 2,137

Generating Capacity
620,000 kw (1984)

Nuclear Power Plants and Output
None (1986)

Crude Oil Production
None (1986)

Natural Gas Production
None (1986)

CZECHOSLOVAKIA
Czechoslovak Socialist Republic

Budget
Revenues
1982: $52,800,000,000
1981: $26,632,000,000
Expenditures
1982: $52,700,000,000
1981: $26,575,000,000

External Public Debt
None (1985)

Gross National Product
$1,471,000,000 (1982)
GNP per capita: $9,550

Gross Domestic Product by Sector (1983)

Agriculture, forestry, and fishing	8.70%
Mining, manufacturing, and utilities	61.80%
Construction	10.50%
Commerce	14.50%
Transportation and communication	4.20%
Other	0.40%

Consumer Price Change (Inflation)
1982: 8.00%
1981: 0.80%
1979: 3.70%

Total Imports
1982: $16,219,000,000
1981: $15,275,000,000

Total Exports
1982: $16,265,000,000
1981: $15,544,000,000

Trading Partners
Imports (1983)

USSR	39.80%
East Germany	8.60%
Poland	6.60%
Hungary	5.10%
West Germany	4.50%

Exports (1983)

USSR	46.20%
East Germany	10.30%
Poland	6.20%
Hungary	4.90%
West Germany	4.40%

Tourists
Total: 14,300,000 (1983)

Labor Profile (1982)

Agriculture, forestry, and fishing	13.30%
Manufacturing	40.00%
Transportation and communication	6.30%
Trade	8.40%
Civil service	1.60%
Services	3.40%
Construction	9.20%
Other	17.80%

Agricultural Products
Wheat, rye, oats, corn, barley, potatoes, sugar beets, hogs, cattle, horses

Industrial Products
Iron and steel products, machinery and equipment, cement, sheet glass, motor vehicles, arms and armament, chemicals, textiles, footwear, glassware, clothing, ceramics, wood and paper products

Natural Resources
Coal/coke, timber, lignite, uranium, magnesite

Electric Power Generation
78,578,000,000 kwh
kwh per capita: 5,080

Generating Capacity
19,800,000 kw (1984)

Nuclear Power Plants and Output
Three plants in operation; total output, 1,194 mwe (1984)

Crude Oil Production
96,000 metric tons; 703,680 barrels (1984)

Natural Gas Production
25,404 terajoules; 2,281,279 cubic feet (1984)

DENMARK
Kingdom of Denmark

Budget
Revenues
1984: $18,500,000,000
Expenditures
1984: $24,800,000,000

Economic Aid Received
None

Gross National Product
$56,400,000,000 (1983)
GNP per capita: $11,026

Gross Domestic Product by Sector (1982)

Agriculture and fishing	5.30%
Mining	0.10%
Manufacturing	17.10%
Utilities	2.00%
Construction	5.00%
Commerce	12.00%
Transportation and communication	7.00%
Other	5.20%

Consumer Price Change (Inflation)
1984: 8.30%

Imports
Industrial raw materials, fuel, machinery and equipment, transportation equipment, consumer goods

Total Imports
1984: $14,800,000,000

Exports
Farm products (including canned goods), manufactured goods, fish, furs

Total Exports
1984: $14,500,000,000

Trading Partners
Imports (1984)

West Germany	20.40%
Sweden	13.90%
United Kingdom	9.00%
Netherlands	5.00%
USA	5.00%

Exports (1984)

West Germany	16.00%
United Kingdom	12.90%
Sweden	11.30%
USA	9.80%
Norway	6.40%

Tourists
Total: 9,171,000 (1983)
Revenue: $1,308,000
Country of origin

West Germany	30.00%
Others	40.00%

Balance of Payments
1984: $1,734,000

Labor Profile (1983)

Agriculture, forestry, and fishing	7.40%
Manufacturing	20.20%
Mining	0.10%
Construction	6.20%
Commerce	13.20%
Transportation	7.00%
Services	45.90%

Agricultural Products
Meath, dairy products, fish, fur

Industrial Products
Industrial and construction equipment, electronics, furniture, textiles

Natural Resources
Oil and gas, zinc, lead, iron ore, coal, molybdenum, cryolite, uranium

Electric Power Generation
21,900,000 kwh (1984)
kwh per capita: 4,279

Generating Capacity
9,119,00 kw

Nuclear Power Plants and Output
Four nuclear power plants are in the planning stage, each with 1,300 net mwe nuclear generating capacity; none is expected to be "on line" until 1988

Crude Oil Production
None

Natural Gas Production
None

DJIBOUTI
Republic of Djibouti

Budget
Revenues
1984: $120,000,000
1983: $118,000,000
Expenditures
1984: $120,000,000
1983: $152,000,000
Deficit
9.21% of GDP (1983)

Expenditures by Function

General public services	19.60%
Defense	27.94%
Education	6.86%
Health	5.88%
Social security and welfare	9.31%
Housing and community amenities	3.92%
Other community and social services	1.25%
Economic services	14.70%
Agriculture, forestry, fishing and hunting	1.10%
Roads	3.43%
Other transportation and communication	2.25%
Other	4.90%

Economic Aid Extended
None

External Public Debt
$32,900,000

Gross Domestic Product (GDP)
$369,000,000 (1983)
GDP per capita: $1,168

Gross Domestic Product by Sector (1983)

Agriculture, forestry, and fishing	4.30%
Manufacturing	8.18%
Utilities	3.19%
Construction	7.58%
Commerce	15.68%
Transportation and communication	9.83%
Other	51.22%

Imports
Machinery and electrical equipment, vehicles, textiles, foodstuffs

Total Imports
1983: $179,000,000
1981: $152,000,000

Exports
Hides, leather, shoes

Total Exports
1983: $108,000,000
1981: $ 66,000,000

Trading Partners
Imports (1985)

France	25.41%
Bahrain	15.51%
Japan	7.92%
Kenya	7.59%
Italy	7.49%

Exports (1985)

Somalia	31.79%
South Yemen	19.47%
Seychelles	13.33%
Italy	12.05%
North Yemen	10.25%

Agricultural Products
Camel, sheep and goat herding, fish

Industrial Products
Leather tanning and shoes

Natural Resources
Negligible

Electric Power Generation
88,000,000 kwh
kwh per capita: 47

Generating Capacity
50,000 kw (1984)

Nuclear Power Plants and Output
None

Crude Oil Production
None (1986)

Natural Gas Production
None (1986)

DOMINICAN REPUBLIC

Budget
Revenues
1983: $999,300,000
1982: $823,900,000
Expenditures
1983: $1,400,000,000
1982: $2,800,000,000
Deficit
25% of GDP (1982)

Expenditures by Function (1982)

General public services	13.50%
Defense	9.60%
Education	15.60%
Health	10.40%
Social security and welfare	8.20%
Housing and community amenities	5.70%
Other community and social services	0.08%
Economic services	29.20%
Agriculture, forestry, fishing and hunting	10.50%
Roads	1.40%
Other transportation and communication	8.90%
Other	4.60%

Economic Aid Extended
None

Economic Aid Received
Total: $809,000,000 (1970-83)
USA only: $599,000,000

External Public Debt
$2,202,300,000 (1983)
Service payments: 19.50% of exports of goods and services

Gross National Product (GNP)
$7,600,000,000 (1982)
GNP per capita: $1,400

Gross Domestic Product (GDP)
$7,917,500,000 (1982)
GDP per capita: $1,379

Gross Domestic Product by Sector (1982)

Agriculture, forestry, and fishing	17.90%
Mining	2.40%
Manufacturing	18.40%
Utilities	1.00%
Construction	7.00%
Transportation and communication	5.00%
Commerce	16.70%
Other	31.00%

International Liquidity
Reserves (minus gold): $353,500,000
Gold reserves: 0.018 fine troy ounces (1984)

Consumer Price Change (Inflation)
1984: 32.70%
1983: 5.50%
1982: 8.30%

Imports
Foodstuffs, machinery, iron and steel, chemicals

Total Imports
1984: $1,252,900,000
1983: $1,271,200,000
1982: $1,255,800,000

Exports
Sugar, coffee, cocoa, tobacco

Total Exports
1984: $865,700,000
1983: $781,700,000
1982: $767,700,000

Trading Partners

Imports (1984)

USA	43.10%
Venezuela	16.10%
Mexico	10.20%
Japan	5.30%
Spain	2.50%

Exports (1984)

USA	80.90%
USSR	3.40%
Spain	2.40%
Canada	2.00%
Belgium	1.80%

Tourists
Total: 598,581 (1983)

Balance of Payments
1982: -$441,900,000
1981: -$405,900,000
1980: -$669,800,000

Labor Profile (1985)

Agriculture, forestry, and fishing	47%
Manufacturing and trade	23%
Civil service	16%
Services	14%

Agricultural Products
Sugar, coffee, cocoa, tobacco, bananas

Industrial Products
Sugar refining, food products, chemicals

Natural Resources
Bauxite, nickel, iron ore

Electric Power Generation
3,100,000,000 kwh
kwh per capita: 483

Generating Capacity
1,360,000 kw (1984)

Nuclear Power Plants and Output
None

Crude Oil Production
None (1985)

Natural Gas Production
None (1985)

EAST GERMANY

See Germany (East)

ECUADOR
Republic of Ecuador

Budget
Revenues
1984: $1,480,000,000
Expenditures
1984: $1,590,000,000

External Public Debt
$6,239,000,000 (1983)
Service payments: 32.50% of exports of goods and services

Gross National Product (GNP)
$10,570,000,000 (1984)
GNP per capita: 1,174

Gross Domestic Product (GDP)
$11,680,000,000 (1984)
GDP per capita: $1,297

Gross Domestic Product by Sector (1983)

Agriculture, forestry, and fishing	13.50%
Extractive industries	14.40%
Manufacturing	17.90%
Utilities	0.60%
Construction	7.30%
Transportation and communication	8.40%

Consumer Price Change (Inflation)
1984: 60.80%

Imports
Raw materials, machinery

Total Imports
1984: $1,460,000,000

Exports
Petroleum, bananas, coffee, sugar

Total Exports
1984: $2,580,000,000

Trading Partners
Imports (1984)

USA	34.70%
Japan	13.90%
Brazil	9.50%
West Germany	7.10%
Colombia	3.00%

Exports (1984)

USA	61.50%
Asia	10.20%
Panama	6.90%
South Korea	4.90%
Colombia	2.50%

Tourists
Total: 217,008 (1982)

Balance of Payments
1984: -$248,000,000

Labor Profile (1983)

Agriculture, forestry, and fishing	47.00%
Mining	0.30%
Manufacturing	11.00%
Utilities	5.00%
Construction	1.00%
Commerce	11.00%
Transportation and communication	2.00%
Finance	10.00%
Services	12.70%

Agricultural Products
Bananas, coffee, sugar, cacao, rice, corn, livestock

Industrial Products
Food products, textiles, other consumer products

Natural Resources
Petroleum, fisheries, forest (hardwood and balsa)

Electric Power Generation
3,400,000,000 kwh (1984)
kwh per capita: 390

Generating Capacity
1,716,000 kw

Nuclear Power Plants and Output
None

Crude Oil Production
13,010,000 metric tons; 96,050,000 barrels (1984)

Natural Gas Production
1,404 terajoules; 1,621,000,000,000 cubic feet

EGYPT
Arab Republic of Egypt

Budget
Revenues
1984: $17,500,000,000
1983: $15,260,000,000
Expenditures
1984: $18,060,000,000
1983: $15,680,000,000
Deficit
1.30% of GDP (1984)

Expenditures by Function (1984)

General public services	7.15%
Defense	16.59%
Education	10.85%
Health	2.68%
Social security and welfare	11.62%
Housing and community amenities	2.81%
Other community and social services	7.82%
Economic services	8.83%
Agriculture, forestry, fishing and hunting	4.49%
Roads	1.24%
Other transportation and communication	0.50%
Other	31.00%

Economic Aid Extended
None (1986)

External Public Debt
$15,228,700 (1983)
Service payments: 18.90% of exports of goods and services

Gross National Product (GNP)
$20,000,000,000 (1983)
GNP per capita: $437

Gross Domestic Product (GDP)
$38,633,000,000 (1984)
GDP per capita: $839

Gross Domestic Product by Sector (1980)

Agriculture, forestry, and fishing	19.00%
Mining	17.00%
Manufacturing	12.00%
Utilities	0.60%
Construction	4.40%
Commerce	13.00%
Transportation and communication	7.00%
Other	26.00%

International Liquidity
Reserves (minus gold): $799,000,000 (1986)
Gold reserves: 2,432,000 fine troy ounces

Consumer Price Change (Inflation)
1985: 13.30%
1984: 17.10%
1983: 16.10%

Imports
Foodstuffs, capital goods

Total Imports
1985: $10,766,000,000
1984: $10,275,000,000
1983: $ 9,078,000,000

Exports
Cotton, rice, petroleum, manufactured goods

Total Exports
1985: $3,140,000,000
1984: $3,214,000,000
1983: $3,120,000,000

Trading Partners
Imports (1984)

USA	20.00%
West Germany	8.27%
Japan	7.58%
Italy	7.31%
France	7.17%

Exports (1984)

Italy	29.78%
France	10.64%
West Germany	8.51%
Romania	6.38%
Spain	5.32%

Tourists
Total: 1,497,925 (1983)

Balance of Payments
1984: -$2,081,000,000
1983: -$ 411,000,000
1982: -$1,852,000,000

Labor Profile (1982)

Agriculture, forestry, and fishing	52.00%
Manufacturing	12.40%
Transportation and communication	5.33%
Construction	5.27%
Other	25.00%

Agricultural Products
Cotton, wheat, rice, corn

Industrial Products
Textiles, processed foods, tobacco manufacturers, chemicals, fertilizers, petroleum and petroleum products

Natural Resources
Petroleum, phosphate, iron ore, salt, manganese, limestone

Electric Power Generation
35,931,000,000 kwh (1984)
kwh per capita: 763

Generating Capacity
6,836,000 kw (1984)

Nuclear Power Plants and Output
None (1984)

Crude Oil Production
41,100,000 metric tons; 301,263,000 barrels (1984)

Natural Gas Production
None (1986)

EL SALVADOR
Republic of El Salvador

Budget
Revenues
1984: $629,500,000
Expenditures
1984: $728,300,000

Economic Aid Received
Total: $785,000,000 (1970-83)
USA only: $690,000,000

External Public Debt
$1,000,000,000 (1983)

Gross National Product (GNP)
$3,800,000,000 (1983)
GNP per capita: $724

Gross Domestic Product (GDP)
$4,300,000,000 (1984)
GDP per capita: $872

Gross Domestic Product by Sector (1983)

Agriculture, forestry, and fishing	21.60%
Mining	0.20%
Manufacturing	15.60%
Utilities	2.40%
Construction	3.50%
Commerce	25.50%
Transportation and communication	4.00%
Other	27.00%

Consumer Price Change (Inflation)
1984: 16.80%

Imports
Foodstuffs, oil, machinery, chemicals, vehicles, metals

Total Imports
1983: $892,000,000

Exports
Coffee, cotton, sugar, woods

Total Exports
1983: $737,000,000

Trading Partners

Imports (1984)

USA	42.00%
Guatemala	16.70%
Mexico	7.70%
Costa Rica	4.10%
Japan	4.10%

Exports (1984)

USA	39.20%
West Germany	18.40%
Guatemala	15.40%
Nicaragua	4.90%
Costa Rica	2.60%

Balance of Payments
1983: -$65,000,000

Labor Profile (1984)

Agriculture	25%
Manufacturing	16%
Commerce	16%
Public and private services	28%
Other	15%

Agricultural Products
Coffee, livestock, cotton, corn, poultry, sugar, sorghum

Industrial Products
Food and beverages, textiles, footwear and clothing, chemicals, petroleum products

Natural Resources
Agricultural products, various mineral deposits, including quartz, diatomaceous earth, kaolin, gypsum

Electric Power Generation
1,700,000,000 kwh (1984)
kwh per capita: 340

Generating Capacity
700,000 kw

Nuclear Power Plants and Output
None

Crude Oil Production
None

ENGLAND

See United Kingdom

EQUATORIAL GUINEA

Republic of Equatorial Guinea

Budget

Revenues
1982: $9,800,000

Expenditures
1982: $13,280,000

Economic Aid Extended
None

Economic Aid Received
Total: $2,000,000 (1954-83)

External Public Debt
$102,900,000

Gross National Product (GNP)
$71,000,000 (1983)
GNP per capita: $417

Imports
Foodstuffs, beverages, tobacco, textiles, machinery

Total Imports
1982: $41,500,000
1981: $26,200,000
1980: $37,100,000

Exports
Cacao, wood, coffee, bananas, palm oil

Total Exports
1982: $16,900,000
1981: $ 8,200,000
1980: $13,300,000

Trading Partners

Imports (1984)

France	29.65%
Spain	26.85%
China	8.57%
Hong Kong	6.86%
Italy	6.57%

Exports (1984)

Spain	23.88%
Netherlands	18.80%
West Germany	16.20%
Italy	9.91%
France	8.77%

Balance of Payments

1981: -$17,588,900

Labor Profile (1982)

Agriculture, forestry, and fishing	73.21%
Other	26.79%

Agricultural Products

Cacao, wood, coffee

Industrial Products

Sawmilling

Natural Resources

Wood, petroleum (under exploration)

Electric Power Generation

17,000,000,000 kwh

kwh per capita: 61

Generating Capacity

10,000 kw (1984)

Nuclear Power Plants and Output

None (1986)

Crude Oil Production

None (1986)

Natural Gas Production

None (1986)

ETHIOPIA

Budget

Revenues

1984: $1,100,000,000

1983: $ 922,000,000

Expenditures

1984: $1,467,000,000

1983: $1,275,000,000

Deficit

3.70% of GDP (1984)

Expenditures by Function

General public services and defense	44.40%
Education	9.80%
Health	3.70%
Other community and social services	4.00%
Economic services	21.80%
Agriculture, forestry, fishing and hunting	9.70%
Roads	5.80%
Other transportation and communication	2.80%
Other	14.20%

Economic Aid Extended

None

Economic Aid Received

Total: $600,000,000 (1946-83)

USA only: $388,000,000

External Public Debt

$1,222,600,000 (1983)

Service payments: 11.50% of exports of goods and services

Gross National Product (GNP)

$4,850,241,546 (1984)

GNP per capita: $138

Gross Domestic Product (GDP)

$4,830,917,874 (1984)

GDP per capita: $138

Gross Domestic Product by Sector (1981)

Agriculture, forestry, and fishing	45.00%
Mining	0.20%
Manufacturing	10.00%

Utilities	1.00%
Construction	4.00%
Transportation and communication	4.00%
Commerce	10.00%
Other	27.00%

International Liquidity
Reserves (minus gold): $44,300,000 (1984)
Gold reserves: 209,000 fine troy ounces

Consumer Price Change (Inflation)
1984: 9.40%
1983: 15.40%
1982: 9.50%

Imports
Manufactured goods, transportation equipment, foodstuffs, fuels, textiles

Total Imports
1984: $876,000,000
1983: $876,000,000
1982: $786,000,000

Exports
Coffee, pulses, hides, skins and meat

Total Exports
1984: $417,000,000
1983: $403,000,000
1982: $402,000,000

Trading Partners

Imports (1984)

USA	20.80%
Italy	10.60%
United Kingdom	9.90%
West Germany	9.80%
Japan	5.90%

Exports (1984)

USA	20.40%
West Germany	17.60%
Japan	7.60%
France	7.50%
Italy	7.10%

Tourists
Total: 58,000 (1982)
Revenue: $12,077,000 (1983)

Balance of Payments
1984: -$202,900,000
1983: -$170,400,000
1982: -$195,200,000

Labor Profile (1975)

Agriculture, forestry, and fishing	84.20%
Manufacturing	5.80%
Services	10.00%

Agricultural Products
Cereals, feed grains, livestock and dairy products, wine, fruits, vegetables

Industrial Products
Chemicals, automobiles, processed foods, iron and steel, aircraft, textiles, clothing

Natural Resources
Coal, iron ore, bauxite, fish, forests

Electric Power Generation
902,000,000 kwh
kwh per capita: 26

Generating Capacity
412,000 kw (1984)

Nuclear Power Plants and Output
None

Crude Oil Production
None (1985)

Natural Gas Production
None (1985)

FEDERAL REPUBLIC OF GERMANY

See Germany (West)

FIJI

Budget

Revenues

1982: $256,550,000
1981: $259,000,000

Expenditures

1982: $317,490,000
1981: $239,000,000

Expenditures by Function (1982)

General public services	18.74%
Defense	4.37%
Education	20.78%
Health	8.18%
Social security and welfare	3.02%
Housing and community amenities	1.19%
Other community and social services	.56%
Economic services	36.80%
Agriculture, forestry, fishing and hunting	6.29%
Roads	6.08%
Other transportation and communication	1.25%
Other	6.61%

Economic Aid Extended

None

Economic Aid Received

Total: $438,000,000 (1980-82)
USA only: None

External Public Debt

$291,600,000 (1983)
Service payments: 7.30% of exports of goods and services

Gross National Product (GNP)

1983: $1,099,880,000
GNP per capita: $1,604

Gross Domestic Product (GDP)

1983: $1,075,780,000
GDP per capita: $1,604

Gross Domestic Product by Sector (1983)

Agriculture, forestry, and fishing	16.63%
Mining	0.61%
Manufacturing	8.23%
Utilities	2.36%
Construction	6.56%
Commerce	16.02%
Transportation and communication	8.58%
Other	40.98%

International Liquidity

Reserves (minus gold): $125,230,000 (1986)
Gold reserves: 11,000 fine troy ounces

Consumer Price Change (Inflation)

1985: 4.40%
1984: 5.30%
1983: 6.70%

Imports

Machinery, manufactured goods, electronic equipment, fuel, food

Total Imports

1984: $232,780,800
1983: $400,444,000
1982: $406,490,000

Exports

Sugar, coconut products, bananas, gold

Total Exports

1984: $243,721,800
1983: $232,845,000
1982: $267,560,000

Trading Partners

Imports (1984)

Australia	17.20%
Japan	16.22%
New Zealand	16.11%
Singapore	5.55%
United Kingdom	5.11%

Exports (1984)

United Kingdom	28.78%
Australia	13.72%
USA	9.80%
Malaysia	8.23%
New Zealand	3.92%

Tourists

Total: 191,616 (1983)

Balance of Payments
1984: -$26,900,000
1983: -$64,600,000
1982: -$92,800,000

Labor Profile (1976)

Agriculture, forestry, and fishing	43.70%
Manufacturing	7.40%
Transportation and communication	5.10%
Trade	9.80%
Civil service and services	16.47%
Construction	6.30%
Other	11.23%

Agricultural Products
Sugar, copra, bananas, ginger

Industrial Products
Sugar refining, gold, lumber, small industries

Natural Resources
Timber, fish, gold, copper

Electric Power Generation
223,000,000 kwh
kwh per capita: 325

Generating Capacity
210,000 kw (1984)

Nuclear Power Plants and Output
None (1986)

Crude Oil Production
None (1986)

Natural Gas Production
None (1986)

FINLAND
Republic of Finland

Budget
Revenues
1984: $11,624,000,000
1983: $11,131,000,000
Expenditures
1984: $11,717,000,000
1983: $12,059,000,000
Deficit
0.20% of GDP (1983)

Expenditures by Function (1983)

General public services	7.10%
Defense	5.50%
Education	13.80%
Health	10.60%
Social security and welfare	30.10%
Housing and community amenities	1.80%
Other community and social services	1.40%
Economic services	25.10%
Agriculture, forestry, fishing and hunting	11.50%
Roads	4.20%
Other transportation and communication	3.90%
Other	4.40%

Economic Aid Extended
$652,000,000 (1970-82)

Economic Aid Received
None

External Public Debt
None (1985)

Gross National Product (GNP)
$46,300,000,000 (1984)
GNP per capita: $9,489

Gross Domestic Product (GDP)
$47,366,153,850 (1984)
GDP per capita: $9,706

Gross Domestic Product by Sector (1983)

Agriculture, forestry, and fishing	7.50%
Mining	3.40%
Manufacturing	23.40%
Utilities	3.00%
Construction	7.40%
Commerce	10.10%
Transportation and communication	6.90%
Other	41.10%

International Liquidity
Reserves (minus gold): $3,720,800,000 (1985)
Gold reserves: 1,591,000 fine troy ounces

Consumer Price Change (Inflation)
1984: 7.10%
1983: 8.40%
1982: 9.30%

Imports
Raw materials, consumer goods, machinery and equipment

Total Imports
1984: $12,433,000,000
1983: $12,819,000,000
1982: $13,401,000,000

Exports
Wood and wood products, paper, metal and agricultural products

Total Exports
1984: $13,471,000,000
1983: $12,538,000,000
1982: $13,088,000,000

Trading Partners

Imports (1984)

USSR	23.40%
West Germany	13.70%
Sweden	12.10%
United Kingdom	7.60%
Japan	7.60%

Exports (1984)

USSR	19.30%
Sweden	12.60%
United Kingdom	11.80%
West Germany	9.60%
USA	8.10%

Tourists
Total: 2,060,562
Revenue: $508,035,714 (1983)
Country of origin (1983)

Sweden	28.20%
West Germany	12.80%
USSR	12.30%

Balance of Payments
1984: -$936,000,000
1983: -$753,000,000
1982: -$373,000,000

Labor Profile (1983)

Agriculture, forestry, and fishing	12.10%
Manufacturing	22.70%
Transportation and communication	7.10%
Trade	13.50%
Civil service	25.80%
Services	5.40%
Construction	7.30%
Other	6.10%

Agricultural Products
Dairy goods, wheat and other grains, livestock, potatoes, sugar beets, furs, berries

Industrial Products
Timber and forest products, machinery, ships, clothing, transportation equipment, food products

Natural Resources
Timber and some ores

Electric Power Generation
43,390,000,000 kwh
kwh per capita: 8,905

Generating Capacity
11,859,000 kw

Nuclear Power Plants and Output
Four in operation; 2,310 mwe (1984)

Crude Oil Production
None (1985)

Natural Gas Production
None (1985)

FRANCE
French Republic

Budget

Revenues

1985: $ 93,152,173,190
1984: $815,500,000,000

Expenditures

1985: $108,152,173,000
1984: $937,800,000,000

Deficit

0.02% of GDP (1985)

Expenditures by Function (1982)

General public services	6.42%
Defense	7.32%
Education	8.15%
Health	14.57%
Social security and welfare	44.19%
Housing and community amenities	3.40%
Other community and social services	0.64%
Economic services	6.87%
Agriculture, forestry, fishing and hunting	1.15%
Roads	0.83%
Other transportation and communication	1.28%
Other	8.35%

Economic Aid Extended

$29,700,000,000 (1970-82)

Economic Aid Received

None

External Public Debt

None

Gross National Product (GNP)

$427,800,000,000 (1983)
GNP per capita: $7,821

Gross Domestic Product (GDP)

$446,145,833,300 (1984)
GDP per capita: $8,119

Gross Domestic Product by Sector (1984)

Agriculture, forestry, and fishing	3.93%
Mining	0.75%
Manufacturing	25.44%
Utilities	2.54%
Construction	5.63%
Commerce	11.78%
Transportation and communication	5.21%
Other	44.72%

International Liquidity

Reserves (minus gold): $26,589,000,000 (1985)
Gold reserves: 81,850,000 fine troy ounces

Consumer Price Change (Inflation)

1985: 5.80%
1984: 7.40%
1983: 9.60%

Imports

Machinery and equipment, crude petroleum, iron and steel products, textiles, fibers

Total Imports

1985: $107,768,000,000
1984: $103,739,000,000
1983: $105,416,000,000

Exports

Textiles and clothing, iron and steel products, textile equipment, wine, agricultural products

Total Exports

1985: $101,674,000,000
1984: $ 97,566,000,000
1983: $ 94,943,000,000

Trading Partners

Imports (1984)

West Germany	16.29%
Italy	9.83%
Belgium	8.19%
United Kingdom	8.00%
USA	7.70%

Exports (1984)

West Germany	14.05%
Italy	10.45%
Belgium	8.20%
USA	7.69%
United Kingdom	7.58%

Tourists
Total: 33,466 (1982)
Revenue: $3,452,923
Country of origin

West Germany	25.15%
United Kingdom	17.36%
Netherlands	11.37%

Balance of Payments
1984: -$ 907,000,000
1983: -$ 5,766,000,000
1982: -$12,082,000,000

Labor Profile (1982)

Agriculture, forestry, and fishing	40.43%
Manufacturing	7.39%
Transportation and communication	5.91%
Trade	1.48%
Civil service	25.65%
Services	6.80%
Construction	7.52%
Other	45.25%

Agricultural Products
Cereals, feed grains, livestock and dairy products, wine, fruits, vegetables

Industrial Products
Chemicals, automobiles, processed foods, iron and steel, aircraft, textiles, clothing

Natural Resources
Coal, corn ore, bauxite, fish, forests

Electric Power Generation
320,035,000,000 kwh
kwh per capita: 5,832

Generating Capacity
88,446,000 kw (1984)

Nuclear Power Plants and Output
41 power plants; 32,993 mwe (1984)

Crude Oil Production
2,064,000 metric tons; 15,129,120 barrels (1984)

Natural Gas Production
378,984 terajoules; 3,403,276,320 cubic feet (1983)

GABON
Gabonese Republic

Budget
Revenues
1982: $1,400,000,000
1981: $1,300,000,000
Expenditures
1982: $1,100,000,000
1981: $1,100,000,000

Economic Aid Extended
None

External Public Debt
$728,900,000 (1983)
Service payments: 9.40% of exports of goods and services

Gross National Product (GNP)
$2,726,500,000 (1979)
GNP per capita: $2,726

Gross Domestic Product (GDP)
$3,400,000,000 (1983)
GDP per capita: $3,692

Gross Domestic Product by Sector (1979)

Agriculture, forestry, and fishing	5.50%
Mining	41.90%
Manufacturing	6.60%
Utilities	1.60%
Construction	7.70%
Commerce	7.20%
Transportation and communication	4.70%
Other	24.80%

International Liquidity
Reserves (minus gold): $199,450,000 (1984)
Gold reserves: 13,000 fine troy ounces

Consumer Price Change (Inflation)
1984: 5.80%
1983: 10.40%
1982: 16.70%

Imports
Foodstuffs and machinery, finished manufactured goods, textiles

Total Imports
1984: $888,000,000
1983: $878,000,000
1982: $860,000,000

Exports
Wood, petroleum, manganese, uranium, iron ore

Total Exports
1984: $559,000,000
1983: $498,000,000
1982: $873,000,000

Trading Partners

Imports (1985)

France	55.12%
Japan	5.38%
Italy	5.12%
USA	4.98%
West Germany	4.59%

Exports (1985)

USA	31.35%
France	18.96%
Spain	11.41%
United Kingdom	4.04%
West Germany	3.94%

Tourists
Revenue: $13,000,000 (1980)

Balance of Payments
1983: $ 74,800,000
1982: $313,100,000
1981: $405,700,000

Labor Profile (1972)

Agriculture, forestry, and construction	70.00%
Manufacturing and trade	2.15%
Civil service	2.09%
Other	25.76%

Agricultural Products
Cocoa, coffee

Industrial Products
Petroleum, lumber, minerals

Natural Resources
Wood, petroleum, iron ore, manganese, uranium

Electric Power Generation
735,000,000 kwh
kwh per capita: 767

Generating Capacity
280,000 kw (1984)

Nuclear Power Plants and Output
None

Crude Oil Production
7,620,000 metric tons; 55,854,600 barrels (1984)

Natural Gas Production
6,000 terajoules; 5,388,000 cubic feet (1983)

GAMBIA

Republic of the Gambia

Budget

Revenues
1983: $44,200,000
1982: $52,700,000

Expenditures
1983: $54,600,000
1982: $83,800,000

Deficit
5.80% of GDP (1983)

Expenditures by Function

General public services	25.00%
Education	6.50%
Health	6.20%
Social security and welfare	2.00%
Housing and community amenities	2.10%
Other community and social services	1.00%
Economic services	52.00%
Agriculture, forestry, fishing and hunting	22.00%
Roads	5.30%
Other transportation and communication	18.70%
Other	4.80%

Economic Aid Extended
None

Economic Aid Received
Total: $242,000,000 (1970-83)
USA only: $42,000,000

External Public Debt
$161,700,000 (1983)
Service payments: 4.10% of exports of goods and services

Gross Domestic Product (GDP)
$138,000,000 (1984)
GDP per capita: $190

Gross Domestic Product by Sector (1977)

Agriculture	58.30%
Manufacturing	2.70%
Construction	4.00%
Utilities	0.80%
Transportation and communication	2.60%
Public administration	6.60%

International Liquidity
Reserves (minus gold): $2,260,000 (1984)

Consumer Price Change (Inflation)
1984: 22.10%
1983: 10.60%
1982: 10.90%

Imports
Rice, wheat and foodstuffs, petroleum, textiles

Total Imports
1984: $69,621,000
1983: $93,686,000
1982: $75,632,000

Exports
Peanuts and peanut products

Total Exports
1984: $37,391,000
1983: $45,684,000
1982: $39,404,000

Trading Partners
Imports (1984)

USA	13.50%
United Kingdom	12.70%
France	8.50%
China	7.40%
Thailand	6.10%

Exports (1984)

France	22.20%
Switzerland	21.10%
Belgium	14.50%
United Kingdom	9.60%
Italy	6.50%

Tourists
Total: 41,950 (1984)

Balance of Payments
1981: -$49,700,000
1980: -$75,080,000
1979: -$33,160,000

Labor Profile (1982)

Agriculture, forestry, and fishing	77%
Other	23%

Agricultural Products
Grain, sorghum, rice, peanuts

Industrial Products
Peanut oil refining, cotton weaving, garment making, softdrink bottling, fishing

Natural Resources
No known minerals of value

Electric Power Generation
64,000,000 kwh
kwh per capita: 88

Generating Capacity
30,000 kw (1984)

Nuclear Power Plants and Output
None

Crude Oil Production
None (1985)

Natural Gas Production
None (1985)

GERMANY (EAST)
German Democratic Republic

Budget
Revenues
1983: $78,530,000,000
Expenditures
1983: $78,240,000,000

External Public Debt
$3,600,000,000 (1981)

Gross National Product (GNP)
$166,600,000,000 (1982)
GNP per capita: $9,916

Gross Domestic Product by Sector (1983)

Agriculture, forestry, and fishing	7.40%
Mining, manufacturing, and utilities	74.50%
Construction	0.20%
Commerce	9.70%
Transportation and communication	4.40%
Other	3.20%

Imports
Coal, coke, iron ore, oil, foodstuffs

Total Imports
1982: $22,400,000,000

Exports
Lignite, manufactured goods

Total Exports
1982: $24,200,000,000

Trading Partners
Bilateral (1982)

USSR	38.00%
West Germany	8.60%
Czechoslovakia	7.20%
Hungary	5.20%
Poland	4.90%

Tourists
Total: 933,889 (1983)

Labor Profile (1982)

Agriculture	10.60%
Industry and fishing	41.00%
Construction	7.00%
Commerce	10.20%
Transportation and communication	7.40%
Other	23.60%

Agricultural Products
Beet sugar, barley, oats, potatoes, rye, meat and dairy products

Industrial Products
Steel, chemicals, machinery, electical and precision engineering products

Natural Resources
Brown coal, potash, uranium

Electric Power Generation
109,200,000 kwh (1983)
kwh per capita: 6,529

Generating Capacity
23,010,000 kw (1984)

Nuclear Power Plants and Output
1,594 mwe nuclear generating capacity; 5 nuclear plants are in operation, 8 are under construction

Crude Oil Production
439,800 barrels (1976)

Natural Gas Production
5,930,000,000 cubic meters (1981)

GERMANY (WEST)
Federal Republic of Germany

Budget
Revenues
1984: $80,700,000,000
Expenditures
1984: $90,100,000,000

Economic Aid Extended
$3,900,000,000 (1976)

Gross National Product (GNP)
$580,100,000,000 (1984)
GNP per capita: $9,417

Gross Domestic Product by Sector (1983)

Agriculture, forestry, and fishing	2.00%
Manufacturing	31.80%
Construction	6.00%
Transportation and communication	5.80%

Consumer Price Change (Inflation)
1984: 2.80%

Imports
Raw materials, fuels, machinery

Total Imports
1984: $153,000,000,000

Exports
Chemicals, motor vehicles, iron and steel products

Total Exports
1984: $171,700,000,000

Trading Partners

Imports (1983)

Netherlands	12.00%
France	11.00%
Italy	8.10%
USA	7.10%
United Kingdom	6.90%

Exports (1983)

France	13.00%
Netherlands	8.00%
Italy	7.00%
Belgium	7.40%
United Kingdom	8.20%

Tourists
Total: 9,800,000
Revenue: $5,500,000,000 (1983)

Country of origin

USA	8.60%
United Kingdom	9.80%
France	5.00%
Benelux region	4.10%

Balance of Payments
1984: $6,440,000,000

Labor Profile (1982)

Agriculture, forestry, and fishing	5.00%
Utilties and mining	2.40%
Manufacturing	32.70%
Construction	7.70%
Trade and finance	20.50%
Transportation and communication	5.70%
Services	25.90%

Agricultural Products
Grains, potatoes, sugar beets, wine

Industrial Products
Iron, steel, coal, cement, chemicals, ships, vehicles

Natural Resources
Iron, coal, potash

Electric Power Generation
394,115,000,000 kwh (1984)
kwh per capita: 6,420

Generating Capacity
93,095,000 kw (1985)

Nuclear Power Plants and Output
9,831 mwe nuclear generating capacity (on line by December 1982); 15 nuclear plants are in operation, 9 are on order

Crude Oil Production
4,000,000 metric tons; 29,700,000 barrels (1984)

Natural Gas Production
587,184 terajoules; 52,700,000,000 cubic feet (1984)

GHANA

Republic of Ghana

Budget

Revenues
1982: $2,078,000,000
1981: $1,192,000,000

Expenditures
1982: $3,610,000,000
1981: $3,216,000,000

Expenditures by Function (1984)

General public services	21.72%

Defense	5.99%
Education	20.22%
Health	8.61%
Social security and welfare	4.12%
Housing and community amenities	2.13%
Other community and social services	2.21%
Economic services	18.72%
Agriculture, forestry, fishing and hunting	4.86%
Roads	7.11%
Other transportation and communication	1.87%
Other	15.73%

Economic Aid Extended
None (1986)

Economic Aid Received
Total: $681,000,000 (1946-83)
USA only: $428,000,000

External Public Debt
$1,095,100,000 (1983)
Service payments: 14.10% of exports of goods and services

Gross National Product (GNP)
$10,500,000,000 (1982)
GNP per capita: $875

Gross Domestic Product (GDP)
$13,800,000,000 (1984)
GDP per capita: $1,053

Gross Domestic Product by Sector (1981)

Agriculture, forestry, and fishing	50.90%
Mining	0.50%
Manufacturing	5.90%
Utilities	4.70%
Construction	1.93%
Commerce	30.00%
Transportation and communication	2.10%
Other	3.97%

International Liquidity
Reserves (minus gold): $462,900,000 (1986)
Gold reserves: 259,000 fine troy ounces

Consumer Price Change (Inflation)
1985: 10.30%
1984: 39.70%
1983: 122.90%

Imports
Petroleum, food, industrial raw materials, machinery, transportation equipment

Total Imports
1984: $579,000,000
1983: $576,000,000
1982: $705,000,000

Exports
Cocoa beans and products, logs and timber

Total Exports
1984: $559,000,000
1983: $498,000,000
1982: $873,000,000

Trading Partners

Imports (1984)

Nigeria	22.76%
United Kingdom	18.61%
West Germany	8.15%
USA	7.84%
Japan	5.07%

Exports (1984)

USSR	25.37%
United Kingdom	12.43%
Japan	10.75%
USA	7.73%
West Germany	7.05%

Tourists
Total: 44,000

Balance of Payments
1984: -$ 61,300,000
1983: -$174,100,000
1982: -$108,600,000

Labor Profile (1971)

Agriculture, forestry, and fishing	11.40%
Manufacturing	6.00%
Transportation and communication	2.10%
Construction	19.30%
Other	61.20%

Agricultural Products
Cocoa, timber, coffee, subsistence crops, rubber

Industrial Products
Mining, lumber, light manufacturing, fishing, aluminum

Natural Resources
Gold, diamonds, bauxite, manganese, fish

Electric Power Generation
2,102,000,000 kwh (1984)
kwh per capita: 152

Generating Capacity
1,200,000 kw (1984)

Nuclear Power Plants and Output
None (1986)

Crude Oil Production
None (1986)

Natural Gas Production
None (1986)

GREAT BRITAIN
See United Kingdom

GREECE
Hellenic Republic

Budget
Revenues
1984: $7,094,687,000
1983: $7,357,000,000
Expenditures
1984: $9,784,000,000
1983: $10,306,122,000
Deficit
9.10% of GDP (1984)

Expenditures by Function (1981)

General public services	1.60%
Defense	1.20%
Education	16.60%
Health	5.90%
Social security and welfare	0.40%
Housing and community amenities	9.00%
Other community and social services	3.20%
Economic services	61.40%
Agriculture, forestry, fishing and hunting	13.60%
Roads	21.20%
Other transportation and communication	7.70%

Economic Aid Extended
None

Economic Aid Received
Total: $1,885,000,000 (1970-83)
USA only: $525,000,000 (1970-82)

External Public Debt
$8,193,500,000 (1983)
Service payments: 16.30% of exports of goods and services

Gross National Product (GNP)
$29,468,750,000 (1984)
GNP per capita: $2,977

Gross Domestic Product (GDP)
$29,468,750,000 (1984)
GDP per capita: $2,977

Gross Domestic Product by Sector (1983)

Agriculture, forestry, and fishing	15.50%
Mining	1.70%
Manufacturing	16.10%
Utilities	1.80%
Construction	6.20%
Transportation and communication	7.20%
Commerce	11.50%
Other	39.90%

International Liquidity
Reserves (minus gold): $954,200,000
Gold reserves: 4,106,000 fine troy ounces

Consumer Price Change (Inflation)
1984: 15.50%
1983: 12.50%
1982: 24.80%

Imports
Crude petroleum and petroleum products, nonelectric machinery, transportation equipment, chemicals

Total Imports
1984: $ 9,435,000,000
1983: $ 9,500,000,000
1982: $10,026,000,000

Exports
Fruits and vegetables, tobacco, petroleum products, cement, iron and steel

Total Exports
1984: $4,811,000,000
1983: $4,413,000,000
1982: $4,298,000,000

Trading Partners

Imports (1984)

West Germany	17.70%
Italy	10.80%
Saudi Arabia	8.90%
France	7.40%
Netherlands	6.70%

Exports (1984)

West Germany	19.50%
Italy	14.70%
USA	7.80%
France	7.30%
United Kingdom	5.80%

Tourists
Total: 5,258,372
Revenue: $1,175,727
Country of origin

United Kingdom	18.50%
West and East Germany	15.20%
USA	8.40%

Balance of Payments
1984: -$2,132,000,000
1983: -$1,878,000,000
1982: -$1,892,000,000

Labor Profile (1981)

Agriculture, forestry, and fishing	28.10%
Manufacturing	19.20%
Transportation and communication	7.70%
Trade	12.60%
Civil service	15.40%
Services	3.70%
Construction	9.40%
Other	3.90%

Agricultural Products
Tobacco, cotton, wheat, raisins, currants, fruit, olives

Industrial Products
Chemicals, petroleum and aluminum refining, textiles

Natural Resources
Lignite, bauxite, iron, nickel, iron ore, chromite, barite, magnesite

Electric Power Generation
24,613,000,000 kwh
kwh per capita: 2,485

Generating Capacity
9,928,000 kw (1984)

Nuclear Power Plants and Output
None

Crude Oil Production
1,308,000 metric tons; 9,587,640 barrels (1984)

Natural Gas Production
None (1984)

GRENADA

Budget
Revenues
1982: $27,000,000
1980: $39,000,000
Expenditures
1982: $62,000,000
1980: $40,000,000

Expenditures by Function (1977)

General public services	2.13%
Defense	5.43%
Education	6.36%
Health	5.41%
Social security and welfare	1.75%
Housing and community amenities	0.43%
Other community and social services	0.23%
Economic services	11.82%
Agriculture, forestry, fishing and hunting	1.74%
Roads	3.06%
Other	1.21%

Gross National Product (GNP)
$56,000,000 (1982)
GNP per capita: $622

Gross Domestic Product (GDP)
$119,000,000 (1983)
GDP per capita: $1,337

Gross Domestic Product by Sector (1976)

Agriculture, forestry, and fishing	30.10%
Mining	0.10%
Manufacturing	5.10%
Utilities	1.70%
Construction	3.90%
Commerce	19.90%
Transportation and communication	9.80%
Other	28.90%

International Liquidity
Reserves (minus gold): $19,260,000 (1985)

Consumer Price Change (Inflation)
1984: 5.60%
1983: 6.10%
1982: 7.80%

Imports
Food, machinery, petroleum, consumer goods

Total Imports
1983: $50,577,777
1982: $50,803,704
1981: $49,396,296

Exports
Nutmeg, cacao beans, bananas, fish, mace

Total Exports
1983: $18,922,222
1982: $18,551,800
1981: $19,000,000

Trading Partners

Imports (1985)

United Kingdom	30.76%
Trinidad and Tobago	25.64%
Japan	7.69%
Hong Kong	5.13%
Guyana	2.82%

Exports (1985)

United Kingdom	43.12%
Trinidad and Tobago	22.50%
West Germany	10.62%
Spain	5.00%
Netherlands	4.81%

Tourists
Total: 82,676 (1983)

Balance of Payments
1983: -$16,390,000
1982: -$17,000,000
1981: -$ 8,300,000

Labor Profile (1983)

Agriculture, forestry, and fishing	20.00%
Manufacturing	4.00%
Services	38.00%
Construction	11.00%
Other	27.00%

Agricultural Products
Bananas, cocoa, nutmeg, mace, lime oil

Industrial Products
Tourist trade

Electric Power Generation
26,000,000 kwh
kwh per capita: 300

Generating Capacity
12,000 kw (1984)

Nuclear Power Plants and Output
None (1986)

Crude Oil Production
None (1986)

Natural Gas Production
None (1986)

GUATEMALA
Republic of Guatemala

Budget
Revenues
1983: $704,000,000
Expenditures
1983: $1,300,000,000

Economic Aid Received
USA only: $30,000,000 (1983)

External Public Debt
$1,400,000,000 (1983)

Gross National Product (GNP)
$8,610,000,000 (1982)
GNP per capita: $1,164

Gross Domestic Product (GDP)
$8,900,000,000 (1983)
GDP per capita: $1,136

Gross Domestic Product by Sector (1983)

Agriculture, forestry, and fishing	25.10%
Mining	0.40%
Manufacturing	15.80%
Utilities	1.70%
Construction	2.60%
Commerce	26.00%
Transportation and communication	6.80%
Other	21.00%

Consumer Price Change (Inflation)
1982: 5.60%

Imports
Machinery and transportation equipment, manufactured goods, chemicals, fuels, foodstuffs, crude materials, beverages and tobacco

Total Imports
1984: $1,180,000,000

Exports
Coffee, sugar, cotton, bananas, car tires and inner tubes, zinc

Total Exports
1983: $1,190,000,000

Trading Partners
Imports (1984)

USA	32.40%
El Salvador	9.00%
Venezuela	7.20%
Mexico	6.90%
Costa Rica	6.40%

Exports (1984)

USA	36.10%
El Salvador	13.60%
Honduras	4.50%
Costa Rica	4.30%
Nicaragua	4.20%

Tourists
Total: 235,166 (1983)
Revenue: $62,000,000

Balance of Payments
1984: -$224,000,000

Labor Profile (1983)

Agriculture, forestry, and fishing	58.10%
Mining	0.10%
Manufacturing	13.60%
Construction	4.00%
Utilities	0.30%
Commerce	7.30%
Transportation and communication	2.50%
Services	14.10%

Agricultural Products
Corn, beans, coffee, cotton, cattle, bananas, essential oils, timber

Industrial Products
Construction, textiles, prepared foods, tires, pharmaceuticals

Natural Resources
Nickel, timber, fish

Electric Power Generation
1,800,000,000 kwh (1983)
kwh per capita: 235

Generating Capacity
655,000 kw

Nuclear Power Plants and Output
None

Crude Oil Production
None

GUINEA

People's Revolutionary Republic of Guinea

Budget
Revenues
1983: $444,000,000
1982: $818,000,000
Expenditures
1983: $434,000,000
1982: $518,000,000

External Public Debt
$1,621,000,000

Gross Domestic Product (GDP)
$582,000,000,000
GDP per capita: $102

Imports
Petroleum, production materials, transportation equipment

Total Imports
1984: $403,000,000
1982: $296,200,000
1981: $385,000,000

Exports
Bauxite, alumina, pineapple, bananas, palm kernals, coffee

Total Exports
1984: $537,000,000
1982: $410,900,000
1981: $385,000,000

Trading Partners
Imports (1984)

France	31.84%
Brazil	12.11%
USA	11.46%
West Germany	6.87%
Spain	5.28%

Exports (1984)

USA	27.59%
West Germany	18.81%
Spain	16.19%
Ireland	10.06%
Italy	5.79%

Labor Profile (1978)

Agriculture	84.00%
Industry and commerce	9.00%
Other	7.00%

Agricultural Products
Rice, cassava, millet, corn

Industrial Products
Bauxite, alumina

Natural Resources
Bauxite, iron ore, diamonds, gold

Electric Power Generation
220,000,000 kwh (1985)
kwh per capita: 38

Generating Capacity
100,600 kw (1985)

Nuclear Power Plants and Output
None (1986)

Crude Oil Production
None (1986)

Natural Gas Production
None (1986)

GUINEA-BISSAU
Republic of Guinea-Bissau

Budget
Revenues
1983: $12,200,000
1979: $27,400,000
Expenditures
1983: $ 55,300,000
1979: $153,100,000
Deficit
28.00% of GDP (1983)

Expenditures by Function (1979)

Finance	16.30%
Defense	15.58%
Education	13.29%
Interior	11.59%
Health and social welfare	9.49%
Rural development	4.98%
Public works, construction, and urban affairs	3.01%
Other	25.76%

Gross Domestic Product (GDP)
$154,000,000 (1983)
GDP per capita: $180

Imports
Foodstuffs, fuels, transport equipment, manufactured goods

Total Imports
1984: $46,149,000
1983: $63,938,000
1982: $59,800,000

Exports
Peanuts, palm kernals, shrimp, fish, lumber

Total Exports
1984: $21,746,000
1983: $22,708,000
1982: $11,305,000

Trading Partners
Imports (1984)

Portugal	29.70%
Italy	14.73%
Spain	9.05%
West Germany	5.60%
Netherlands	5.30%

Exports (1984)

Romania	45.05%
Portugal	29.04%
China	7.80%
France	5.15%
Belgium	3.80%

Labor Profile (1986)

Agriculture, forestry, and fishing	90.00%
Industry, services, and commerce	5.00%
Government	5.00%

Agricultural Products
Rice, vegetables and melons, peanuts, palm products, root crops, coconuts, wood

External Public Debt
$138,200,200 (1983)
Service payments: 19.70% of exports of goods and services

Industrial Products
Agricultural processing, beer, beverages

Natural Resources
Bauxite, phosphates, potential petroleum

Electric Power Generation
38,000,000 kwh (1985)
kwh per capita: 44 kwh

Generating Capacity
20,200 kw (1985)

Nuclear Power Plants and Output
None (1986)

Crude Oil Production
None (1986)

Natural Gas Production
None (1986)

GUYANA

Cooperative Republic of Guyana

Budget

Revenues

1984: $138,500,000

1983: $200,000,000

Expenditures

1984: $197,250,000

1983: $381,000,000

Deficit

13.82% of GDP (1984)

Expenditures by Function (1984)

Defense	5.28%
Education	7.28%
Health	3.64%
Social security and welfare	2.64%
Housing and community amenities	0.21%
Economic services	15.36%
Agriculture, forestry, fishing and hunting	4.92%
Roads	0.12%
Other transportation and communication	0.12%

Economic Aid Extended

None (1986)

External Public Debt

$662,800,000 (1983)

Service payments: 24.50% of exports of goods and services

Gross National Product (GNP)

$464,250,000 (1985)

GNP per capita: $4,939

Gross Domestic Product (GDP)

$491,000,000 (1985)

GDP per capita: $5,223

Gross Domestic Product by Sector (1984)

Agriculture, forestry, and fishing	20.41%
Mining	3.82%
Manufacturing and utilities	10.76%
Construction	5.88%
Commerce	7.35%
Transportation and communication	5.88%
Other	45.88%

International Liquidity

Reserves (minus gold): $2,850,000 (1985)

Consumer Price Change (Inflation)

1983: 13.30%

1982: 20.20%

1981: 24.70%

Imports

Foodstuffs, fuel, consumer goods, capital goods, machinery and transportation equipment

Total Imports

1983: $223,333,000

1982: $283,000,000

1981: $339,000,000

Exports

Bauxite/alumina, sugar, rice

Total Exports

1983: $269,333,333

1982: $241,000,000

1081: $241,333,333

Trading Partners

Imports (1984)

Trinidad and Tobago	34.19%
USA	24.24%
United Kingdom	9.52%
Barbados	7.36%
Tunisia	3.46%

Exports (1984)

USA	25.47%
United Kingdom	22.29%
Venezuela	16.56%
Canada	6.36%
Trinidad and Tobago	6.27%

Balance of Payments

1983: -$157,500,000

1982: -$142,300,000

1981: -$184,500,000

Labor Profile (1980)

Agriculture, forestry, and fishing	20.30%
Manufacturing	11.66%

Transportation and communication	3.80%
Construction	2.71%
Other	61.53%

Agricultural Products
Sugar, rice

Industrial Products
Bauxite mining, alumina production

Natural Resources
Bauxite, gold, diamonds, hardwood timber, shrimp

Electric Power Generation
266,000,000 kwh (1984)
kwh per capita: 335

Generating Capacity
200,000 kw (1984)

Nuclear Power Plants and Output
None (1986)

Crude Oil Production
None (1986)

Natural Gas Production
None (1986)

HAITI
Republic of Haiti

Budget
Revenues
1984: $219,700,000
1983: $200,540,000
Expenditures
1984: $357,080,000
1983: $416,480,000
Deficit
7.50% of GDP (1984)

Economic Aid Extended
None

Economic Aid Received
Total: $613,000,000 (1970-83)
USA only: $317,000,000

External Public Debt
$433,500,000 (1983)
Service payments: 3.80% of exports of goods and services

Gross National Product (GNP)
$1,616,000,000 (1983)
GNP per capita: $323

Gross Domestic Product (GDP)
$1,820,800,000 (1984)
GDP per capita: $350

Gross Domestic Product by Sector (1983)

Agriculture, forestry, and fishing	31.80%
Mining	0.09%
Manufacturing	17.40%
Utilities	0.80%
Construction	5.70%
Transportation and communication	2.10%
Commerce	18.10%
Other	23.90%

International Liquidity
Reserves (minus gold): $13,000,000 (1984)
Gold reserves: 18,000 fine troy ounces

Consumer Price Change (Inflation)
1984: 6.40%
1983: 10.20%
1982: 7.40%

Total Imports
1982: $284,000,000
1981: $400,600,000
1980: $326,400,000

Total Exports
1984: $179,220,000
1983: $166,000,000
1982: $177,680,000

Trading Partners
Imports (1984)

USA	66.90%
Netherlands Antilles	5.00%
Japan	4.70%
Argentina	3.00%
France	2.70%

Exports (1984)

USA	79.70%
West Germany	3.40%
France	3.30%
Canada	2.90%
Italy	2.80%

Tourists

Total: 221,094 (1983)

Country of origin (1983)

USA	45%

Balance of Payments

1984: -$26,900,000
1983: -$64,600,000
1982: -$92,800,000

Labor Profile (1983)

Agriculture, forestry, and fishing	65.00%
Manufacturing	17.10%
Transportation and communication	2.00%
Trade	18.10%
Civil service	0.20%
Services	6.90%
Construction	1.20%
Other	1.80%

Agricultural Products

Coffee, rice, sugar, sisal, cotton, corn

Industrial Products

Processing of coffee, sugar cane, sisal and edible oils, light industrial products, textiles, soap, cement

Natural Resources

Bauxite, copper, deposits of gold, silver, antimony, tin, sulphur, coal, nickel, gypsum

Electric Power Generation

314,000,000 kwh
kwh per capita: 54

Generating Capacity

184,000 kw (1984)

Nuclear Power Plants and Output

None

Crude Oil Production

None (1985)

Natural Gas Production

None (1985)

HONDURAS

Republic of Honduras

Budget

Revenues

1984: $475,000,000

Expenditures

1984: $614,100,000

Economic Aid Received

Total: $818,000,000 (1970-83)
USA only: $485,000,000 (1970-83)

External Public Debt

$1,650,000,000 (1982)

Gross National Product (GNP)

$3,000,000,000 (1984)
GNP per capita: $714

Gross Domestic Product (GDP)

$3,200,000,000 (1984)
GDP per capita: $753

Gross Domestic Product by Sector (1983)

Agriculture, forestry, and fishing	24.60%
Mining	2.00%
Manufacturing	13.30%
Utilities	2.20%
Construction	5.40%
Commerce	11.70%
Transportation and communication	6.80%
Other	34.00%

Consumer Price Change (Inflation)

1984: 6.10%

Imports

Machinery, transportation equipment, manufactured foods, fuels and lubricants, chemicals, foodstuffs

Total Imports

1983: $705,000,000

Exports
Bananas, coffee, lumber, refrigerated meat, metals

Total Exports
1983: $675,000,000

Trading Partners
Imports (1984)

USA	41.60%
Guatemala	7.20%
Mexico	5.20%
Japan	4.90%
Brazil	3.90%

Exports (1984)

USA	52.60%
Japan	7.10%
West Germany	5.70%
Guatemala	3.10%
Canada	3.00%

Tourists
Total: 157,715 (1983)

Balance of Payments
1984: -$225,200,000

Labor Profile (1983)

Agriculture, forestry, and fishing	53.20%
Mining	0.30%
Manufacturing	13.20%
Construction	4.30%
Financial	0.90%
Transportation and communication	4.00%
Commerce	9.60%
Other	14.50%

Agricultural Products
Corn, beans, bananas, coffee, lumber, rice, livestock, cotton

Industrial Products
Light consumer goods, processing of sugar, fruit juices, vegetable oils, meat packing

Natural Resources
Large forests, both hard and soft wood; unexploited agricultural lands; commercially exploitable quantities of gold, silver, lead, zinc, and antimony

Electric Power Generation
1,100,00 kwh (1984)
kwh per capita: 250

Generating Capacity
255,000 kw

Nuclear Power Plants and Output
None

Crude Oil Production
None

Natural Gas Production
None

HONG KONG

Budget
Revenues
1985: $4,640,256,000
1084: $3,897,307,000
Expenditures
1985: $4,786,153,000
1984: $4,281,154,000
Deficit
0.44% of GDP (1985)

Economic Aid Extended
None (1986)

Economic Aid Received
USA only: None (1986)

External Public Debt
None (1986)

Gross National Product (GNP)
$21,900,000,000 (1981)
GNP per capita: $4,340

Gross Domestic Product (GDP)
$33,300,000,000 (1985)
GDP per capita: $6,064

Gross Domestic Product by Sector (1983)

Agriculture, forestry, and fishing	0.59%
Mining	0.15%
Manufacturing	21.18%

Utilities 2.27%
Construction 5.88%
Commerce 18.18%
Transportation and
communication 7.66%
Other 44.09%

Consumer Price Change (Inflation)
1984: 11.20%
1983: 9.60%
1982: 12.50%

Imports
Raw materials, meats, other foodstuffs

Total Imports
1984: $28,600,000,000
1983: $24,000,000,000
1982: $23,500,000,000

Exports
Textiles, electronic products, plastics

Total Exports
1984: $28,400,000,000
1983: $21,900,000,000
1982: $21,000,000,000

Trading Partners
Imports (1984)
China 24.91%
Japan 23.50%
USA 10.87%
Singapore 5.47%
United Kingdom 3.85%

Exports (1984)
USA 33.57%
China 17.85%
United Kingdom 5.21%
West Germany 4.82%
Japan 4.46%

Tourists
Total: 3,400,000
Revenue: $1,897,435,000 (1985)
Country of origin
Japan 19.80%
USA 14.50%

Labor Profile (1981)
Agriculture, forestry, and
fishing 2.10%
Manufacturing and
transportation 50.40%
Construction 7.75%
Other 39.75%

Agricultural Products
Vegetables, pigs, chickens, fish

Industrial Products
Textiles, clothing, plastic toys, radios, electronic components

Natural Resources
None

Electric Power Generation
17,803,000,000 kwh (1985)
kwh per capita: 3,290

Generating Capacity
6,142,000 kw (1985)

Nuclear Power Plants and Output
None (1986)

Crude Oil Production
None (1986)

Natural Gas Production
None (1986)

HUNGARY
Hungarian People's Republic

Budget
Revenues
1984: $11,235,294,000
1983: $12,044,444,444
Expenditures
1984: $11,313,725,490
1983: $12,200,000,000
Deficit
0.30% of GDP (1984)

External Public Debt
$6,176,600,000 (1983)
Service payments: 18.80% of exports of goods and services

Gross National Product (GNP)
$17,066,666,667 (1983)
GNP per capita: $1,596

Gross Domestic Product (GDP)
$19,184,313,730 (1984)
GDP per capita: $1,799

Gross Domestic Product by Sector (1983)

Agriculture, forestry, and fishing	13.30%
Mining	0.00%
Manufacturing	37.50%
Utilities	0.00%
Construction	10.70%
Commerce	11.00%
Transportation and communication	7.80%
Other	19.60%

International Liquidity
Reserves (minus gold): $2,573,000,000 (1985)
Gold reserves: 2,352,000 fine troy ounces

Consumer Price Change (Inflation)
1984: 8.20%
1983: 7.30%
1982: 6.90%

Imports
Cotton, steel, oil, wheat, coal and iron ore

Total Imports
1984: $8,091,000,000
1983: $8,509,000,000
1982: $8,819,000,000

Exports
Machinery and tools, industrial and consumer goods, raw materials

Total Exports
1984: $8,563,000,000
1983: $8,702,000,000
1982: $8,773,000,000

Trading Partners

Imports (1984)

USSR	36.60%
West Germany	10.70%
East Germany	6.40%
Czechoslovakia	5.00%
Austria	5.00%

Exports (1984)

USSR	30.10%
West Germany	7.50%
East Germany	5.90%
Austria	5.30%
Czechoslovakia	5.20%

Tourists
Total: 10,500,000
Revenue: $413,333,337 (1983)

Balance of Payments
1984: +$271,000,000
1983: +$ 35,000,000
1982: -$429,000,000

Labor Profile (1984)

Agriculture, forestry, and fishing	21.70%
Manufacturing	32.80%
Transportation and communication	8.00%
Trade	10.20%
Services	19.90%
Construction	7.30%
Other	0.10%

Agricultural Products
Corn, wheat, potatoes, sugar beets, vegetables, fruits

Industrial Products
Precision equipment, pharmaceuticals, textiles, transportation equipment

Natural Resources
Some bauxite and brown coal

Electric Power Generation
26,709,000 kwh
kwh per capita: 2,513

Generating Capacity
6,530,000 kw (1984)

Nuclear Power Plants and Output
Two in operation; total output, 805 mwe (1984)

Crude Oil Production
2,004,000 metric tons; 14,700,000 barrels (1984)

Natural Gas Production
249,000 terajoules; 2,240,976,900 cubic feet (1984)

ICELAND
Republic of Iceland

Budget
Revenues
1984: $619,600,000
1982: $648,614,458
Expenditures
1984: $619,300,000
1982: $629,698,795
Deficit
None (1984)

Expenditures by Function (1982)

General public services	9.56%
Education	12.91%
Health	21.05%
Social security and welfare	16.25%
Housing and community amenities	2.33%
Other community and social services	1.78%
Economic services	28.71%
Agriculture, forestry, fishing and hunting	12.44%
Roads	7.65%
Other transportation and communication	1.90%
Other	7.22%

Economic Aid Extended
None

Economic Aid Received
Total: $19,100,000 (1970-81)

External Public Debt
None (1983)

Gross National Product (GNP)
$2,039,150,000 (1984)
GNP per capita: $8,604

Gross Domestic Product (GDP)
$1,925,300,000 (1984)
GDP per capita: $8,122

International Liquidity
Reserves (minus gold): $175,800,000 (1986)
Gold reserves: 49,000 fine troy ounces

Consumer Price Change (Inflation)
1985: 32.00%
1984: 30.80%
1983: 85.00%

Imports
Consumer goods, fuels, intermediate goods, capital equipment

Total Imports
1985: $813,857,000
1984: $608,625,000
1983: $645,931,034

Exports
Fish, aluminum, agricultural products

Total Exports
1985: $805,380,952
1984: $588,925,000
1983: $664,285,700

Trading Partners
Imports (1984)

West Germany	12.83%
Finland	9.14%
USSR	8.91%
Sweden	8.43%
United Kingdom	8.19%

Exports (1984)

USA	27.95%
United Kingdom	13.17%
West Germany	10.88%
USSR	7.93%
Spain	4.56%

Tourists

Total: 77,592 (1983)

Country of origin (1983)

USA	32.25%
United Kingdom	11.35%
West Germany	11.22%

Balance of Payments

1984: -$131,300,000
1983: -$ 56,900,000
1982: -$263,200,000

Labor Profile (1982)

Agriculture, forestry, and fishing	12.19%
Manufacturing	23.07%
Transportation and communication	7.02%
Trade	3.59%
Civil service	24.12%
Services	5.61%
Construction	12.26%
Other	2.04%

Agricultural Products

Livestock, hay, fodder, cheese

Industrial Products

Fish, aluminum

Natural Resources

Fish, diatomite, hydroelectric power

Electric Power Generation

4,226,000,000 kwh
kwh per capita: 17,682

Generating Capacity

913,000 kw (1984)

Nuclear Power Plants and Output

None (1986)

Crude Oil Production

None (1986)

Natural Gas Production

None (1986)

INDIA

Republic of India

Budget

Revenues

1984: $18,480,000,000

Expenditures

1984: $25,470,000,000

External Public Debt

$23,000,000,000 (1982)

Gross National Product (GNP)

185,770,000,000 (1983)
GNP per capita: $253

Gross Domestic Product (GDP)

$186,420,000,000 (1983)
GDP per capita: $255

Gross Domestic Product by Sector (1982)

Agriculture, forestry, and fishing	29.30%
Mining	2.70%
Manufacturing	14.40%
Utilities	1.60%
Construction	4.00%
Commerce	14.70%
Transportation and communication	5.60%
Other	27.40%

Consumer Price Change (Inflation)

1984: 11.40%

Imports

Petroleum, machinery, food grains, raw cotton, metals

Total Imports

1984: $15,000,000,000

Exports

Tea, sugar, jute, cotton fabrics, iron ore

Total Exports

1984: $9,400,000,000

Trading Partners

Imports (1984)

USA	9.90%
Japan	7.30%
Saudi Arabia	6.80%
United Kingdom	6.60%
USSR	6.20%

Exports (1984)

USA	24.20%
USSR	12.40%
Japan	10.00%
United Kingdom	6.80%
West Germany	4.50%

Tourists

Total: 884,731 (1983)

Balance of Payments

1982: -$2,520,000,000

Labor Profile (1971)

Agriculture	72.00%
Mining	0.50%
Manufacturing	9.40%
Utilities	0.30%
Construction	1.20%
Commerce	5.50%
Transportation and communication	2.40%
Finance	0.60%
Services	0.40%

Agricultural Products

Rice, pulses, oilseeds, cotton, jute, tea, wheat

Industrial Products

Textiles, refined sugar

Natural Resources

Iron ore, coal, manganese, mica, zinc, limestone

Electric Power Generation

144,000,000,000 kwh (1984)
kwh per capita: 194

Generating Capacity

40,000,000 kw (1985)

Nuclear Power Plants and Output

1,020 mwe nuclear generating capacity (on line by Dec 1984); 5 nuclear plants are in operation, 5 are under construction

Crude Oil Production

279,480,000 metric tons; 204,860,000 barrels (1984)

Natural Gas Production

124,940 terajoules; 11,219,000,000,000 cubic feet (1984)

INDONESIA

Republic of Indonesia

Budget

Revenues
1984: $16,248,600,000
1983: $15,663,481,000

Expenditures
1984: $16,711,359,400
1983: $16,711,267,610

Deficit
0.50% of GDP (1984)

Expenditures by Function (1983)

General public services	31.70%
Defense	11.60%
Education	9.10%
Health	2.20%
Housing and community amenities	1.40%
Other community and social services	0.90%
Economic services	38.00%
Agriculture, forestry, fishing and hunting	6.90%
Roads	0.30%
Other transportation and communication	6.80%
Other	4.40%

Economic Aid Extended

None

Economic Aid Received

Total: $6,600,000,000 (1982-83)
USA only: $25,000,000

External Public Debt
$21,685,300,000 (1983)
Service payments: 12.80% of exports of goods and services

Gross National Product (GNP)
$68,590,543,260 (1983)
GNP per capita: $438

Gross Domestic Product (GDP)
$79,994,413,400 (1984)
GDP per capita: $500

Gross Domestic Product by Sector (1983)

Agriculture, forestry, and fishing	26.40%
Mining	19.40%
Manufacturing	12.50%
Utilities	0.70%
Construction	6.20%
Commerce	15.30%
Transportation and communication	4.70%
Other	14.80%

International Liquidity
Reserves (minus gold): $5,094,000,000 (1985)
Gold reserves: 3,104,000 fine troy ounces

Consumer Price Change (Inflation)
1984: 10.50%
1983: 11.80%
1982: 9.50%

Imports
Foods, chemicals, textiles, iron, steel

Total Imports
1984: $13,882,000,000
1983: $16,352,000,000
1982: $16,859,000,000

Exports
Rubber, oil, nickel, tin

Total Exports
1984: $21,902,000,000
1983: $22,293,000,000
1982: $22,260,000,000

Trading Partners

Imports (1984)

Japan	23.60%
USA	18.60%
Singapore	12.80%
Saudi Arabia	9.60%
West Germany	5.90%

Exports (1984)

Japan	47.30%
USA	20.50%
Singapore	9.50%
Saudi Arabia	2.70%
West Germany	1.50%

Tourists
Total: 638,900,000
Revenue: $440,000,000 (1983)

Balance of Payments
1984: -$2,114,000,000
1983: -$6,338,000,000
1982: -$5,324,000,000

Labor Profile (1980)

Agriculture, forestry, and fishing	55.00%
Manufacturing	13.00%
Transportation and communication	5.00%
Trade	13.00%
Civil service	13.90%
Services	0.50%
Construction	6.00%
Other	6.60%

Agricultural Products
Rice, cassava, corn, copra, sweet potatoes, rubber

Industrial Products
Textiles, food, beverages, light manufacturing, cement, fertilizer

Natural Resources
Oil, timber, nickel, natural gas, tin, bauxite, copper

Electric Power Generation
24,300,000,000 kwh
kwh per capita: 144

Generating Capacity
9,100,000,000 kw

Nuclear Power Plants and Output
None (1985)

Crude Oil Production
69,120,000 metric tons; 506,649,600 barrels (1984)

Natural Gas Production
1,668,900 terajoules; 1,498,672,200 cubic feet (1984)

IRAN
Islamic Republic of Iran

Budget
Revenues
1984: $39,000,000,000
1983: $34,000,000,000
Expenditures
1984: $42,000,000,000
1983: $42,000,000,000
Deficit
6.85% of GDP (1983)

Expenditures by Function (1983)

General public services	0.09%
Defense	0.40%
Education	6.36%
Health	2.81%
Social security and welfare	0.20%
Housing and community amenities	0.81%
Other community and social services	0.82%
Economic services	64.45%
Agriculture, forestry, fishing and hunting	6.66%
Roads	8.00%
Other transportation and communication	6.90%
Other	8.81%

Economic Aid Extended
None (1986)

Economic Aid Received
Total: $8,999,000,000 (1946-83)
USA only: $766,000,000

External Public Debt
None (1984)

Gross National Product (GNP)
$118,000,000,000 (1984)
GNP per capita: $2,681

Gross Domestic Product (GDP)
$156,238,000,000 (1983)
GDP per capita: $3,714

Gross Domestic Product by Sector (1982)

Agriculture, forestry, and fishing	17.77%
Mining	17.92%
Manufacturing	8.31%
Utilities	0.91%
Construction	6.36%
Commerce	15.83%
Transportation and communication	6.59%
Other	26.26%

International Liquidity
Reserves (minus gold): $5,701,000,000
Gold reserves: 5,932,000 fine troy ounces (1982)

Consumer Price Change (Inflation)
1985: 4.40%
1984: 12.70%
1983: 19.70%

Imports
Machinery, iron and steel products, transportation equipment, cereals, sugar and honey, textiles, chemicals

Total Imports
1984: $14,840,000,000
1983: $18,327,000,000
1982: $14,164,000,000

Exports
Oil, cotton, fruit and vegetables, crude fertilizers and minerals, naturalgums, resins, balsam and lacs

Total Exports
1984: $13,220,000,000
1983: $20,211,000,000
1982: $19,430,000,000

Trading Partners

Imports (1984)

West Germany	16.33%
Japan	12.15%
Italy	6.53%
United Kingdom	6.52%
Turkey	6.33%

Exports (1984)

Japan	17.21%
Italy	11.25%
Netherlands	10.59%
Turkey	8.60%
Spain	7.28%

Tourists

Total: 157,000 (1984)

Balance of Payments

1983: $ 74,800,000
1982: $313,100,000
1981: $405,700,000

Labor Profile (1977)

Agriculture, forestry, and fishing	48.50%
Manufacturing	18.60%
Transportation and communication	3.80%
Construction	7.00%
Other	22.10%

Agricultural Products

Wheat, barley, rice, sugar beets, cotton, dates, raisins, tea

Industrial Products

Oil, petrochemicals, textiles, cement, steel, aluminum

Natural Resources

Petroleum, natural gas, iron, copper

Electric Power Generation

35,363,000,000 kwh
kwh per capita: 807 (1984)

Generating Capacity

11,212,000 kw (1984)

Nuclear Power Plants and Output

None (1986)

Crude Oil Production

112,956,000 metric tons; 827,967,000 barrels (1985)

Natural Gas Production

264,000 terajoules; 2,370,720,000 cubic feet (1983)

IRAQ

Republic of Iraq

Budget

Revenues
1981: $62,192,000,000
Expenditures
1981: $63,200,000,000

External Public Debt

$1,221,000,000 (1978)
Service payments: 1.10% of exports of goods and services

Gross National Product (GNP)

$27,000,000,000 (1984)
GNP per capita: $1,800

Gross Domestic Product by Sector (1976)

Agriculture, forestry, and fishing	7.50%
Mining	53.10%
Manufacturing	6.90%
Utilities	0.50%
Construction	7.60%
Transportation and communication	5.70%
Commerce	4.30%
Other	15.40%

Consumer Price Change (Inflation)

1984: 7.50%
1983: 3.10%
1982: 0.90%

Imports

Manufactured goods, foodgrains, machinery, construction materials, livestock.

Total Imports
1984: $11,178,000,000
1983: $12,275,000,000
1982: $21,728,000,000

Exports
Petroleum, dates, raw wool, hides and skins

Total Exports
1983: $ 9,785,000,000
1982: $10,250,000,000
1981: $10,530,000,000

Trading Partners

Imports (1984)

West Germany	16.30%
Japan	11.70%
Italy	6.50%
United Kingdom	6.50%
Turkey	6.30%

Exports (1984)

Japan	19.70%
Netherlands	12.10%
Turkey	9.70%
Spain	8.30%
Italy	2.90%

Tourists
Total: 719,823 (1978)

Labor Profile (1977)

Agriculture, forestry, and fishing	30.10%
Manufacturing	7.90%
Transportation and communication	0.70%
Trade	7.20%
Civil service	30.50%
Services	9.80%
Construction	10.30%
Other	3.50%

Agricultural Products
Livestock, wheat, barley, cotton, fruits, vegetables

Industrial Products
Petroleum, cement, textiles

Natural Resources
Oil, natural gas, phosphates, sulphur

Electric Power Generation
14,590,000,000 kwh
kwh per capita: 972

Generating Capacity
4,759,000 kw (1984)

Nuclear Power Plants and Output
None

Crude Oil Production
59,448,000 metric tons; 435,753,840 barrels (1984)

Natural Gas Production
None (1985)

IRELAND

Budget
Revenues
1984: $6,075,000,000
Expenditures
1984: $7,880,000,000

Economic Aid Received
None

Gross National Product (GNP)
$15,100,000,000 (1983)
GNP per capita: 4,272

Gross Domestic Product by Sector (1981)

Agriculture	10%
Mining, manufacturing, utilities, and construction	28%
Commerce, transportation, and communication	17%

Consumer Price Change (Inflation)
1982: 13.40%

Imports
Grains, foodstuffs, coal, petroleum products, machinery, electrical goods, transportation equipment, chemicals, textile yarn

Total Imports
1984: $8,320,000,000

Exports
Livestock, food, beverages, machinery, transportation equipment, chemicals, textiles

Total Exports
1984: $8,810,000,000

Trading Partners
Imports (1983)

United Kingdom	46.00%
USA	14.60%
West Germany	7.90%
France	4.60%
Netherlands	3.70%

Exports (1983)

United Kingdom	36.80%
West Germany	9.90%
France	8.20%
USA	8.10%
Netherlands	5.80%

Tourists
Total: 2,690,000
Revenue: $613,000,000
Country of origin (1983)

United Kingdom	46.20%
Northern Ireland	24.40%
USA	12.60%
West Germany	4.10%
France	3.60%
Netherlands	1.30%

Balance of Payments
1982: -$1,846,000,000

Labor Profile (1985)

Agriculture, forestry, and fishing	16.80%
Manufacturing	19.50%
Construction	7.60%
Commerce	18.80%
Transportation and communication	6.20%
Public administration and defense	6.40%

Agricultural Products
Cattle and dairy products, potatoes, barley, sugar beets, turnips, hay

Industrial Products
Tobacco, food processing, vehicle assembly, metals, textiles, chemicals, brewing

Natural Resources
Zinc, lead, silver

Electric Power Generation
10,944,000,000 (1984)
kwh per capita: 3,115

Generating Capacity
3,300,000 kw (1984)

Nuclear Power Plants and Output
One nuclear plant is in the planning stage

Crude Oil Production
None

Natural Gas Production
91,500 terajoules; 82,200,000,000 cubic feet (1984)

ISRAEL
State of Israel

Budget
Revenues
1983: $9,209,642,857
1982: $4,858,541,667
Expenditures
1983: $9,605,410,714
1982: $9,280,416,667
Deficit
1.60% of GDP (1983)

Expenditures by Function (1982)

General public services	3.00%
Defense	25.30%
Education	6.70%
Health	3.60%
Social security and welfare	18.00%
Housing and community amenities	0.10%
Other community and social services	0.60%
Economic services	6.20%

Agriculture, forestry, fishing and hunting	0.40%
Roads	0.10%
Other transportation and communication	1.60%
Other	35.00%

Economic Aid Extended
None

Economic Aid Received
USA only: $7,149,000,000 (1946-83)

External Public Debt
$15,148,800,000 (1983)
Service payments: 19.60% of exports of goods and services

Gross National Product (GNP)
$24,500,000,000 (1984)
GNP per capita: $6,093

Gross Domestic Product (GDP)
$25,250,339,290 (1983)
GDP per capita: $6,313

Gross Domestic Product by Sector (1983)

Agriculture, forestry, and fishing	5.30%
Mining and manufacturing	19.90%
Utilities	2.20%
Construction	6.70%
Commerce	12.60%
Transportation and communication	7.20%
Other	46.00%

International Liquidity
Reserves (minus gold): $2,886,900,000 (1985)
Gold reserves: 1,017,000 fine troy ounces

Consumer Price Change (Inflation)
1984: 373.80%
1983: 145.60%
1982: 120.40%

Imports
Fuel, machines, rough diamonds, food and consumer durables

Total Imports
1984: $9,889,000,000
1983: $9,660,000,000
1982: $9,597,000,000

Exports
Diamonds, chemicals, citrus, textiles, minerals

Total Exports
1984: $5,804,000,000
1983: $5,108,000,000
1982: $5,255,000,000

Trading Partners

Imports (1984)

USA	17.20%
West Germany	10.10%
Belgium	8.30%
United Kingdom	7.40%
Switzerland	4.80%

Exports (1984)

USA	27.50%
United Kingdom	8.20%
West Germany	6.10%
Netherlands	4.50%
France	4.20%

Tourists
Total: 1,166,820

Balance of Payments
1984: -$1,544,000,000
1983: -$2,325,000,000
1982: -$2,187,000,000

Labor Profile (1983)

Agriculture, forestry, and fishing	5.30%
Manufacturing	21.30%
Transportation and communication	6.20%
Trade	12.10%
Civil service	28.00%
Services	5.50%
Construction	6.10%
Other	15.50%

Agricultural Products
Citrus fruit, wheat, grains, vegetables, dairy products

Industrial Products
Diamonds, food processing, textiles, electronics, chemicals, petroleum refining

Natural Resources
Agricultural products, potash, phosphate, bromine, copper, iron, ceramic clays, glass sand

Electric Power Generation
15,305,000,000 kwh
kwh per capita: 3,810

Generating Capacity
3,585,000 kw (1984)

Nuclear Power Plants and Output
None (1985)

Crude Oil Production
12,000 metric tons; 87,000 barrels (1983)

Natural Gas Production
2,568 terajoules; 2,329,800,000 cubic feet (1983)

ITALY
Italian Republic

Budget
Revenues
1983: $119,640,000,000
Expenditures
1983: $167,090,000,000

Economic Aid Received
None

Gross National Product (GNP)
$350,000,000,000 (1982)
GNP per capita: $6,142

Gross Domestic Product by Sector (1983)

Agriculture, forestry, and fishing	5.80%
Mining, manufacturing, and utilities	32.00%
Construction	7.70%
Commerce	15.50%
Transportation and communication	6.50%
Other	32.30%

Consumer Price Change (Inflation)
1983: 14.70%

Imports
Crude oil, machinery and transportation equipment, foodstuffs, ferrous and nonferrous metals, wool, cotton

Total Imports
1983: $80,360,000,000

Exports
Machinery and transportation equipment, textiles, foodstuffs, chemicals, footwear

Total Exports
1983: $72,680,000,000

Trading Partners
Imports (1980)

West Germany	21%
France	18%
USA	9%
Saudi Arabia	8%
Netherlands	5%

Exports (1980)

West Germany	18%
France	15%
USA	5%
United Kingdom	6%
Netherlands	4%

Tourists
Total: 48,300,000
Revenue: $8,300,000,000 (1982)
Country of origin

West Germany	21.30%
Switzerland	21.00%
France	18.00%
Austria	9.00%
Yugoslavia	6.00%

Balance of Payments
1983: -$641,000,000

Labor Profile (1981)

Agriculture	12.20%
Mining	1.00%
Manufacturing and utilities	27.00%

Construction	9.90%
Commerce and public services	18.00%
Transportation and communication	5.60%
Finance and insurance	2.10%
Private services and public administration	20.40%

Agricultural Products
Sugar beet, wheat, maize, olives, potatoes, grapes, tomatoes.

Industrial Products
Automobiles, machinery, chemicals, textiles, iron and steel, food processing, footwear

Natural Resources
Fish, dwindling natural gas reserves, mercury, small quantities of iron ore, lignite, pyrites, sulphur

Electric Power Generation
181,700,000 kwh (1983)
kwh per capita: 3,225

Generating Capacity
50,558,700 kw (1984)

Nuclear Power Plants and Output
Three nuclear plants are in operation, 4 are under construction; 1,232 mwe nuclear generating capacity (on line by December 1981)

Crude Oil Production
2,200,000 metric tons; 16,100,000 barrels (1983)

Natural Gas Production
498,000 terjoules; 447,200,000,000 cubic feet (1983)

IVORY COAST
Republic of the Ivory Coast

Budget
Revenues
1985: $907,006,650
1984: $900,945,378
Expenditures
1985: $907,006,650
1984: $900,945,378
Deficit
0.02% of GDP (1982)

Expenditures by Function (1980)

General public services	21.26%
Defense	3.91%
Education	16.34%
Health	3.95%
Social security and welfare	3.05%
Housing and community amenities	1.26%
Other community and social services	1.38%
Economic services	13.41%
Agriculture, forestry, fishing and hunting	3.40%
Roads	1.99%
Other transportation and communication	4.26%
Other	7.95%

Economic Aid Extended
None

Economic Aid Received
Total: $2,700,000,000 (1970-82)
USA only: $340,000,000

External Public Debt
$4,824,200,000 (1983)
Service payments: 31.00% of exports of goods and services

Gross Domestic Product (GDP)
$7,600,000,000 (1982)
GDP per capita: $871

Gross Domestic Product by Sector (1979)

Agriculture, forestry, and fishing	27.24%
Mining	2.57%
Manufacturing	11.11%
Utilities	1.20%
Construction	8.21%
Commerce	20.77%
Transportation and communication	7.35%
Other	23.84%

International Liquidity
Reserves (minus gold): $5,400,000 (1985)
Gold reserves: 45,000 fine troy ounces

Consumer Price Change (Inflation)
1984: 4.30%
1982: 7.30%

Imports
Machinery, cement, wine, fuel, oils

Total Imports
1982: $1,850,000,000
1981: $2,700,000,000
1980: $2,615,000,000

Exports
Coffee, cocoa, wood, ore, palm oil, bananas

Total Exports
1982: $2,450,000,000
1981: $3,200,000,000
1980: $3,110,000,000

Trading Partners

Imports (1985)

France	34.00%
Nigeria	5.00%
USA	4.00%
Netherlands	4.00%
China	3.00%

Exports (1985)

France	18.00%
USA	16.00%
West Germany	9.00%
Italy	8.00%
Netherlands	7.00%

Tourists
Total: 194,101 (1980)

Balance of Payments
1983: -$1,004,900,000
1982: -$1,103,400,000
1981: -$1,659,900,000

Labor Profile (1965)

Agriculture, forestry, and fishing	86.48%
Manufacturing	.83%
Transportation and communication	2.26%
Trade	6.75%
Services	2.21%
Construction	0.89%
Other	0.58%

Agricultural Products
Yams, cassava, rice (paddy), coffee, bananas, pineapples, taro, maize, coconuts, cotton, rubber, corn

Industrial Products
Shoes and sandals, petroleum products, hydroelectric power, textiles and clothing, auto, truck, bus assembly

Natural Resources
Small deposits of diamonds and manganese, iron ore

Electric Power Generation
2,133,000,000 kwh
kwh per capita: 220

Generating Capacity
974,000 kw (1984)

Nuclear Power Plants and Output
None (1986)

Crude Oil Production
200,000 metric tons; 1,466,000 barrels (1981)

JAMAICA

Budget

Revenues
1983: $ 558,787,878
1982: $1,000,000,000

Expenditures
1983: $ 850,303,030
1982: $1,600,000,000

Deficit
13.64% of GDP (1983)

Expenditures by Function (1977)

General public services	13.20%
Defense	2.80%
Education	19.57%
Health	8.35%
Social security and welfare	3.51%
Housing and community amenities	6.22%
Other community and social services	3.13%

Economic services	24.27%
Agriculture, forestry, fishing and hunting	7.15%
Roads	3.96%
Other transportation and communication	2.70%
Other	25.37%

Economic Aid Extended
None

External Public Debt
$1,949,900,000 (1983)
Service payments: 14.90% of exports of goods and services

Gross National Product (GNP)
$1,634,800,000 (1984)
GNP per capita: $711

Gross Domestic Product (GDP)
$1,873,600,000 (1984)
GDP per capita: $815

Gross Domestic Product by Sector (1982)

Agriculture, forestry, and fishing	7.03%
Mining	5.94%
Manufacturing	1.63%
Utilities	1.69%
Construction	8.23%
Commerce	23.52%
Transportation and communication	5.73%
Other	31.52%

International Liquidity
Reserves (minus gold): $121,000,000 (1986)

Consumer Price Change (Inflation)
1985: 25.70%
1984: 27.80%
1983: 11.60%

Imports
Fuels, basic manufactures, foodstuffs, chemicals, machinery and transportation equipment

Total Imports
1985: $1,124,000,000
1984: $1,130,000,000
1983: $1,480,000,000

Exports
Alumina, bauxite, sugar, bananas, chemicals

Total Exports
1985: $549,000,000
1984: $714,000,000
1983: $713,000,000

Trading Partners

Imports (1984)

USA	41.85%
Netherlands Antilles	14.00%
Venezuela	10.92%
United Kingdom	5.38%
Canada	4.92%

Exports (1984)

USA	47.66%
Canada	13.52%
United Kingdom	12.13%
Trinidad and Tobago	4.04%
Norway	2.40%

Tourists
Total: 775,797 (1983)

Balance of Payments
1984: -$312,100,000
1983: -$358,600,000
1982: -$408,500,000

Labor Profile (1982)

Agriculture, forestry, and fishing	30.02%
Manufacturing	11.77%
Transportation and communication	4.42%
Trade	13.39%
Civil service	14.48%
Services	19.33%
Construction	4.97%
Other	1.62%

Agricultural Products
Sugar, bananas, coconuts, coffee, pimento, allspice

Industrial Products
Food sugar, rum, molasses, cement, textiles, metal, paper, chemical products

Natural Resources
Bauxite gypsum, limestone

Electric Power Generation
800,000,000 kwh
kwh per capita: 754

Generating Capacity
1,030,000 kw (1984)

Nuclear Power Plants and Output
None (1986)

Crude Oil Production
None (1986)

Natural Gas Production
None (1986)

JAPAN

Budget
Revenues
1985: $144,000,000,000
1984: $148,000,000,000
Expenditures
1985: $211,000,000,000
1984: $202,000,000,000
Deficit
10.69% of GDP (1985)

Economic Aid Extended
$31,500,000,000 (1970-83)

Economic Aid Received
None (1986)

External Public Debt
None (1986)

Gross National Product (GNP)
$1,189,597,610,000 (1984)
GNP per capita: $9,913

Gross Domestic Product (GDP)
$1,187,585,000 (1984)
GDP per capita: $9,891

Gross Domestic Product by Sector (1983)

Agriculture, forestry, and fishing	3.31%
Mining	0.40%
Manufacturing	30.49%
Utilities	3.27%
Construction	7.88%
Commerce	12.19%
Transportation and communication	6.49%
Other	35.48%

International Liquidity
Reserves (minus gold): $28,096,000,000 (1986)
Gold reserves: 24,230,000 fine troy ounces

Consumer Price Change (Inflation)
1985: 2.00%
1984: 2.23%
1983: 1.80%

Imports
Metal ores, fuels, chemicals, machine equipment, foodstuffs

Total Imports
1985: $130,488,000,000
1984: $136,176,000,000
1983: $126,437,000,000

Exports
Machinery, textiles, iron and steel, optical instruments, ships, motor vehicles

Total Exports
1985: $177,164,000,000
1984: $169,700,000,000
1983: $146,900,000,000

Trading Partners
Imports (1984)

USA	38.97%
Saudi Arabia	10.80%
Indonesia	8.16%
United Arab Emirates	5.66%
Australia	5.29%

Exports (1984)

USA	35.59%
South Korea	4.24%
China	4.18%
West Germany	3.88%
Hong Kong	3.80%

Tourists
Total: 2,000,000
Revenue: $825,000,000 (1983)

Balance of Payments
1984: $35,000,000,000
1983: $20,700,000,000
1982: $ 6,850,000.000

Labor Profile (1983)

Agriculture, forestry, and fishing	8.23%
Manufacturing	24.43%
Transportation and communication	6.11%
Construction	9.42%
Other	51.81%

Agricultural Products
Rice, wheat, barley, vegetables, fruits

Industrial Products
Machinery and equipment, metals, ships, autos, textiles, electronics

Natural Resources
Negligible mineral resources, fish

Electric Power Generation
609,000,000 kwh (1984)
kwh per capita: 5,075

Generating Capacity
168,700,000 kw (1984)

Nuclear Power Plants and Output
31 power plants; total output, 21,751 mwe (1984)

Crude Oil Production
528,000 metric tons; 3,870,000 barrels (1984)

Natural Gas Production
98,544 terajoules; 88,492,512,000 cubic feet (1985)

JORDAN
Hashemite Kingdom of Jordan

Budget
Revenues
1984: $1,080,000,000
Expenditures
1984: $1,640,000,000

External Public Debt
$2,276,000,000 (1981)

Gross National Product (GNP)
$4,650,000,000 (1984)
GNP per capita: $1,126

Gross Domestic Product by Sector

Agriculture	6.70%
Mining	3.50%
Manufacturing	14.10%
Utilities	1.60%
Construction	8.50%
Commerce	15.40%
Transportation and communication	10.80%
Other	39.20%

Consumer Price Change (Inflation)
1984: 4.70%

Imports
Machinery, transportation equipment, cereals, petroleum products

Total Imports
1984: $2,400,000,000

Exports
Fruits, vegetables, phosphates

Total Exports
1984: $717,000,000

Trading Partners
Imports (1983)

China	16.20%
Saudi Arabia	16.10%
USA	9.60%
West Germany	6.00%
United Kingdom	5.20%

Exports (1983)

Syria	16.40%
Saudi Arabia	14.90%
Iraq	11.40%
Romania	3.80%
United Kingdom	0.50%

Tourists
Total: 2,075,502 (1982)

Balance of Payments
1983: -$390,700,000

Labor Profile (1976)
Agriculture 20%
Industry 20%
Trade and services 60%

Agricultural Products
Wheat, fruits, vegetables, olive oil

Industrial Products
Phosphates, petroleum refining, cement production

Natural Resources
Phosphate, potash

Electric Power Generation
1,518,000,000 kwh
467 kwh per capita

Generating Capacity
577,600 kw

Nuclear Power Plants and Output
None

Crude Oil Production
None

Natural Gas Production
None

KAMPUCHEA
Democratic Kampuchea

Economic Aid Received
Total: $936,000,000
USA only: $227,000,000

Gross National Product (GNP)
$570,000,000 (1978)
GNP per capita: $70

Gross Domestic Product by Sector (1966)
Agriculture, forestry, and fishing 40.90%
Mining, manufacturing, utilities and construction 16.90%
Commerce, transportation and communication, other 42.20%

Imports
Foodstuffs, fuels, machinery, textiles, pharmaceuticals and chemicals

Total Imports
1983: $30,000,000

Exports
Rice, natural rubber, pepper, wood

Total Exports
1983: $10,000,000

Labor Profile (1975)
Agriculture, forestry, and fishing 78.20%
Manufacturing 4.20%
Other 18.00%

Agricultural Products
Rice, corn, sugar palm, rubber, sugar cane

Industrial Products
Cement, paper, plywood, textiles

Natural Resources
Undeveloped deposits of phosphate, iron ore and limestone

Electric Power Generation
144,000,000 kwh (1982)
kwh per capita: 23

Generating Capacity
120,000 kw (1979)

Nuclear Power Plants and Output
None

Crude Oil Production
None

Natural Gas Production
None

KENYA

Republic of Kenya

Budget

Revenues

1984: $1,136,560,000

1983: $1,146,423,358

Expenditures

1984: $1,354,076,000

1983: $1,294,452,555

Deficit

3.98% of GDP (1984)

Expenditures by Function (1983)

General public services	13.06%
Defense	13.56%
Education	20.60%
Health	7.03%
Social security and welfare	0.13%
Housing and community amenities	0.54%
Other community and social services	3.15%
Economic services	26.62%
Agriculture, forestry, fishing and hunting	10.05%
Roads	6.53%
Other transportation and communication	0.37%
Other	16.58%

Economic Aid Extended

None

Economic Aid Received

Total: $49,000,000 (1954-83)

External Public Debt

$2,387,000,000 (1983)

Service payments: 21.50% of exports of goods and services

Gross National Product (GNP)

$5,276,942,675 (1984)

GNP per capita: $336

Gross Domestic Product (GDP)

$5,470,127,389 (1984)

GDP per capita: $281

Gross Domestic Product by Sector (1984)

Agriculture, forestry, and fishing	26.73%
Mining	1.90%
Manufacturing	10.74%
Utilities	1.53%
Construction	5.37%
Commerce	11.27%
Transportation and communication	5.10%
Other	39.03%

International Liquidity

Reserves (minus gold): $357,900,000 (1986)

Gold reserves: 80,000 fine troy ounces

Consumer Price Change (Inflation)

1984: 10.20%

1983: 11.50%

1982: 20.40%

Imports

Crude oil, industrial machinery, motor vehicles, iron and steel, fertilizers, pharmaceuticals, paper, food, live animals, beverages and tobacco

Total Imports

1984: $1,529,000,000

1983: $1,357,000,000

1982: $1,673,000,000

Exports

Coffee, tea, petroleum, sisal, hides and skins, pyrethrum, cement, fruit and vegetables and soda ash

Total Exports

1984: $1,084,000,000

1983: $ 983,000,000

1982: $1,045,000,000

Trading Partners

Imports (1984)

United Kingdom	15.36%
Saudi Arabia	12.62%
Japan	9.83%
West Germany	7.62%
United Arab Emirates	6.96%

Exports (1984)

United Kingdom	20.37%
West Germany	11.49%
Uganda	8.55%
Pakistan	5.70%
USA	5.13%

Tourists

Total: 339,000

Revenue: $8,133,333 (1983)

Country of origin

West Germany	18.58%
United Kingdom	12.39%
USA and Canada	11.50%

Balance of Payments

1984: -$138,400,000
1983: -$120,900,000
1982: -$518,000,000

Labor Profile (1982)

Agriculture, forestry, and fishing	21.53%
Manufacturing	14.16%
Transportation and communication	5.11%
Trade	7.22%
Civil service	40.26%
Services	4.23%
Construction	5.78%
Other	1.71%

Agricultural Products

Corn, wheat, rice, sugarcane, coffee, tea, sisal, pyrethrum, pineapple, wattle

Industrial Products

Petroleum products, cement, beverages

Natural Resources

Wildlife, land

Electric Power Generation

1,686,000,000 kwh
kwh per capita: 87

Generating Capacity

550,000 kw (1984)

Nuclear Power Plants and Output

None (1986)

Crude Oil Production

None (1986)

Natural Gas Production

None (1986)

KIRIBATI

Budget

Revenues

1982: $17,610,000

Expenditures

1982: $18,820,000

Economic Aid Received

Western (non-USA): $46,000,000 (1979)

Gross Domestic Product (GDP)

$36,000,000 (1979)
GDP per capita: $630

Gross Domestic Product by Sector (1978)

Agriculture	18.50%
Mining	42.60%
Manufacturing	1.70%
Utilities	1.50%
Construction	7.80%
Commerce	6.10%
Transportation	2.50%

Imports

Foodstuffs, fuel

Total Imports

1979: $15,000,000

Exports

Phosphate, copra

Total Exports

1979: $20,000,000

Agricultural Products

Coconuts, breadfruit, pandanus, bananas, paw paw

Industrial Products

Copra

Natural Resources

Fish, phosphate rock

Electric Power Generation
6,000,000 kwh (1981)
kwh per capita: 102

Generating Capacity
2,000 kw

Nuclear Power Plants and Output
None

Crude Oil Production
None

Natural Gas Production
None

KOREA, NORTH
Democratic People's Republic of Korea

Budget
Revenues
1985: $13,040,000,000
1984: $12,526,000,000
Expenditures
1985: $13,040,000,000
1984: $12,456,000,000

Economic Aid Received
USA only: None (1986)

Gross National Product (GNP)
$16,900,000,000 (1984)
GNP per capita: $998

Imports
Machinery and equipment, fuel

Total Imports
1983: $1,500,000,000
1982: $1,000,000,000
1981: $1,645,000,000

Exports
Machinery and equipment, iron, steel and other metals, mineral ores

Total Exports
1983: $1,400,000,000
1982: $ 725,100,000
1981: $1,410,000,000

Trading Partners
Imports (1982)
Japan 34.40%
China 30.60%

Exports (1982)
China 37.70%
West Germany 19.00%
Japan 18.90%

Labor Profile (1970)
Agriculture, forestry, and fishing 54.60%
Manufacturing 27.60%
Other 17.80%

Agricultural Products
Rice, corn, vegetables

Industrial Products
Machines, electric power, chemicals, minerals, metals, textiles

Natural Resources
Coal, iron ore, graphite, zinc, lead, copper, manganese, cobalt

Electric Power Generation
35,500,000,000 kwh (1984)
kwh per capita: 1,810

Generating Capacity
6,500,000 kw (1984)

Nuclear Power Plants and Output
None (1986)

Crude Oil Production
None (1986)

Natural Gas Production
None (1986)

KOREA, SOUTH
Republic of Korea

Budget
Revenues
1983: $14,500,000,000

Expenditures
1983: $13,430,000,000

Economic Aid Received
Total: $19,300,000,000

External Public Debt
$42,000,000,000 (1984)

Gross National Product (GNP)
$79,980,000,000 (1984)
GNP per capita: $1,880

Gross Domestic Product (GDP)
$81,060,000,000 (1984)
GDP per capita: $1,930

Gross Domestic Product by Sector (1983)

Agriculture, forestry, and fishing,	13.90%
Mining	1.40%
Manufacturing	27.20%
Utilities	2.10%
Construction	8.40%
Commerce	14.20%
Transportation and communication	8.50%
Other	24.10%

Consumer Price Change (Inflation)
1984: 3.10%

Imports
Petroleum and petroleum products, machinery, wood, organic chemicals, iron and steel, grain

Total Imports
1984: $27,660,000,000

Exports
Textiles, electrical machinery, transportation equipment, footwear, fish

Total Exports
1984: $28,490,000,000

Trading Partners

Imports (1984)

Japan	24.80%
USA	22.50%
Saudi Arabia	4.80%
Australia	3.50%
Malaysia	3.40%

Exports (1984)

USA	34.90%
Japan	15.30%
Hong Kong	4.20%
Saudi Arabia	3.40%
India	3.40%

Tourists
Total: 1,300,000 (1984)
Revenue: $460,000,000 (1981)

Balance of Payments
1983: -$1,607,000,000

Labor Profile (1983)

Agriculture, forestry, and fishing	29.70%
Mining and manufacturing	23.30%
Construction	5.60%
Trade	22.30%
Services	11.50%
Other	7.60%

Agricultural Products
Rice, barley, wheat

Industrial Products
Textiles, clothing, food processing, chemical fertilizers, chemicals, plywood, coal, electronics, steel

Natural Resources
Anthracite coal, tungsten, iron ore, lead, amorphous graphite, silver, zinc

Electric Power Generation
5,300,000 kwh (1984)
kwh per capita: 1,261

Generating Capacity
13,970,000 kw (1985)

Nuclear Power Plants and Output
Three reactors in operation (near Pusan), 6 under construction; nuclear generating capacity (installed as of December 1984) 1,790 mwe

Crude Oil Production
None

Natural Gas Production
None

KUWAIT
State of Kuwait

Budget
Revenues
1982/83: $14,900,000,000
Expenditures
1982/83: $11,100,000,000

Economic Aid Extended
$3,550,000,000 (1960-76)

Gross Domestic Product (GDP)
$21,140,000,000 (1983)
GDP per capita: $25,850

Gross Domestic Product by Sector (1983)

Extractive industries	49.70%
Agriculture and fishing	0.54%
Manufacturing	6.40%
Utilities	0.50%
Construction	4.60%
Commerce	8.50%
Transportation and communication	3.10%
Other	26.40%

Consumer Price Change (Inflation)
1983: 4.70%

Imports
Foodstuffs, automobiles, building materials, machinery, textiles

Total Imports
1983: $8,270,000,000

Exports
Crude and refined petroleum, shrimp

Total Exports
1983: $11,760,000,000

Trading Partners
Imports (1981)

Japan	23.20%
USA	14.30%
West Germany	12.30%
United Kingdom	8.00%
Italy	5.90%
France	3.50%

Exports (1981)

Japan	22.20%
Taiwan	11.60%
South Korea	8.20%
Netherlands	6.70%
United Kingdom	4.30%
Singapore	3.60%

Balance of Payments
1982: $5,780,000,000

Labor Profile (1980)

Agriculture and fishing	1.80%
Extractive industries	1.30%
Manufacturing	8.40%
Utilities	1.60%
Construction	20.00%
Commerce	12.10%
Transportation and communication	6.20%
Business services	2.60%

Agricultural Products
Fruit and vegetables

Industrial Products
Oil industry

Natural Resources
Crude oil and natural gas

Electric Power Generation
10,385,000,000 kwh (1982)
kwh per capita: 6,684

Generating Capacity
3,387,300 kw (1984)

Nuclear Power Plants and Output
None

Crude Oil Production
52.78 metric tons, 386,900,000 barrels

Natural Gas Production
75.204 terajoules; 67,000,000,000 cubic feet (1982)

LAOS
Lao People's Democratic Republic

Budget
Revenues
1981: $26,600,000
Expenditures
1981: $61,700,000

Economic Aid Received
Total: $665,000,000
USA only: $272,300,000

Gross National Product (GNP)
$525,000,000 (1983)
GNP per capita: $144

Imports
Foodstuffs, petroleum, manufactured foods

Total Imports
1983: $125,000,000

Exports
Timber

Total Exports
1983: $52,000,000

Trading Partners

Imports (1984)

Thailand	48.00%
Singapore	14.30%
Japan	5.70%
United Kingdom	2.20%
Vietnam	1.60%

Exports (1984)

China	43.10%
USA	17.70%
Thailand	7.90%
Iran	5.70%
United Kingdom	2.90%

Labor Profile (1975)

Agriculture	79%
Industry	5%
Services	16%

Agricultural Products
Rice, corn, coffee, cotton, tea, tobacco

Industrial Products
Light consumer goods

Natural Resources
Tin, iron ore, gold, copper, manganese

Electric Power Generation
900,000,000 kwh (1984)
kwh per capita: 240

Generating Capacity
175,000 kw

Nuclear Power Plants and Output
None

LEBANON
Republic of Lebanon

Budget
Revenues
$500,000,000
Expenditures
$1,300,000,000

Economic Aid Extended
None

External Public Debt
$350,000,000 (1982)

Gross National Product (GNP)
$3,000,000,000 (1973)
GNP per capita: $1,163

Gross Domestic Product (GDP)
$4,200,000,000 (1982)
GDP per capita: $1,590

Gross Domestic Product by Sector (1977)

Agriculture and livestock	8.50%
Energy and water	5.40%
Industry	13.00%
Construction	3.40%
Transportation and communication	7.70%
Services	23.40%
Commerce	28.30%
Administration	10.20%

Consumer Price Change (Inflation)
1984: -2.40%

Imports
Precious stones and metals, textiles, foodstuffs, machinery

Total Imports
1983: $3,300,000,000

Exports
Fruit, coins, wool, vegetables

Total Exports
1983: $690,000,000

Trading Partners

Imports

Italy	15.30%
USA	10.80%
France	9.20%
Romania	7.40%
West Germany	6.40%

Exports

Saudi Arabia	28.80%
Kuwait	8.40%
United Arab Emirates	5.90%
Egypt	4.80%
Switzerland	4.40%

Tourists
Total: 3,008,391 (1974)

Agricultural Products
Citrus fruits, sugar beets, apples, grapes, potatoes, grain, olives

Industrial Products
Timber, tobacco manufactures, electricity, cement, petroleum

Natural Resources
Small deposits of bitumen, iron ore, lime, salt

Electric Power Generation
1,212,000,000 kwh (1984)
kwh per capita: 465

Generating Capacity
922,000 kw

Nuclear Power Plants and Output
None

Crude Oil Production
None

Natural Gas Production
None

LESOTHO
Kingdom of Lesotho

Budget

Revenues
1984: $160,000,000
1983: $269,200,000

Expenditures
1984: $200,000,000
1983: $269,200,000

Deficit
None (1983)

Expenditures by Function (1983)

General public services	27.00%
Education	17.40%
Health	7.20%
Social security and welfare	1.00%
Housing and community amenities	0.20%
Other community and social services	0.40%
Economic services	29.20%
Agriculture, forestry, fishing and hunting	8.20%
Roads	7.30%
Other transportation and communication	6.70%
Other	10.30%

Economic Aid Extended
None

External Public Debt
$145,200,000 (1983)
Service payments: 2.50% of exports of goods and services

Gross National Product (GNP)
$640,000,000 (1982)
GNP per capita: $455

Gross Domestic Product (GDP)
$345,280,000 (1983)
GDP per capita: $240

Gross Domestic Product by Sector (1981)

Agriculture, forestry, and fishing	19.20%
Mining	4.50%
Manufacturing	5.20%
Utilities	0.40%
Construction	9.10%
Transportation and communication	1.30%
Commerce	11.40%
Other	49.00%

International Liquidity
Reserves (minus gold): $48,580,000 (1984)

Consumer Price Change (Inflation)
1984: 16.90%
1983: 21.20%
1982: 11.00%

Imports
Foodstuffs, clothing, machinery and transportation equipment, petroleum products, chemicals

Total Imports
1984: $345,000,000
1983: $484,000,000
1982: $486,000,000

Exports
Wool, mohair, diamonds, live animals

Total Exports
1984: $20,150,000
1983: $26,520,000
1983: $35,154,000

Trading Partners

Imports (1979)

South African Customs Union	97.40%
EEC	1.70%
Other	0.80%

Exports (1979)

South African Customs Union	33.30%
EEC	9.50%
Other European	5.60%
Other	0.80%

Tourists
Total: 150,000 (1980)

Balance of Payments
1984: +$31,000,000
1983: -$ 8,000,000
1982: -$37,000,000

Labor Profile (1981)

Agriculture and forestry	37.40%
Mining	3.50%
Manufacturing	12.10%
Utilities	1.60%
Construction	11.10%
Distribution	8.20%
Transportation and storage	5.10%
Finance	1.90%
Social services	18.90%
Other	3.60%

Agricultural Products
Mohair, corn, wheat, sorghum, peas, beans, potatoes, asparagus

Industrial Products
Carpet weaving, woolen apparel, candlemaking, pottery, tapestry

Natural Resources
Diamonds, water

Electric Power Generation
1,000,000 kwh
kwh per capita: 6

Generating Capacity
2,000 kw (1984)

Nuclear Power Plants and Output
None (1985)

Crude Oil Production
None (1985)

Natural Gas Production
None (1985)

LIBERIA
Republic of Liberia

Budget
Revenues
1985: $315,000,000
1984: $306,000,000
Expenditures
1985: $371,000,000
1984: $213,000,000
Deficit
11% of GDP (1982)

Expenditures by Function (1984)

General public services	19.50%
Defense	7.70%
Education	14.70%
Health	6.40%
Social security and welfare	.80%
Housing and community amenities	0.70%
Other community and social services	2.70%
Economic services	27.00%
Agriculture, forestry, fishing and hunting	5.70%
Roads	7.70%
Other transportation and communication	1.10%
Other	21.50%

Economic Aid Extended
None

Economic Aid Received
Total: $854,800,000 (1970-83)
USA only: $377,000,000

External Public Debt
$699,100,000 (1983)
Service payments: 6.60% of exports of goods and services

Gross National Product (GNP)
$1,885,000,000 (1982)
GNP per capita: $845

Gross Domestic Product (GDP)
$1,060,000,000 (1982)
GDP per capita: $492

Gross Domestic Product by Sector (1981)

Agriculture, forestry, and fishing	13.50%
Mining	15.00%
Manufacturing	7.80%
Utilities	2.20%
Construction	3.40%
Transportation and communication	6.50%
Commerce	8.50%
Other	42.80%

International Liquidity
Reserves (minus gold): $3,480,000 (1984)

Consumer Price Change (Inflation)
1984: 1.20%
1983: 2.70%
1982: 6.00%

Imports
Machinery, transportation equipment, foodstuffs, manufactured goods

Total Imports
1984: $335,180,000
1983: $374,690,000
1982: $371,910,000

Exports
Iron ore, diamonds, rubber, coffee, palm kernels, cocoa

Total Exports
1984: $452,120,000
1983: $427,600,000
1982: $477,440,000

Trading Partners
Imports (1984)

Singapore	13.80%
South Korea	12.60%
Spain	10.30%
West Germany	8.30%
Norway	7.40%

Exports (1984)

West Germany	19.80%
USA	12.60%
South Korea	12.30%
Italy	11.70%
Japan	10.60%

Tourists
Total: 6,000 (1976)

Balance of Payments
1984: -$ 77,000,000
1983: -$136,000,000
1982: -$ 67,000,000

Labor Profile (1980)

Agriculture, forestry, fishing and hunting	71.60%
Manufacturing	1.30%
Transportation and communication	1.40%
Trade	3.80%
Services	5.80%
Construction	0.90%
Other	15.20%

Agricultural Products
Rubber, palm kernels, coffee, rice, casava

Industrial Products
Iron ore, rubber, frozen fish

Natural Resources
Iron ore, rubber, timber, diamonds

Electric Power Generation
1,134,000,000 kwh
kwh per capita: 525

Generating Capacity
370,000 kw (1984)

Nuclear Power Plants and Output
None

Crude Oil Production
None (1985)

Natural Gas Production
None (1985)

LIBYA
Socialist People's Libyan Arab Jamahiriya

Budget
Revenues
1984: $10,500,000,000
1983: $140,000,000,000
Expenditures
1984: $16,400,000,000
1983: $19,200,000,000
Deficit
21.93% of GDP (1984)

Economic Aid Extended
None

Economic Aid Received
USA only: $212,000,000 (1946-83)

Gross Domestic Product (GDP)
$26,900,000,000 (1984)
GDP per capita: $7,175

Gross Domestic Product by Sector

Agriculture, forestry, and fishing	2.45%
Mining	48.21%
Manufacturing	3.44%
Utilities	0.78%
Construction	11.91%
Commerce	5.91%
Transportation and communication	4.37%
Other	22.89%

International Liquidity
Reserves (minus gold): $6,075,000 (1986)
Gold reserves: 3,600,000 fine troy ounces

Consumer Price Change (Inflation)
1983: 9.00%
1982: 6.00%
1981: 4.00%

Imports
Machinery, manufactured goods, foodstuffs

Total Imports
1984: $6,732,000,000
1983: $7,392,000,000
1982: $7,175,000,000

Exports
Crude petroleum, groundnuts, leather hides

Total Exports
1985: $10,929,000,000
1984: $11,140,000,000
1983: $11,089,000,000

Trading Partners
Imports (1984)

Italy	26.47%
West Germany	13.01%
Japan	16.69%
United Kingdom	5.31%
Spain	4.31%

Exports (1984)

Italy	22.72%
West Germany	17.27%
Spain	8.81%
France	6.84%
Turkey	5.95%

Tourists
Total: 126,000 (1980)

Balance of Payments
1982: -$ 72,700,000
1981: -$ 88,700,000
1980: -$206,700,000

Labor Profile (1978)

Agriculture, forestry, and fishing	19.14%
Manufacturing	6.10%
Transportation and communication	8.79%
Trade	6.21%
Civil services	24.71%
Services	1.16%
Construction	2.12%
Other	31.07%

Agricultural Products
Cereals, dates, olives, peanuts, citrus fruits, livestock

Industrial Products
Crude petroleum, processed foods, textiles

Natural Resources
Petroleum, naturalgas

Electric Power Generation
11,870,000,000 kwh
kwh per capita: 3,170

Generating Capacity
3,872,600 kw (1984)

Nuclear Power Plants and Output
None

Crude Oil Production
65,748,000 metric tons; 481,932,840 barrels (1984)

Natural Gas Production
None (1986)

LIECHTENSTEIN
Principality of Liechtenstein

Budget
Revenues
1985: $126,827,000
1984: $ 94,690,800
Expenditures
1985: $102,859,000
1984: $ 76,440,000

Economic Aid Extended
None (1986)

Economic Aid Received
Total: $14,400,000
USA only: None (1980-83)

External Public Debt
None (1986)

Gross National Product
$400,200,000 (1984)
GNP per capita: $15,000

Imports
Raw materials, machinery, processed foods and goods

Total Imports
1984: $66,000,000

Exports
Metal manufactures, machines and instruments, textiles, chemical products, furniture

Total Exports
1984: $440,000,000
1983: $512,287,396
1981: $441,000,000

Trading Partners
Exports (1984)

EC	39.00%
EFTA	32.00%
Switzerland	24.00%

Tourists
Total: 83,589 (1984)
Country of origin

West Germany	27.10%
Switzerland	22.40%

Labor Profile

Agriculture, forestry, and fishing	2.97%
Manufacturing and construction	44.14%
Other	52.89%

Agricultural Products
Livestock, vegetables, corn, wheat, potatoes, grapes

Industrial Products
Light industries including textiles, ceramics, steel screws, precision instruments, pharmaceutical products

Natural Resources
Timber, hydroelectric power, some quarrying

Electric Power Generation
150,000,000 kwh (1985)
kwh per capita: 5.35

Generating Capacity
23,000 kwh (1985)

Nuclear Power Plants and Output
None (1986)

Crude Oil Production
None (1986)

Natural Gas Production
None (1986)

LUXEMBOURG
Grand Duchy of Luxembourg

Budget
Revenues
1984: $1,180,000,000
1983: $1,220,000,000
Expenditures
1984: $1,170,000,000
1983: $1,340,000,000
Deficit
0.40% of GDP (1983)

Expenditures by Function (1983)

General public services	10.00%
Defense	0.30%
Education	5.07%
Health	6.86%
Social security and welfare	4.66%
Housing and community amenities	5.64%
Other community and social services	7.69%
Economic services	61.53%
Agriculture, forestry, fishing and hunting	3.07%
Roads	23.53%
Other transportation and communication	5.84%
Other	3.07%

Economic Aid Extended
None (1986)

Gross National Product (GNP)
$4,200,000,000 (1983)
GNP per capita: $11,350

Gross Domestic Product (GDP)
$3,438,849,000 (1983)
GDP per capita: $7,867

Gross Domestic Product by Sector (1982)

Agriculture, forestry, and fishing	3.41%
Mining and manufacturing	28.74%
Utilities	2.81%
Construction	6.37%

Commerce	17.41%
Transportation and communication	4.80%
Other	36.46%

International Liquidity
Reserves (minus gold): $13,960,000 (1986)
Gold reserves: 429,000 fine troy ounces

Consumer Price Change (Inflation)
1985: 4.10%
1984: 5.60%
1983: 8.70%

Imports
Coal, machinery, textiles, transportation equipment, plastics

Total Imports
1984: $2,446,043,165
1983: $2,659,574,446
1982: $2,921,052,632

Exports
Iron and steel products

Total Exports
1984: $2,005,395,683
1983: $2,170,212,766
1982: $2,328,947,368

Tourists
Total: 420,674 (1984)

Labor Profile (1984)

Agriculture, forestry, and fishing	4.81%
Manufacturing	25.75%
Transportation and communication	6.77%
Construction	9.87%
Other	52.80%

Agricultural Products
Barley, potatoes, oats, wheat, wine grapes, rye, cattle, horses

Industrial Products
Pig iron, steel ingots and castings, chemicals, rubber, fertilizer, food processing

Natural Resources
Iron ore, slate

Electric Power Generation
956,000,000 kwh (1985)
kwh per capita: 2,605

Generating Capacity
1,497,000 kw (1985)

Nuclear Power Plants and Output
None (1986)

Crude Oil Production
None (1986)

Natural Gas Production
None (1986)

MACAO

Budget
Revenues
1983: $128,125,000
1982: $140,400,000
Expenditures
1983: $128,125,000
1982: $140,400,000
Deficit
None (1983)

Economic Aid Extended
None

Gross National Product (GNP)
$640,000,000 (1980)
GNP per capita: $2,560

Imports
Tobacco, pigs, fresh and dried fruit, plastic materials, cotton fabrics, fuel oil, casting, soft iron and steel

Total Imports
1983: $722,400,000
1982: $731,400,000
1981: $705,500,000

Exports
Clothing, knitwear, leather manufactures

Total Exports
1983: $755,900,000
1982: $737,700,000
1981: $686,900,000

Trading Partners
Imports (1983)

Hong Kong	38.88%
China	27.77%
Japan	9.38%
USA	6.70%
United Kingdom	1.87%

Exports (1983)

South Africa	26.54%
Hong Kong	21.94%
West Germany	11.80%
France	10.47%
United Kingdom	6.23%

Tourists
Total: 4,000,000 (1983)

Labor Profile (1960)

Agriculture	5%
Manufacturing	30%
Transportation and communication	8%
Trade	27%
Services	26%
Construction	3%
Other	1%

Agricultural Products
Rice and vegetables (there are food shortages and most foodstuffs are imported)

Industrial Products
Textiles, fishing, fireworks

Natural Resources
Fish

Electric Power Generation
330,000,000 kwh
kwh per capita: 870

Generating Capacity
123,000 kw (1984)

Nuclear Power Plants and Output
None (1986)

Crude Oil Production
None (1986)

Natural Gas Production
None (1986)

MADAGASCAR
Democratic Republic of Madagascar

Budget
Revenues
1981: $310,000,000
Expenditures
1981: $372,000,000

Economic Aid Received
Total: $350,000,000 (through 1980)
USA only: $19,000,000

External Public Debt
$718,800,000 (1981)
Service payments: 3.90% of exports of goods and services

Gross National Product (GNP)
$2,900,000,000 (1979)
GNP per capita: $341

Gross Domestic Product by Sector (1980)

Agriculture, forestry, and fishing	32.49%
Mining, manufacturing, utilities, and construction	18.54%
Commerce, transportation and communication	48.80%

Consumer Price Change (Inflation)
1982: 34.40%

Imports
Machinery and electrical equipment, crude oil, chemical products

Total Imports
1981: $545,000,000

Exports
Coffee, cloves and clove oil, vanilla

Total Exports
1981: $317,000,000

Trading Partners

Imports (1981)

France	38.50%
West Germany	20.20%
Italy	4.70%
USA	4.10%
Netherlands	3.20%

Exports (1981)

France	20.70%
USA	11.90%
Japan	9.10%
West Germany	6.50%
Netherlands	3.40%

Tourists

Total: 13,000 (1980)
Revenue: $5,000,000 (1980)

Balance of Payments

1979: -$197,000,000
1978: -$ 67,000,000
1977: -$ 65,000,000

Labor Profile

Agriculture	26%
Domestic service	17%
Industry	15%
Commerce	14%
Construction	11%
Services	9%
Transportation	6%
Miscellaneous	2%

Agricultural Products

Rice, livestock, coffee, vanilla, sugar, cloves, cotton, peanuts, tobacco

Industrial Products

Processed food, textiles, mining paper, refined petroleum products

Natural Resources

Graphite, chrome, coal, bauxite, ilmenite, semiprecious stones

Electric Power Generation

700,000,000 kwh (1983)
kwh per capita: 75

Nuclear Power Plants and Output

None

Crude Oil Production

None

Natural Gas Production

None

MALAWI

Republic of Malawi

Budget

Revenues

1984: $186,228,000
1983: $291,300,000

Expenditures

1984: $283,832,000
1983: $328,500,000

Deficit

9.19% of GDP (1983)

Expenditures by Function (1983)

General public services	18.79%
Defense	6.26%
Education	13.49%
Health	6.74%
Social security and welfare	1.30%
Housing and community amenities	0.01%
Other community and social services	0.72%
Economic services	35.18%
Agriculture, forestry, fishing and hunting	16.14%
Roads	6.74%
Other transportation and communication	5.30%
Other	14.21%

Economic Aid Extended

None

Economic Aid Received

Total: $1,160,000,000 (1970-82)
USA only: $45,000,000 (1970-83)

External Public Debt

$718,600,000 (1983)
Service payments: 20.30% of exports of goods and services (1982)

Gross National Product (GNP)
$1,025,000,000 (1985)
GNP per capita: $971

Gross Domestic Product (GDP)
$1,077,245,000 (1985)
GDP per capita: $1,020

Gross Domestic Product by Sector (1983)

Agriculture, forestry, and fishing	37.54%
Mining	0.00%
Manufacturing	12.69%
Utilities	2.06%
Construction	4.08%
Commerce	13.29%
Transportation and communication	5.81%
Other	24.64%

International Liquidity
Reserves (minus gold): $39,510,000 (1986)
Gold reserves: 13,000 fine troy ounces

Consumer Price Change (Inflation)
1984: 20.00%
1983: 13.50%
1982: 9.80%

Imports
Fuel, vehicles, garments, agricultural machinery

Total Imports
1984: $214,743,500
1983: $273,500,000
1982: $257,272,000

Exports
Tobacco, tea, sugar, peanuts

Total Exports
1984: $285,897,000
1983: $203,500,000
1982: $233,636,000

Trading Partners

Imports (1984)

United Kingdom	21.33%
Zimbabwe	11.74%
Japan	9.11%
Zambia	7.59%
West Germany	5.69%

Exports (1984)

United Kingdom	31.59%
USA	11.71%
France	8.33%
Netherlands	5.95%
Zimbabwe	5.55%

Tourists
Total: 52,569
Revenue: $10,000,000 (1982)

Balance of Payments
1982: -$ 72,700,000
1981: -$ 88,700,000
1980: -$206,700,000

Labor Profile (1979)

Agriculture, forestry, and fishing	50.76%
Manufacturing	10.91%
Transportation and communication	5.22%
Trade	6.19%
Civil service	13.85%
Services	2.39%
Construction	9.53%
Other	1.15%

Agricultural Products
Tobacco, tea, sugar, peanuts, cotton

Industrial Products
Food, beverages, tobacco, clothing, textiles

Natural Resources
Limestone

Electric Power Generation
458,000,000 kwh
kwh per capita: 67

Generating Capacity
175,000 kw (1984)

Nuclear Power Plants and Output
None (1986)

Crude Oil Production
None (1986)

Natural Gas Production
None (1986)

MALAYSIA

Budget

Revenues
1984: $8,668,750,000
1983: $8,090,434,000

Expenditures
1984: $10,035,416,670
1983: $10,506,956,520

Deficit
4.20% of GDP (1984)

Expenditures by Function (1981)

General public services	4.50%
Defense	15.00%
Education	15.90%
Health	4.40%
Social security and welfare	4.00%
Housing and community amenities	6.50%
Other community and social services	1.20%
Economic services	29.00%
Agriculture, forestry, fishing and hunting	8.20%
Roads	4.50%
Other transportation and communication	7.50%
Other	21.40%

Economic Aid Extended
None

Economic Aid Received
USA only: $22,300,000 (1974)

External Public Debt
$10,665,200 (1983)
Service payments: 5.90% of exports of goods and services

Gross National Product (GNP)
$29,706,250,000 (1984)
GNP per capita: $1,980

Gross Domestic Product (GDP)
$31,875,000,000 (1984)
GDP per capita: $2,125

Gross Domestic Product by Sector (1983)

Agriculture, forestry, and fishing	22.00%
Mining	4.40%
Manufacturing	18.00%
Utilities	2.50%
Construction	5.30%
Transportation and communication	7.80%
Commerce	13.50%
Other	26.40%

International Liquidity
Reserves (minus gold): $3,723,000,000 (1984)
Gold reserves: 2,330,000 fine troy ounces

Consumer Price Change (Inflation)
1984: 4.40%
1983: 11.30%
1982: 11.00%

Imports
Machinery and transportation equipment, manufactures, food, beverages, tobacco

Total Imports
1984: $14,051,000,000
1983: $13,262,000,000
1982: $12,418,000,000

Exports
Crude oil, manufactures, rubber, palm oil, sawlogs, tin

Total Exports
1984: $16,484,000,000
1983: $14,104,000,000
1982: $12,030,000,000

Trading Partners

Imports (1984)

Japan	26.40%
USA	16.40%
Singapore	14.20%
West Germany	4.10%
Australia	3.90%

Exports (1984)

Japan	22.40%
Singapore	20.60%
USA	13.30%
South Korea	4.80%
Netherlands	3.60%

Tourists
Total: 2,093,101
Revenue: $443,478,260

Balance of Payments
1984: $1,696,000,000
1983: $3,379,000,000
1982: $3,601,000,000

Labor Profile (1985)

Agriculture, forestry, and fishing	35.50%
Manufacturing	15.70%
Transportation and communication	4.90%
Civil service	16.10%
Trade and services	13.90%
Construction	6.90%
Other	7.00%

Agricultural Products
Rubber, palm oil, timber, cocoa, rice, pepper

Industrial Products
Steel, automobiles, electronics

Natural Resources
Tin, oil, copper, timber, natural rubber

Electric Power Generation
10,516,000,000 kwh
kwh per capita: 806

Generating Capacity
2,500,000 kw (1984)

Nuclear Power Plants and Output
None

Crude Oil Production
14,420,000 metric tons; 105,720,000 barrels (1982)

Natural Gas Production
34,944 terajoules; 3,137,971 cubic feet (1982)

MALDIVES
Republic of Maldives

Budget
Revenues
1983: $22,700,000
1982: $19,600,000
Expenditures
1983: $41,650,000
1982: $32,200,000
Deficit
24.64% of GDP (1983)

Expenditures by Function (1983)

General public services	21.71%
Education	1.80%
Health	0.47%
Social security and welfare	1.04%
Housing and community amenities	26.46%
Economic services	48.19%
Agriculture, forestry, fishing and hunting	32.85%
Other transportation and communication	15.04%

Economic Aid Extended
None (1986)

External Public Debt
$46,500,000 (1983)
Service payments: 5.50% of exports of goods and services

Gross Domestic Product (GDP)
$76,714,285 (1984)
GDP per capita: $451 (1986)

Gross Domestic Product by Sector (1983)

Agriculture, forestry, and fishing	30.25%
Mining	1.33%
Manufacturing and utilities	4.93%
Construction	7.33%
Commerce	10.81%
Transportation and communication	6.26%
Other	39.27%

International Liquidity
Reserves (minus gold): $6,440,000 (1986)

Consumer Price Change (Inflation)
1982: 22.00%
1981: 47.20%
1980: 42.90%

Imports
Rice, manufactured goods

Total Imports
1984: $51,720,000
1983: $38,472,000
1982: $39,282,000

Exports
Fish, copra, ambergris, postage stamps

Total Exports
1984: $17,625,000
1983: $13,379,000
1982: $ 9,798,000

Trading Partners

Imports (1984)

Singapore	49.71%
Japan	16.28%
South Korea	7.57%
Sri Lanka	6.42%
India	4.14%

Exports (1984)

Thailand	38.46%
Sri Lanka	12.31%
Pakistan	9.23%
West Germany	9.23%
South Africa	6.15%

Tourists
Total: 74,000 (1983)
Revenue: $18,300,000 (1981)

Balance of Payments
1984: -$16,500,000
1983: -$24,200,000
1982: -$19,100,000

Labor Profile (1985)

Fishing	80%
Other	20%

Agricultural Products
Coconuts, millet, corn, pumpkins, sweet potatoes

Industrial Products
Canned and dried fish, electrical parts, coir (rope), woven mats

Natural Resources
Extensive fishing grounds

Electric Power Generation
9,000,000 kwh
kwh per capita: 54 (1984)

Generating Capacity
4,690 kw (1984)

Nuclear Power Plants and Output
None (1986)

Crude Oil Production
None (1986)

Natural Gas Production
None (1986)

MALI
Republic of Mali

Budget

Revenues
1983: $261,391,000
1982: $154,000,000

Expenditures
1983: $621,103,100
1982: $169,000,000

Deficit
1.50% of GDP (1982)

Expenditures by Function (1983)

General public services	10.40%
Defense	7.70%
Education	10.70%
Health	2.50%
Social security and welfare	4.60%
Housing and community amenities	0.04%
Other community and social services	7.60%
Economic services	0.10%
Agriculture, forestry, fishing and hunting	4.20%
Roads	2.20%
Other transportation and communication	0.10%
Other	3.00%

Economic Aid Extended
None

Economic Aid Received
Total: $145,000,000 (1954-83)
USA only: None

External Public Debt
$880,800,000
Service payments: 5.20% of exports of goods and services

Gross Domestic Product (GDP)
$1,000,000,000 (1982)
GDP per capita: $138

Gross Domestic Product by Sector (1982)

Agriculture, forestry, and fishing	53.10%
Mining and manufacturing	7.40%
Utilities	0.60%
Construction	5.70%
Commerce	16.50%
Transportation and communication	3.40%
Other	13.30%

International Liquidity
Reserves (minus gold): $39,000,000 (1985)
Gold reserves: 19,000 fine troy ounces

Imports
Food, machinery, vehicles, petroleum products, chemicals

Total Imports
1983: $232,613,909
1982: $232,600,000
1981: $270,383,375

Exports
Meat, livestock, baskets, cotton, fish, peanuts, tannery products

Total Exports
1983: $152,398,082
1982: $145,800,000
1981: $146,341,463

Trading Partners

Imports (1984)

France	29.50%
Ivory Coast	25.10%
West Germany	4.90%
Senegal	4.20%
Italy	3.40%

Exports (1984)

France	18.70%
Belgium	18.50%
West Germany	14.90%
USSR	7.20%
United Kingdom	6.20%

Tourists
Total: 22,000 (1979)
Revenue: $9,000,000 (1980)

Balance of Payments
1984: -$127,200,000
1983: -$107,000,000
1982: -$115,200,000

Labor Profile (1976)

Agriculture, forestry, and fishing	82.00%
Manufacturing	0.80%
Transportation and communication	0.50%
Trade	2.00%
Civil service	7.60%
Services	0.10%
Construction	0.30%
Other	5.70%

Agricultural Products
Sorghum, millet, livestock, cotton, fishing, peanuts, rice

Industrial Products
Textiles, food processing

Natural Resources
Iron ore, bauxite, uranium, copper, manganese, phosphate

Electric Power Generation
161,000,000 kwh
kwh per capita: 21

Generating Capacity
92,000 kw (1984)

Nuclear Power Plants and Output
None (1985)

Crude Oil Production
None (1985)

Natural Gas Production
None (1985)

MALTA
Republic of Malta

Budget

Revenues

1983: $317,224,336
1982: $447,240,000

Expenditures

1983: $396,682,000
1982: $420,048,000

Deficit

7.90% of GDP (1985)

Expenditures by Function (1983)

General public services	9.70%
Defense	3.00%
Education	8.60%
Health	10.30%
Social security and welfare	35.40%
Housing and community amenities	1.30%
Other community and social services	1.20%
Economic services	24.60%
Agriculture, forestry, fishing and hunting	2.10%
Roads	5.60%
Other transportation and communication	1.10%
Other	6.50%

Economic Aid Extended

None

External Public Debt

$108,800,000 (1983)
Service payments: 1.20% of exports of goods and services

Gross National Product (GNP)

$1,012,000,000 (1984)
GNP per capita: $2,663

Gross Domestic Product (GDP)

$922,200,000 (1984)
GDP per capita: $2,427

Gross Domestic Product by Sector (1983)

Agriculture, forestry, and fishing	4.20%
Mining	5.20%
Manufacturing	26.30%
Utilities	4.60%
Transportation and communication	5.30%
Commerce	14.00%
Other	40.70%

International Liquidity

Reserves (minus gold): $990,200,000 (1984)
Gold reserves: 466,000 fine troy ounces

Consumer Price Change (Inflation)

1984: -4.00%
1983: -9.00%
1982: +5.80%

Imports

Machinery and transportation equipment, textiles, foodstuffs, chemicals

Total Imports

1984: $595,480,000
1983: $627,527,000
1982: $702,864,000

Exports

Clothing, scientific instruments and watches, machinery and transportation equipment

Total Exports

1984: $362,720,000
1983: $344,850,000
1982: $405,696,000

Trading Partners

Imports (1984)

Italy	30.70%
United Kingdom	18.00%
West Germany	17.30%
USA	6.00%
France	3.60%

Exports (1984)

West Germany	31.20%
United Kingdom	14.90%
Italy	10.40%
Libya	9.10%
Netherlands	5.30%

Tourists

Total: 490,812 (1983)

Balance of Payments
1984: -$16,500,000
1983: -$24,200,000
1982: -$19,100,000

Labor Profile (1983)

Agriculture, forestry, and fishing	5.00%
Manufacturing	30.70%
Transportation and communication	5.50%
Trade	10.10%
Civil service	24.10%
Services	14.10%
Construction	5.50%
Other	5.00%

Agricultural Products
Fodder crops, potatoes, onions, other vegetables and fruits

Industrial Products
Textiles, yarn, knitted wear, processed food, electronic components

Natural Resources
Limestone, salt

Electric Power Generation
703,000,000 kwh
kwh per capita: 1,972

Generating Capacity
157,000 kw (1984)

Nuclear Power Plants and Output
None

Crude Oil Production
None (1985)

Natural Gas Production
None (1985)

MAURITANIA
Islamic Republic of Mauritania

Budget
Revenues
1984: $184,000,000
1983: $195,000,000
Expenditures
1984: $225,000,000
1983: $231,000,000

Expenditures by Function (1979)

General public services	22.72%
Defense	29.09%
Education	10.36%
Health	2.81%
Social security and welfare	3.84%
Housing and community amenities	0.11%
Other community and social services	1.45%
Economic services	13.45%
Agriculture, forestry, fishing and hunting	7.10%
Roads	2.37%
Other transportation and communication	1.69%
Other	5.70%

Economic Aid Extended
None

Economic Aid Received
Total: $9,000,000 (1954-83)
USA only: None

External Public Debt
$1,171,100 (1983)
Service payments: 9.90% of exports of goods and services

Gross National Product (GNP)
$730,000,000 (1982)
GNP per capita: $460

Gross Domestic Product (GDP)
$689,739,000 (1980)
GDP per capita: $431

Gross Domestic Product by Sector (1980)

Agriculture, forestry, and fishing	21.60%
Mining	12.60%
Manufacturing and utilities	5.80%
Construction	7.30%
Commerce	10.70%
Transportation and communication	8.10%
Other	33.50%

International Liquidity
Reserves (minus gold): $50,700,000 (1986)
Gold reserves: 11,000 fine troy ounces

Consumer Price Change (Inflation)
1984: 7.00%
1983: 0.90%
1982: 12.60%

Imports
Machinery, motor vehicles, electrical equipment, railway vehicles, sugar, honey

Total Imports
1985: $204,649,350
1984: $158,507,464
1983: $193,210,500

Exports
Iron ore, fish, copper concentrates

Total Exports
1985: $375,156,000
1984: $276,074,637
1983: $280,385,965

Trading Partners
Imports (1983)

France	19.20%
Other EEC	12.00%
Spain	7.20%
Senegal	6.40%

Exports (1983)

Other EEC	36.47%
France	27.05%
Spain	11.36%
Senegal	0.23%

Tourists
Revenue: $6,000,000 (1980)

Balance of Payments
1983: -$196,100,000
1982: -$262,400,000
1981: -$269,900,000

Labor Profile (1978)

Agriculture, forestry, and fishing	92.30%
Manufacturing and services	4.80%
Civil service	2.80%
Other	0.10%

Agricultural Products
Livestock, millet, maize, wheat, dates, rice

Industrial Products
Iron mining, fish processing

Natural Resources
Iron ore, gypsum, fish

Electric Power Generation
114,000,000 kwh
kwh per capita: 70

Generating Capacity
131,000 kw (1984)

Nuclear Power Plants and Output
None (1986)

Crude Oil Production
None (1986)

Natural Gas Production
None (1986)

MAURITIUS

Budget
Revenues
1984: $245,000,000
1983: $248,000,000
Expenditures
1984: $276,000,000
1983: $323,000,000
Deficit
3.41% (1984)

Expenditures by Function (1984)

General public services	16.29%
Defense	0.97%
Education	15.13%
Health	8.19%
Social security and welfare	16.21%
Housing and community amenities	2.00%
Other community and social services	0.67%
Economic services	10.45%
Agriculture, forestry, fishing and hunting	6.22%

Roads	0.41%
Other transportation and communication	0.75%
Other	31.08%

Economic Aid Extended
None

External Public Debt
$332,500,000 (1983)
Service payments: 16.40% of exports of goods and services

Gross National Product (GNP)
$873,333,333 (1984)
GNP per capita: $891

Gross Domestic Product (GDP)
$908,974,359 (1984)
GDP per capita: $927

Gross Domestic Product by Sector (1984)

Agriculture, forestry, and fishing	12.28%
Mining	0.13%
Manufacturing	14.88%
Utilities	19.93%
Construction	4.82%
Commerce	11.47%
Transportation and communication	9.28%
Other	45.12%

International Liquidity
Reserves (minus gold): $44,400,000 (1986)
Gold reserves: 38,000 fine troy ounces (1986)

Consumer Price Change (Inflation)
1985: 6.70%
1984: 7.40%
1983: 5.60%

Imports
Petroleum products, machinery, iron and steel, textiles, cement

Total Imports
1984: $1,529,000,000
1983: $1,357,000,000
1982: $1,673,000,000

Exports
Sugar, clothing, electronic goods, molasses, tea

Total Exports
1984: $372,000,000
1983: $366,000,000
1982: $366,000,000

Trading Partners
Imports (1984)

Bahrein	13.25%
France	11.91%
United Kingdom	7.92%
Hong Kong	7.00%
Japan	5.73%

Exports (1984)

United Kingdom	49.43%
France	16.01%
USA	12.84%
West Germany	5.61%
Italy	3.37%

Tourists
Total: 123,800
Revenue: $42,820,500 (1983)

Balance of Payments
1984: -$ 857,200,000
1983: -$1,160,100,000
1982: -$1,388,400,000

Labor Profile (1972)

Agriculture, forestry, and fishing	32.73%
Manufacturing	13.45%
Transportation and communication	6.72%
Trade	9.42%
Civil service	24.66%
Services	1.34%
Construction	9.59%
Other	2.09%

Agricultural Products
Sugar, tea, tobacco

Industrial Products
Sugar products, molasses

Natural Resources
None except local stone

Electric Power Generation
464,000,000 kwh
kwh per capita: 455

Generating Capacity
212,000 kw (1984)

Nuclear Power Plants and Output
None (1986)

Crude Oil Production
None (1986)

Natural Gas Production
None (1986)

MEXICO

United Mexican States

Budget
Revenues
1983: $52,800,000,000
Expenditures
1983: $51,900,000,000

Economic Aid Received
$3,547,000,000 (1970-82)
USA only: $2,800,000,000 (1970-83)

External Public Debt
$89,800,000,000 (1984)

Gross National Product (GNP)
$168,000,000,000 (1982)
GNP per capita: $2,520

Gross Domestic Product (GDP)
$121,200,000,000 (1983)
GDP per capita: $1,601

Gross Domestic Product by Sector (1982)

Agriculture, forestry, and fishing	7%
Mining	10%
Manufacturing	21%
Utilities	1%
Construction	6%
Commerce	23%
Transportation and communication	6%
Other	2%

Consumer Price Change (Inflation)
1984: 53%

Imports
Machinery and mechanical equipment, motor vehicle parts, maize, wool, sorghum

Total Imports
1984: $8,620,000,000

Exports
Cotton, coffee, sugar, lead, copper, zinc, fuel oil, cattle and meat products

Total Exports
1984: $21,200,000,000

Trading Partners
Imports (1983)

USA	60.40%
West Germany	4.50%
Japan	4.40%
Canada	2.80%
United Kingdom	2.10%

Exports (1983)

USA	58.20%
Spain	7.60%
Japan	7.10%
France	3.90%
Brazil	3.00%

Tourists
Total: 4,700,000
Revenue: $1,630,000,000 (1983)

Balance of Payments
$5,208,000,000

Agricultural Products
Livestock, wheat, corn, sugar, fruits, coffee, cotton, seafood

Industrial Products
Cars, household machinery, petrochemicals, steel, copper, cement, beverages, tobacco

Natural Resources
Petroleum, silver, sulphur, lead, zinc, coal, tin, antimony, mercury, copper, iron ore

Electric Power Generation
67,800,000,000 kwh (1984)
kwh per capita: 873

Generating Capacity
18,650,000 kw (1984)

Nuclear Power Plants and Output
Two nuclear plants are under construction and 2 are in the planning stage. The first nuclear plant is due to begin operations in 1986, the second in 1988

Crude Oil Production
138,580,000 metric tons; 1,015,800,000 barrels (1983)

Natural Gas Production
89,800,000,000 cubic feet (1984)

MONACO
Principality of Monaco

Budget
Revenues
1983: $204,337,349
1982: $213,432,835
Expenditures
1983: $203,493,975
1982: $174,925,373

Economic Aid Extended
None

Tourists
Total: 241,664 (1983)

Industrial Products
Tourism, gambling, chemicals, plastics, precision instruments

Electric Power Generation
None

Generating Capacity
8,000 kw (1983)

Nuclear Power Plants and Output
None (1986)

Crude Oil Production
None (1986)

Natural Gas Production
None (1986)

MONGOLIA
Mongolian People's Republic

Budget
Revenues
1986: $1,628,888,000
1985: $1,620,000,000
Expenditures
1986: $1,626,666,000
1985: $1,523,333,333

Economic Aid Extended
None (1986)

Gross National Product (GNP)
$1,470,000,000 (1978)
GNP per capita: $970

Gross Domestic Product (GDP)
$1,200,000,000 (1976)

Imports
Machinery and equipment, processed foods, chemicals, sugar and tea

Total Imports
1983: $808,600,000
1982: $689,000,000
1981: $613,600,000

Exports
Livestock, animal products, nonferrous metals

Total Exports
1983: $531,700,000
1982: $488,800,000
1981: $408,200,000

Trading Partners

Soviet Union	85%

Tourists
Total: 10,000 (1984)

Labor Profile (1983)

Agriculture, forestry, and fishing	10.59%
Manufacturing	22.09%
Transportation and communication	11.53%
Construction	7.09%
Other	48.70%

Agricultural Products
Wheat, oats, barley and animal husbandry (sheep, goats, camels, yaks, horses)

Industrial Products
Livestock processing, building materials, mining

Natural Resources
Coal, petroleum, gold, tungsten, lead, copper, uranium

Electric Power Generation
2,100,000,000 kwh (1985)
1,110 kwh per capita

Generating Capacity
645,000 kw (1985)

Nuclear Power Plants and Output
None (1986)

Crude Oil Production
None (1986)

Natural Gas Production
None (1986)

MOROCCO
Kingdom of Morocco

Budget
Revenues
1984: $4,500,000,000
1983: $5,500,000,000
Expenditures
1984: $5,600,000,000
1983: $6,400,000,000
Deficit
17.60% of GDP (1984)

Expenditures by Function (1983)

General public services	15.60%
Defense	14.70%
Education	18.80%
Health	2.80%
Social security and welfare	5.90%
Housing and community amenities	1.10%
Other community and social services	1.00%
Economic services	28.70%
Agriculture, forestry, fishing and hunting	5.30%
Roads	1.70%
Other transportation and communication	9.30%
Other	10.90%

Economic Aid Extended
None

Economic Aid Received
Total: $3,569,500,000
(1954-83) USA only: $1,142,000,000

External Public Debt
$9,445,300,000 (1983)
Service payments: 29.10% of exports of goods and services

Gross National Product (GNP)
$9,942,708,333 (1983)
GNP per capita: $452

Gross Domestic Product (GDP)
$11,900,000,000 (1984)
GDP per capita: $500

Gross Domestic Product by Sector (1981)

Agriculture, forestry, and fishing	14.30%
Mining	5.60%
Manufacturing	17.50%
Construction	7.00%
Commerce	14.30%
Transportation and communication	4.40%
Other	36.90%

International Liquidity
Reserves (minus gold): $92,000,000 (1985)
Gold reserves: 704,000 fine troy ounces

Consumer Price Change (Inflation)
1984: 12.40%
1983: 6.20%
1982: 10.50%

Imports
Industrial capital goods, foodstuffs, fuels, consumer goods, raw materials

Total Imports
1984: $3,911,000,000
1983: $3,592,000,000
1982: $4,315,000,000

Exports
Phosphates, foodstuffs, finished products

Total Exports
1984: $2,171,000,000
1983: $2,006,000,000
1982: $2,062,000,000

Trading Partners

Imports (1984)

France	19.70%
Saudi Arabia	13.60%
USA	11.90%
Spain	8.20%
Iraq	7.70%

Exports (1984)

France	47.90%
Spain	8.40%
West Germany	8.20%
India	7.30%
Italy	5.50%

Tourists
Total: 1,646,610 (1981)

Balance of Payments
1984: -$ 988,000,000
1983: -$ 892,000,000
1982: -$1,878,000,000

Labor Profile (1971)

Agriculture, forestry, and fishing	54.60%
Manufacturing	10.10%
Transportation and communication	3.00%
Trade	0.20%
Civil service	12.60%
Services	1.30%
Construction	4.70%
Other	13.50%

Agricultural Products
Wheat, barley, citrus, grapes, sugar beets

Industrial Products
Coal, electric power, phosphates, iron ore, lead, zinc

Natural Resources
Phosphates, iron, manganese, lead, zinc

Electric Power Generation
6,438,000 kwh
kwh per capita: 273

Generating Capacity
2,100,000 kw (1984)

Nuclear Power Plants and Output
None (1985)

Crude Oil Production
24,000 metric tons; 175,920 barrels (1983)

Natural Gas Production
None (1985)

MOZAMBIQUE
People's Republic of Mozambique

Budget

Revenues
1982: $500,000,000
1981: $488,000,000

Expenditures
1982: $600,000,000
1981: $523,000,000

Gross National Product (GNP)
$2,000,000,000 (1983)
GNP per capita: $150

Imports
Machines, vehicles, metals, textiles, crude oil, wheat

Total Imports
1983: $608,857,142
1982: $735,000,000
1981: $674,214,285

Exports
Textiles, cashew nuts, cotton, sugar, vegetable oil, wood

Total Exports
1983: $125,880,952
1982: $303,200,000
1981: $236,333,333

Trading Partners
Imports (1984)

Thailand	8.70%
Portugal	8.50%
France	7.80%
Canada	5.50%
USA	4.70%

Exports (1984)

USA	12.80%
Saudi Arabia	10.80%
Indonesia	8.90%
Zimbabwe	7.60%
Japan	7.00%

Tourists
Total: 70,000 (1974)

Balance of Payments
1983: -$189,285,714
1982: -$256,428,571
1981: -$275,000,000

Labor Profile (1980)

Agriculture, forestry, and fishing	83.80%
Manufacturing	6.10%
Transportation and communication	1.40%
Trade	1.90%
Services	4.30%
Construction	7.40%
Other	1.76%

Agricultural Products
Cashews, cotton, sugar, copra, tea

Industrial Products
Processed agricultural products, vegetable oil, oilcakes, soap, paint, petroleum products, beverages, tobacco

Natural Resources
Coal, iron ore, tantalite, flourite, hydroelectric power

Electric Power Generation
9,636,000,000 kwh
kwh per capita: 718

Generating Capacity
2,200,000 kw (1984)

Nuclear Power Plants and Output
None (1986)

Crude Oil Production
None (1986)

Natural Gas Production
None (1986)

NAMIBIA

Budget
Revenues
1985: $519,000,000
1984: $524,193,548
Expenditures
1985: $632,795,699
1984: $556,989,000

Economic Aid Extended
None

Gross Domestic Product (GDP)
$1,500,000 (1983)
GDP per capita: $1,391

Imports
Textiles, foodstuffs, construction equipment, fuels

Exports
Diamonds, fish products, livestock, karakul pelts

Tourists
Total: 400,000

Labor Profile (1981)

Agriculture, forestry, and fishing	60%
Manufacturing and trade	19%
Civil service	7%
Services	8%
Mining	6%

Agricultural Products
Processing of meat and livestock products

Industrial Products
Manufacturing output is negligible

Natural Resources
Diamonds, copper, lead, zinc, tin, vanadium, uranium

Electric Power Generation
1,261,000,000 kwh
kwh per capita: 1,170

Generating Capacity
400,000 kw (1984)

Nuclear Power Plants and Output
None

Crude Oil Production
None (1985)

Natural Gas Production
None (1985)

NATIONALIST CHINA

See China (Taiwan)

NAURU

Republic of Nauru

Budget
Revenues
1981/82: $116,050,000
Expenditures
1981/82: $90,720,000

Gross National Product (GNP)
$155,400,000 (1981)
GNP per capita: $21,400

Imports
Food, water, fuel

Total Imports
1979: $11,830,000

Exports
Phosphate

Total Exports
1979: $76,340,000

Labor Profile (1966)

Mining	57%
Administration	34%
Other	9%

Agricultural Products
Negligible; there is an insignificant amount of arable land on Nauru

Industrial Products
Mined phosphate

Natural Resources
Phosphate

Electric Power Generation
30,000,000 kwh (1981)
3,333 kwh per capita

Generating Capacity
10,000 kw (1984)

Nuclear Power Plants and Output
None

Crude Oil Production
None

Natural Gas Production
None

NEPAL

Kingdom of Nepal

Budget
Revenues
1984: $211,200,000
1983: $217,800,000
Expenditures
1984: $438,300,000
1983: $467,100,000
Deficit
10.80% of GDP (1984)

Expenditures by Function (1982)

General public services	11.50%
Defense	0.53%

Education	9.98%
Health	4.48%
Social security and welfare	0.40%
Housing and community amenities	3.90%
Other community and social services	1.86%
Economic services	51.92%
Agriculture, forestry, fishing and hunting	21.15%
Roads	12.11%
Other transportation and communication	4.28%
Other	9.42%

Economic Aid Extended

None (1986)

External Public Debt

$346,400,000 (1983)

Service payments: 3.00% of exports of goods and services

Gross Domestic Product (GDP)

$2,085,000,000 (1985)

GDP per capita: $129

Gross Domestic Product by Sector (1983)

Agriculture, forestry, and fishing	52.76%
Mining	0.20%
Manufacturing	4.07%
Utilities	0.39%
Construction	6.68%
Commerce	3.57%
Transportation and communication	7.18%
Other	25.15%

International Liquidity

Reserves (minus gold): $75,300,000 (1986)

Gold reserves: 151,000 fine troy ounces

Consumer Price Change (Inflation)

1985: 8.10%
1984: 2.80%
1983: 12.40%

Imports

Basic manufactures, machinery and transportation equipment, mineral fuels, foodstuffs

Total Imports

1985: $398,970,394
1984: $362,261,111
1983: $422,703,947

Exports

Crude materials, basic manufactures, food and live animals

Total Exports

1985: $146,570,000
1984: $117,183,333
1983: $ 89,532,894

Trading Partners

Imports (1984)

India	36.70%
Japan	16.80%
Bangladesh	6.30%
South Korea	5.30%
China	4.70%

Exports (1984)

West Germany	26.90%
India	25.50%
USA	11.90%
United Kingdom	10.00%
Italy	8.50%

Tourists

Total: 176,634

Balance of Payments

1984: -$101,700,000
1983: -$145,300,000
1982: -$ 85,400,000

Labor Profile (1981)

Agriculture, forestry, and fishing	91.10%
Manufacturing	0.50%
Transportation and communication	0.10%
Construction	0.02%
Other	8.28%

Agricultural Products

Rice, jute, wheat, corn, tea, forest products

Industrial Products

Cigarettes, matches, bricks, sugar, lumber, jute, hydroelectric power

Natural Resources
Water, timber, hydroelectric power, copper, iron

Electric Power Generation
395,000,000 kwh
kwh per capita: 24 (1984)

Generating Capacity
160,000 kw (1984)

Nuclear Power Plants and Output
None (1986)

Crude Oil Production
None (1986)

Natural Gas Production
None (1986)

NETHERLANDS
Kingdom of the Netherlands

Budget
Revenues
1984: $37,800,000,000
Expenditures
1984: $44,700,000,000

Economic Aid Received
None

Gross National Product (GNP)
$131,000,000,000 (1983)
GNP per capita: $9,120

Gross Domestic Product by Sector (1983)

Agriculture, forestry, and fishing	3.90%
Mining	0.20%
Manufacturing	27.00%
Construction	6.00%
Commerce	13.00%
Transportation and communication	6.00%
Other	43.00%

Consumer Price Change (Inflation)
1984: 3.60%

Imports
Machinery, transportation equipment, crude petroleum, chemicals, textiles, mineral ores, foodstuffs

Total Imports
1984: $53,000,000,000

Exports
Foodstuffs, machinery, transportaion equipment, natural gas, chemicals, petroleum products, textiles

Total Exports
1984: $59,200,000,000

Trading Partners
Imports (1984)

West Germany	21.80%
Belgium	11.40%
USA	8.90%
United Kingdom	8.70%
France	6.40%

Exports (1984)

West Germany	29.70%
Belgium	13.80%
France	10.40%
United Kingdom	9.50%
Italy	5.60%

Tourists
Total: 3,000,000 (1983)
Country of origin

West Germany	20.00%
United Kingdom	18.00%
USA	16.00%
France	7.00%
Belgium	3.60%

Balance of Payments
1984: $4,900,000,000

Labor Profile

Agriculture, forestry, and fishing	6.00%
Mining and manufacturing	19.50%
Utilities	1.00%
Commerce	18.00%
Transportation and communication	7.00%
Other services	32.50%
Government	16.00%

Agricultural Products
Wheat, barley, sugar beets, fruits, potatoes, oats, flax, bulbs, flowers, meat and dairy products

Industrial Products
Metal fabrication, textile, chemicals, electronics, foodstuffs

Natural Resources
Natural gas, salt, crude oil

Electric Power Generation
61,354,000,000 kwh (1984)
kwh per capita: 4,250

Generating Capacity
19,546,000 kw (1985)

Nuclear Power Plants and Output
Two nuclear plants are in operation with 501 nuclear generating capacity

Crude Oil Production
2,590,000 metric tons; 18,900,000 barrels (1983)

Natural Gas Production
2,444,988 terajoules; 2,190,000,000 cubic feet (1984)

NETHERLANDS ANTILLES

Budget
Revenues
1982: $373,000,000
1979: $119,000,000
Expenditures
1982: $378,000,000
1979: $142,000,000

Expenditures by Function (1979)

General public services	34.37%
Defense	0.04%
Education	5.47%
Health	7.81%
Social security and welfare	11.32%
Housing and community amenities	1.05%
Other community and social services	1.64%
Economic services	11.52%
Agriculture, forestry, fishing and hunting	0.31%
Roads	0.31%
Other transportation and communication	4.76%
Other	17.03%

Economic Aid Extended
None (1986)

Economic Aid Received
Total: $353,000,000 (1970-79)
USA only: None

External Public Debt
None (1986)

Gross National Product (GNP)
$131,600,000,000 (1983)
GNP per capita: $9,140

International Liquidity
Reserves (minus gold): $243,000,000 (1986)
Gold reserves: 548,000 fine troy ounces

Consumer Price Change (Inflation)
1984: 2.10%
1983: 2.80%
1982: 6.10%

Imports
Petroleum and petroleum products

Total Imports
1984: $4,025,000,000
1983: $4,518,000,000
1981: $5,853,000,000

Exports
Crude petroleum, motor spirit, aviation turbine fuel, gas, oil, residual fuel oil

Total Exports
1985: $22,108,000,000
1984: $24,407,000,000
1983: $21,819,000,000

Trading Partners

Imports (1984)

Nigeria	15.49%
USA	12.01%
United Arab Emirates	4.19%
France	2.88%
Saudi Arabia	2.57%

Exports (1984)

USA	54.28%
United Kingdom	7.14%
Jamaica	4.71%
Colombia	4.65%
Netherlands	2.42%

Tourists

Total: 489,400 (1983)

Balance of Payments

1983: $ 90,600,000
1982: $193,900,000
1981: $ 60,000,000

Labor Profile (1982)

Agriculture, forestry, and fishing	0.40%
Manufacturing	10.50%
Transportation and communication	7.37%
Construction	8.75%
Other	72.98%

Agricultural Products

Pigs, goats

Industrial Products

Oil refining

Natural Resources

Phosphate, petroleum

Electric Power Generation

1,517,000,000kwh
kwh per capita: 6,000 (1984)

Generating Capacity

433,000kw (1984)

Nuclear Power Plants and Output

None (1986)

NEW ZEALAND

Budget

Revenues

1984: $6,000,000,000
1983: $7,620,600,000

Expenditures

1984: $7,300,000,000
1983: $9,170,200,000

Deficit

6.80% of GNP (1983)

Expenditures by Function

General public services	7.10%
Defense	5.00%
Education	11.40%
Health	12.80%
Social security and welfare	28.50%
Housing and community amenities	0.90%
Other community and social services	0.30%
Economic services	17.80%
Agriculture, forestry, fishing and hunting	7.10%
Roads	2.40%
Other transportion and communication	1.90%
Other	15.00%

Economic Aid Extended

$338,000,000 (1970-82)

Economic Aid Received

None

External Public Debt

$4,011,000,000
Service payments: 6.70% of exports of goods and services (1981)

International Liquidity

Reserves (minus gold): $1,787,000,000 (1984)
Gold reserves: 22,000 fine troy ounces (1984)

Gross National Product (GNP)

$16,200,000,000 (1984)
GNP per capita: $5,063

Gross Domestic Product (GDP)
$22,707,750,000 (1983)
GDP per capita: $7,096

Gross Domestic Product by Sector (1982)

Agriculture, forestry, and fishing	10.90%
Manufacturing	23.00%
Transportation and communication	7.90%
Trade	16.20%
Civil service	22.30%
Services	7.10%
Construction	6.40%
Other	6.20%

Imports
Machinery and transportion equipment, basic manufactures, fuels, chemicals, foodstuffs and beverages

Total Imports
1984: $4,800,000
1983: $4,700,000
1982: $5,183,000

Exports
Meat, wool, butter, forest, and other animal and primary products

Total Exports
1984: $4,600,000
1983: $5,265,000
1982: $5,402,000

Trading Partners

Imports (1984)

Japan	20.90%
Australia	20.10%
USA	15.40%
United Kingdom	8.60%
West Germany	4.50%

Exports (1984)

Australia	15.10%
Japan	14.90%
USA	13.60%
United Kingdom	10.00%
Iran	4.30%

Tourists
Total: 487,700 (1983)

Consumer Price Change (Inflation)
1984: 8.90%
1983: 9.80%
1982: 18.70%

Balance of Payments
1984: $1,429,000,000
1983: $1,060,000,000
1982: $1,476,000,000

Agricultural Products
Beef, mutton, dairy products, wool

Industrial Products
Processed foods, consumer goods, pulp and paper

Natural Resources
Forests, grasslands, modest mineral deposits

Electric Power Generation
27,008,000 kwh (1984)
kwh per capita: 8,330

Generating Capacity
7,300,000 kw

Nuclear Power Plants and Output
None

Crude Oil Production
744,000 metric tons; 5,453,000 barrels (1984)

Natural Gas Production
87,072 terajoules; 7,819,065 cubic feet (1983)

NICARAGUA
Republic of Nicaragua

Budget
Revenues
1984: $1,100,000,000
Expenditures
1984: $1,900,000,000

External Public Debt
$2,400,000,000 (1981)

Gross National Product (GNP)
$3,500,000,000 (1983)
GNP per capita: $1,166

Gross Domestic Product (GDP)
$3,300,000,000 (1983)
GDP per capita: $1,132

Gross Domestic Product by Sector (1978)

Agriculture, forestry, and fishing	24.70%
Mining	0.30%
Manufacturing	21.00%
Utilities	2.00%
Construction	2.90%
Commerce	23.60%
Transportation and communication	5.30%
Other	20.20%

Consumer Price Change (Inflation)
1984: 72.40%

Imports
Raw materials, consumer goods, crude petroleum, industrial machinery, construction material

Total Imports
1984: $776,000,000

Exports
Coffee, meat, cotton

Total Exports
1982: $753,400,000

Trading Partners

Imports (1984)

USA	15.20%
Mexico	13.10%
Guatemala	7.00%
USSR	5.00%
Costa Rica	4.80%

Exports (1984)

Japan	24.30%
USA	15.90%
Canada	9.00%
West Germany	7.70%
France	6.60%

Balance of Payments
1983: -$443,000,000

Labor Profile (1981)

Agriculture and fishing	42.00%
Mining	0.70%
Manufacturing	13.00%
Construction	3.00%
Utilities	0.70%
Commerce	14.00%
Transportation and communication	3.50%
Services	23.00%

Agricultural Products
Sugarcane, maize, cotton, sorghum, rice, beans, coffee, fish

Industrial Products
Cigarettes, fuel oils, raw sugar, beverages, cement, electric energy

Natural Resources
Copper, gold, silver, tungsten, gypsum, precious stones

Electric Power Generation
1,200,000,000 kwh (1984)
kwh per capita: 410

Generating Capacity
400,000 kw

NIGER
Republic of Niger

Budget

Revenues
1983: $213,301,837
1982: $285,267,478

Expenditures
1983: $213,301,837
1982: $285,267,478

Deficit
None (1983)

Expenditures by Function (1980)

General public services	19.50%
Defense	4.00%
Education	18.10%
Health	4.10%
Social security and welfare	1.60%
Housing and community amenities	2.10%
Other community and social services	2.20%
Economic services	32.60%

Agriculture, forestry, fishing and hunting	6.80%
Roads	10.40%
Other transportation and communication	3.70%
Other	14.70%

Economic Aid Extended
None

Economic Aid Received
Total: $254,900,000 (1946-75)
USA only: $53,500,000

External Public Debt
$631,000,000 (1980)
Service payments: 6.00% of exports of goods and services

Gross National Product (GNP)
$1,671,942,446 (1983)
GNP per capita: $289

Gross Domestic Product (GDP)
$2,000,000,000 (1982)
GDP per capita: $425

Gross Domestic Product by Sector (1980)

Agriculture, forestry, and fishing	42.50%
Mining	12.60%
Manufacturing	3.70%
Utilities	0.40%
Construction	6.00%
Commerce	11.60%
Transportation and communication	4.20%
Other	19.00%

International Liquidity
Reserves (minus gold): $128,000,000 (1985)
Gold reserves: 11,000 fine troy ounces

Consumer Price Change (Inflation)
1984: 8.40%
1983: 2.50%
1982: 11.60%

Imports
Fuels, machinery, transportation equipment, consumer items

Total Imports
1982: $438,000,000
1981: $510,000,000
1980: $801,000,000

Exports
Uranium, peanuts, cattle, cotton

Total Exports
1982: $362,000,000
1981: $455,000,000
1980: $557,900,000

Trading Partners

Imports (1984)

France	30.00%
Nigeria	14.50%
Ivory Coast	6.70%
Asia	5.70%
Ireland	5.10%

Exports (1984)

France	53.60%
Nigeria	21.30%
Libya	18.30%
Asia	2.50%
Japan	1.00%

Tourists
Total: 50,453 (1984)

Balance of Payments
1982: -$ 75,500,000
1981: -$ 54,900,000
1980: +$476,300,000

Labor Profile (1975)

Agriculture, forestry, and fishing	92.80%
Manufacturing	2.10%
Services	4.90%
Other	0.20%

Agricultural Products
Millet, sorghum, peanuts, beans, cotton

Industrial Products
Textiles, cement, agricultural products

Natural Resources
Uranium, coal, iron, tin

Electric Power Generation
96,000,000 kwh
kwh per capita: 15

Generating Capacity
74,000 kw (1984)

Nuclear Power Plants and Output
None (1985)

Crude Oil Production
None (1985)

Natural Gas Production
None (1985)

NIGERIA
Federal Republic of Nigeria

Budget
Revenues
1984: $15,100,000,000
1983: $ 7,153,000,000
Expenditures
1984: $7,000,000,000
1983: $8,000,000,000
Deficit
None (1984)

Expenditures by Function (1978)

General public services	11.57%
Defense	23.53%
Education	4.51%
Health	2.51%
Social security and welfare	2.47%
Housing and community amenities	4.15%
Other community and social services	2.59%
Economic services	32.35%
Agriculture, forestry, fishing and hunting	1.74%
Roads	10.49%
Other transportation and communication	16.47%
Other	16.41%

Economic Aid Extended
None (1986)

Economic Aid Received
Total: $2,170,000,000 (1954-83)
USA only: $406,000,000

External Public Debt
$11,757,200,000 (1983)
Service payments: 18.60% of exports of goods and services

Gross National Product (GNP)
$35,923,000,000 (1983)
GNP per capita: $403

Gross Domestic Product (GDP)
$40,416,666,667 (1984)
GDP per capita: $430

Gross Domestic Product by Sector (1983)

Agriculture, forestry, and fishing	25.00%
Mining	20.30%
Manufacturing	4.90%
Utilities	0.90%
Construction	6.70%
Commerce	21.60%
Transportation and communication	4.40%
Other	15.90%

International Liquidity
Reserves (minus gold): $1,796,000,000 (1986)
Gold reserves: 687,000 fine troy ounces

Consumer Price Change (Inflation)
1984: 63.50%
1983: 30.20%
1982: 10.70%

Imports
Iron and steel products, commercial road vehicles, cereals, pharmaceuticals, passenger cars, textiles, paper products

Total Imports
1983: $13,422,000
1982: $18,658,000
1981: $20,554,000

Exports
Crude petroleum, cocoa beans, palm kernals, tin metal, rubber, hides and skins, timber

Total Exports
1984: $14,525,000
1983: $10,508,000
1982: $12,952,000

Trading Partners

Imports (1984)

United Kingdom	15.71%
France	13.86%
USA	9.00%
Japan	7.14%
West Germany	6.42%

Exports (1984)

USA	16.23%
France	13.69%
West Germany	13.68%
British West Indies	8.90%
Italy	8.00%

Tourists
Total: 113,827 (1976)
Revenue: $50,000,000 (1980)

Balance of Payments
1984: +$ 329,000,000
1983: -$4,189,000,000
1982: -$7,208,000,000

Labor Profile (1975)

Agriculture, forestry, and fishing	62.10%
Manufacturing	13.80%
Services	24.10%

Agricultural Products
Coca, rubber, palm oil, yams, casava, sorghum, millet, corn, rice, livestock

Industrial Products
Petroleum, cotton, rubber, textiles, cement, food products, footwear, metal products, lumber and plywood

Natural Resources
Petroleum, tin, columbite, iron ore, coal, limestone, lead, zinc, forests

Electric Power Generation
8,146,000,000 kwh (1984)
kwh. per capita: 92

Generating Capacity
3,100,000 kw (1984)

Nuclear Power Plants and Output
None (1986)

Crude Oil Production
73,080,000 metric tons; 535,676,400 barrels (1985)

Natural Gas Production
219,996 terajoules; 1,975,564,080 cubic feet (1984)

NORTH KOREA
See Korea (North)

NORTHERN IRELAND
See United Kingdom

NORWAY
Kingdom of Norway

Budget
Revenues
1984: $18,710,000,000
Expenditures
1984: $22,530,000,000

Economic Aid Extended
Total: $2,100,000,000 (1970-82)

Economic Aid Received
None

Gross National Product (GNP)
$47,700,000,000 (1984)
GNP per capita: $11,466

Gross Domestic Product by Sector (1983)

Agriculture, forestry, and fishing	3.20%
Mining	17.00%
Manufacturing	14.00%
Utilities	3.50%

Construction	5.60%
Commerce	11.70%
Transportation and communication	9.00%
Other	36.00%

Consumer Price Change (Inflation)
1984: 16.50%

Imports
Machinery and transportation equipment, foodstuffs, iron and steel, textiles and clothing

Total Imports
1984: $12,100,000,000

Exports
Metals, chemicals, crude oil, pulp and paper

Total Exports
1984: $16,900,000,000

Trading Partners
Imports (1984)

Sweden	17.00%
West Germany	14.40%
United Kingdom	10.30%
USA	9.20%
Japan	4.50%

Exports (1984)

United Kingdom	36.50%
West Germany	16.50%
Sweden	9.90%
USA	5.10%
Denmark	3.50%

Tourists
Total: 4,912,000 (1983)
Revenue: $664,000,000

Balance of Payments
1984: $3,230,000,000

Labor Profile (1983)

Agriculture and forestry	6.60%
Fishing and whaling	0.80%
Extractive industries and manufacturing	19.00%
Construction and utilities	9.00%
Commerce and finance	18.00%
Water transportation	2.30%
Other transportation	6.80%
Government and business services	32.40%
Personal services	3.05%

Agricultural Products
Dairy products, livestock, grain (barley, oats, wheat), potatoes, vegetables, fruits and berries, furs, wood

Industrial Products
Crude oil and natural gas, fish and other food products, pulp and paper, ships, aluminum, ferroalloys, iron and steel, nickel, zinc, nitrogen fertilizers, transportation equipment, hydroelectric power, refinery products.

Natural Resources
Fish, timber, hydroelectric power, ores, crude oil, natural gas

Electric Power Generation
117,882,000,000 kwh (1984)
kwh per capita: 28,440

Generating Capacity
22,915 kw (1985)

Nuclear Power Plants and Output
None

Crude Oil Production
37,770,000 metric tons, 276,900,000 barrels (1984)

Natural Gas Production
1,116,220 terajoules; 1,047,200,000,000 cubic feet (1984)

OMAN
Sultanate of Oman

Budget
Revenues
1984: $3,426,000,000
1983: $3,700,000,000
Expenditures
1984: $4,503,000,000
1983: $4,300,000,000
Deficit
10.59% of GDP (1984)

Expenditures by Function (1984)

General public services	10.60%
Defense	48.53%
Education	7.60%
Health	4.13%
Housing and community amenities	2.33%
Other community and social services	1.54%
Economic services	22.46%
Agriculture, forestry, fishing and hunting	2.20%
Roads	3.46%
Other transportation and communication	1.93%
Other	2.60%

Economic Aid Extended

None (1985)

External Public Debt

$1,125,000,000 (1983)

Service payments: 3.10% of exports of goods and services

Gross National Product (GNP)

$8,770,000,000 (1984)

GNP per capita: $7,308

Gross Domestic Product (GDP)

$10,156,666,666 (1984)

GDP per capita: $8,463

Gross Domestic Product by Sector (1984)

Agriculture, forestry, and fishing	2.92%
Mining	4.75%
Manufacturing	1.08%
Utilities	1.07%
Construction	7.39%
Commerce	13.00%
Transportation and communication	2.75%
Other	23.11%

International Liquidity

Reserves (minus gold): $987,200,000 (1986)

Gold reserves: 289,000 fine troy ounces

Imports

Machinery and transportation equipment, food and live animals, mineral fuels, tobacco

Total Imports

1983: $3,000,000,000

1982: $2,432,000,000

1981: $2,700,000,000

Exports

Oil, dates, dried limes, dried fish, tobacco leaf

Total Exports

1983: $4,300,000,000

1982: $4,185,000,000

1981: $4,700,000,000

Trading Partners

Imports (1984)

Japan	21.66%
United Arab Emirates	18.11%
United Kingdom	16.85%
West Germany	9.70%
USA	7.66%

Exports (1984)

Japan	81.48%
South Korea	14.59%
Singapore	10.48%
USA	5.70%
United Kingdom	3.77%

Balance of Payments

1985: +$ 21,000,000

1984: -$ 70,000,000

1983: +$247,000,000

Labor Profile (1984)

Agriculture, forestry, and fishing	6.20%
Construction	0.30%
Other	93.50%

Agricultural Products

Dates, alfalfa, onions, wheat, tobacco, bananas, mangoes, coconuts, sugarcane, rice

Industrial Products

Petroleum, fish, construction

Natural Resources

Oil, asbestos, marble, copper, limestone, chromium, manganese, iron

Electric Power Generation

2,155,000,000 kwh (1984)

kwh per capita: 1,820

Generating Capacity
984,000 kw (1984)

Nuclear Power Plants and Output
None (1986)

Crude Oil Production
23,880,000 metric tons; 175,040,400 barrels (1985)

Natural Gas Production
None (1986)

OUTER MONGOLIA

See Mongolia

PAKISTAN

Islamic Republic of Pakistan

Budget
Revenues
1983: $4,280,000,000
Expenditures
1983: $5,230,000,000

Economic Aid Received
USA only: $279,000,000 (1983)

External Public Debt
$10,400,000,000 (1983)

Gross National Product (GNP)
$29,970,000,000 (1984)
GNP per capita: $332

Gross Domestic Product (GDP)
$27,330,000,000 (1984)
GDP per capita: $304

Gross Domestic Product by Sector (1984)

Agriculture, forestry, and fishing	21.90%
Mining	1.30%
Manufacturing	17.90%
Utilities	1.90%
Construction	4.60%
Commerce	14.50%
Transportation and communication	6.90%
Other	31.00%

Consumer Price Change (Inflation)
1984: 5.90%

Imports
Capital goods, raw materials, food grains, consumer goods

Total Imports
1984: $4,880,000,000

Exports
Rice, cotton, yarn, textiles, light manufactured products

Total Exports
1984: $2,700,000,000

Trading Partners
Imports (1984)

Japan	14.80%
USA	10.90%
Saudi Arabia	9.60%
United Kingdom	6.50%

Exports (1984)

Iran	10.60%
USA	10.30%
Japan	9.20%
Saudi Arabia	7.40%
United Kingdom	6.10%

Tourists
Total: 313,708 (1982)

Balance of Payments
1983: $25,000,000

Labor Profile (1984)

Agriculture, forestry, and fishing	52.70%
Industry	13.40%
Services	11.00%
Commerce	11.90%
Other	11.00%

Agricultural Products
Wheat, cotton, rice

Industrial Products
Cotton textiles, fertilizers, cement, iron, steel, tires, electrical goods

Natural Resources
Land, extensive natural gas, limited petroleum, poor quality coal, iron ore

Electric Power Generation
19,300,000,000 kwh (1984)
kwh per capita: 200

Generating Capacity
5,068,000 kw (1984)

Nuclear Power Plants and Output
One nuclear plant is in operation, and 1 is in the planning stage; 125 nuclear generating capacity (on line by December 1981)

Crude Oil Production
660,000 metric tons; 4,840,000 barrels (1984)

Natural Gas Production
396,048 terajoules; 333,400,000,000 cubic feet (1984)

PANAMA
Republic of Panama

Budget
Revenues
1984: $1,121,100,000
1983: $1,122,000,000
Expenditures
1984: $1,173,200,000
1983: $1,173,000,000
Deficit
1.20% of GDP

Economic Aid Received
Total: $801,000,000
USA only: $382,000,000 (1970-83)

External Public Debt
$2,986,200,000 (1983)
Service payments: 6.80% of exports of goods and services

Gross National Product (GNP)
$4,381,100,000
GNP per capita: $2,086

Gross Domestic Product (GDP)
$4,379,400,000
GDP per capita: $2,085

Gross Domestic Product by Sector (1983)

Agriculture, forestry, and fishing	9.40%
Mining	2.30%
Manufacturing	8.90%
Utilities	3.50%
Construction	6.10%
Transportation and communication	13.30%
Commerce	14.90%
Other	43.60%

International Liquidity
Reserves (minus gold): $110,400,000 (1984)

Consumer Price Change (Inflation)
1984: 1.80%
1983: 2.30%
1982: 4.60%

Imports
Crude oil, capital goods, food

Total Imports
1984: $1,296,800,000

Exports
Refined petroleum, bananas, shrimp, sugar

Total Exports
1984: $276,030,000

Trading Partners
Imports (1984)

Japan	30.50%
USA	21.00%
Mexico	5.20%
Venezuela	4.60%
Ecuador	3.80%

Exports (1984)

USA	55.40%
Costa Rica	7.50%
West Germany	5.40%
Belgium	4.90%
Italy	4.00%

Tourists
Total: 334,751 (1983)

Balance of Payments
1984: -$116,000,000
1983: +$194,000,000
1982: -$150,000,000

Labor Profile (1983)

Agriculture, forestry, and fishing	28.40%
Manufacturing	10.30%
Transportation and communication	6.10%
Trade	14.50%
Civil service	26.50%
Services	4.70%
Construction	6.00%
Other	3.50%

Agricultural Products
Bananas, corn, sugar, rice, cattle

Industrial Products
Refined petroleum, sugar refining

Natural Resources
Geographic location, copper (yet to be exploited)

Electric Power Generation
2,900,000,000 kwh (1984)
kwh per capita: 1,450

Generating Capacity
1,100,000 kw

Nuclear Power Plants and Output
None

Crude Oil Production
None

Natural Gas Production
None

PAPUA NEW GUINEA

Budget
Expenditures
1983: $1,020,000,000

Economic Aid Received
Total: $1,360,000,000

External Public Debt
$757,000,000 (1981)
Service payments: 6.90% of exports of goods and services

Gross National Product (GNP)
$2,300,000,000 (1982)

Gross Domestic Product by Sector (1976)

Agriculture, forestry, and fishing	35.50%
Mining	9.00%
Manufacturing	8.80%
Utilities	1.30%
Construction	5.70%
Commerce	7.60%
Transportation and communication	4.90%
Other	27.20%

Consumer Price Change (Inflation)
1983: 7.90%

Imports
Food, machinery, transportation equipment, manufactured goods, fuels, chemicals

Total Imports
1982: $1,200,000,000

Exports
Copper, gold and silver concentrates, coffee beans, cocoa beans, copra and copra oil, timber and plywood

Total Exports
1983: $812,000,000

Trading Partners
Imports (1982)

Australia	40.80%
Singapore	14.50%
Japan	14.10%
USA	8.40%

Exports (1982)

Japan	32.80%
West Germany	25.70%
Australia	10.20%
United Kingdom	5.80%
Spain	4.60%

Tourists
Total: 32,505 (1982)

Balance of Payments
1983: -$393,600,000

Labor Profile (1971)

Agriculture	64.00%
Primary production	6.50%
Mining	0.40%
Manufacturing	1.20%
Construction	2.20%
Transportation and communication	1.00%
Commerce	0.90%
Personal service	1.60%

Industrial Products
Palm oil, copra, coffee, timber, cocoa and tea processing; beer, soap, concrete products, clothing, paper products, light fabricated metal

Natural Resources
Copper, gold, silver, timber, tuna

Electric Power Generation
1,400,000,000 kwh (1983)
kwh per capita: 430

Generating Capacity
664,100 kw (1984)

Nuclear Power Plants and Output
None

Crude Oil Production
None

Natural Gas Production
None

PARAGUAY
Republic of Paraguay

Budget
Revenues
1983: $494,000,000
1982: $680,738,095
Expenditures
1983: $741,000,000
1982: $688,214,285
Deficit
3.80% of GDP (1983)

Expenditures by Function (1982)

General public services	16.10%
Defense	12.60%
Education	12.00%
Health	3.40%
Social security and welfare	30.00%
Housing and community amenities	2.50%
Other community and social services	0.20%
Economic services	13.80%
Agriculture, forestry, fishing and hunting	2.10%
Roads	8.60%
Other transportation and communication	0.10%
Other	0.10%

Economic Aid Extended
None

Economic Aid Received
Total: $681,000,000 (1970-83)
USA only: $151,000,000

External Public Debt
$1,161,200,000 (1983)
Service payments: 14.90% of exports of goods and services

Gross National Product (GNP)
$6,489,603,000 (1983)
GNP per capita: $1,870

Gross Domestic Product (GDP)
$2,500,000,000 (1984)
GDP per capita: $900

Gross Domestic Product by Sector (1983)

Agriculture, forestry, and fishing	25.90%
Mining	0.40%
Manufacturing	16.40%
Utilities	2.50%
Construction	6.70%
Transportation and communication	4.20%
Commerce	26.50%
Other	17.30%

International Liquidity
Reserves (minus gold): $666,270,000 (1984)
Gold reserves: 35,000 fine troy ounces

Consumer Price Change (Inflation)
1984: 20.30%
1983: 13.40%
1982: 6.80%

Imports
Crude petroleum, foodstuffs, transportation equipment, machinery

Total Imports
1984: $495,221,000
1983: $553,051,800
1982: $631,388,889

Exports
Sawn timber, cotton, soybeans, vegetable oils

Total Exports
1984: $319,000,000
1093: $342,547,000
1982: $375,031,706

Trading Partners

Imports (1984)

Brazil	37.40%
Argentina	16.10%
USA	9.90%
Japan	5.70%
France	4.80%

Exports (1984)

Brazil	16.40%
West Germany	11.90%
Argentina	10.90%
Netherlands	10.60%
USA	5.60%

Tourists
Total: 147,830 (1983)
Revenue: $44,300,000

Balance of Payments
1984: -$313,200,000
1983: -$247,400,000
1982: -$387,700,000

Labor Profile (1982)

Agriculture, forestry, and fishing	43.00%
Manufacturing	12.40%
Transportation and communication	2.60%
Trade	8.50%
Civil service	16.90%
Services	1.70%
Construction	6.70%
Other	8.20%

Agricultural Products
Wheat, manioc, corn, sweet potatoes, beets, rice, sugarcane, fruits, vegetable oil, meat and meat by-products

Industrial Products
Agricultural processing, wood products, consumer goods, cement, refined oil products, hydroelectric power

Natural Resources
Forests, few minerals

Electric Power Generation
2,900,000,000 kwh
kwh per capita: 800

Generating Capacity
1,100,000 kw (1984)

Nuclear Power Plants and Output
None

Crude Oil Production
None (1985)

Natural Gas Production
None (1985)

PEOPLE'S REPUBLIC OF CHINA

See China

PERU

Republic of Peru

Budget

Revenues
1984: $1,620,000,000

Expenditures
1984: $2,190,000,000

Economic Aid Received
Total: $4,700,000,000
USA only: $2,400,000,000 (1982)

External Public Debt
$7,931,000,000 (1983)
Service payments: 19.60% of exports of goods and services

Gross National Product (GNP)
$16,300,000,000 (1983)
GNP per capita: $875

Gross Domestic Product (GDP)
$11,700,000,000 (1983)
GDP per capita: $624

Gross Domestic Product by Sector (1983)

Agriculture, forestry, and fishing	8.10%
Mining	11.10%
Manufacturing	25.50%
Utilities	1.00%
Construction	3.10%
Commerce	17.00%
Transportation and communication	7.20%
Other	27.00%

Consumer Price Change (Inflation)
1984: 671.20%

Imports
Machinery, cereals, chemicals, pharmaceuticals

Total Imports
1984: $1,070,000,000

Exports
Copper, fish products, cotton, sugar, coffee, lead, silver, zinc, iron ore, wool

Total Exports
1984: $1,920,000,000

Trading Partners

Imports (1984)

USA	38.20%
Japan	8.10%
West Germany	6.70%
Argentina	6.70%
Brazil	6.30%

Exports (1982)

USA	39.40%
Japan	28.30%
United Kingdom	11.20%
West Germany	9.20%
France	8.40%

Tourists
Total: 273,324 (1983)

Balance of Payments
1984: -$253,000,000

Labor Profile (1981)

Agriculture, forestry, and fishing	37.00%
Extractive industries	2.00%
Manufacturing	11.00%
Utilities	0.20%
Construction	4.00%
Commerce	12.00%
Transportation and communication	4.00%
Business services	2.00%
Community, social and personal services	19.00%
Other	8.80%

Agricultural Products
Corn, other grains, sugar, cotton, coffee, wool

Industrial Products
Mineral processing, fishmeal, oil refining, textiles, light engineering, automobile assembly

Natural Resources
Copper, zinc, iron ore, other metals, fish, petroleum, forests

Electric Power Generation
12,700,000,000 kwh (1984)
kwh per capita: 663

Generating Capacity
3,675,000 kw

Nuclear Power Plants and Output
None

Crude Oil Production
9,100,000 metric tons; 66,850,000 barrels (1984)

PHILIPPINES
Republic of the Philippines

Budget
Revenues
1984: $2,922,500,000
1983: $4,100,000,000
Expenditures
1984: $2,649,590,000
1983: $5,700,000,000
Deficit
None (1984)

Expenditures by Function (1983)

General public services	16.60%
Defense	11.30%
Education	21.70%
Health	5.60%
Social security and welfare	2.50%
Housing and community amenities	1.60%
Other community and social services	0.70%
Economic services	37.70%
Agriculture, forestry, fishing and hunting	8.90%
Roads	2.30%
Other transportation and communication	0.04%
Other	9.40%

Economic Aid Extended
None

Economic Aid Received
USA only: $2,326,000,000 (1946-83)

External Public Debt
$10,385,400,000 (1983)
Service payments: 15.10% of exports of goods and services

Gross National Product (GNP)
$27,346,000,000 (1984)
GNP per capita: $513

Gross Domestic Product (GDP)
$27,910,152,280 (1984)
GDP per capita: $523

Gross Domestic Product by Sector (1984)

Agriculture, forestry, and fishing	25.20%
Mining	1.80%
Manufacturing	25.00%
Utilities	1.30%
Construction	5.70%
Commerce	19.40%
Transportation and communication	6.20%
Other	14.40%

International Liquidity
Reserves (minus gold): $615,000,000 (1985)
Gold reserves: 1,478,000 fine troy ounces

Consumer Price Change (Inflation)
1984: 50.30%
1983: 10.00%
1982: 10.20%

Imports
Crude oil, electric machinery, non-electric machinery, transportation equipment, base metals

Total Imports
1984: $6,432,000,000
1983: $7,976,000,000
1982: $8,263,000,000

Exports
Semiconductors, sugar, coconut oil, copper concentrates

Total Exports
1984: $5,274,000,000
1983: $4,890,000,000
1982: $4,968,000,000

Trading Partners
Imports (1984)

USA	26.60%
Japan	13.30%
Saudi Arabia	6.70%
Jordan	6.00%
Malaysia	5.50%

Exports (1984)

USA	37.70%
Japan	18.80%
Singapore	6.10%
Hong Kong	4.40%
United Kingdom	4.20%

Tourists
Total: 860,550 (1983)
Revenue: $464,750,000

Balance of Payments
1984: -$1,253,000,000
1983: -$2,751,000,000
1982: -$3,212,000,000

Labor Profile (1983)

Agriculture, forestry, and fishing	52.30%
Manufacturing	9.10%
Transportation and communication	4.60%
Trade	11.70%
Civil service	16.20%
Services	1.60%
Construction	3.20%
Other	1.30%

Agricultural Products
Rice, corn sugar, copra and coconut oil

Industrial Products
Processed food, beverages, tobacco, rubber products, cement and glass

Natural Resources
Forests, metallic and nonmetallic minerals

Electric Power Generation
23,000,000,000 kwh
kwh per capita: 414

Generating Capacity
6,486,000 kw (1984)

Nuclear Power Plants and Output
None (1985)

Crude Oil Production
None (1986)

Natural Gas Production
None (1986)

POLAND
Polish People's Republic

Budget
Revenues
1983: $26,790,000,000
Expenditures
1983: $27,600,000,000

Gross National Product (GNP)
$186,800,000,000 (1982)
GNP per capita: $5,543

Gross Domestic Product by Sector (1983)

Agriculture, forestry, and fishing	18.30%
Mining, manufacturing, and utilities	50.00%
Construction	11.00%
Commerce	13.50%
Transportation and communication	5.00%
Other	1.70%

Consumer Price Change (Inflation)
1983: 84.50%

Imports
Oil, lignite, coke, railway rolling stock, ships

Total Imports
1983: $10,090,000,000

Exports
Coal, steel products, electric-engineering products, food

Total Exports
1983: $11,020,000,000

Trading Partners
Imports (1983)

USSR	37.00%
East Germany	7.00%
West Germany	6.70%
Czechoslovakia	5.70%
United Kingdom	3.60%

Exports (1983)

USSR	31.20%
Czechoslovakia	5.20%
East Germany	4.70%
West Germany	3.30%
Hungary	3.30%

Tourists

Total: 2,402,000 (1983)

Country of origin

East Germany	15.30%
Czechoslovakia	15.30%
Soviet Union	35.00%
Hungary	3.90%
West Germany	9.40%

Labor Profile (1978)

Agriculture, forestry, and fishing	30.00%
Mining, manufacturing and utilities	29.00%
Construction	8.00%
Trade and restaurants	8.00%
Transportation and communication	7.00%
Finance, business, services	0.20%
Community, social and personal services	13.00%

Agricultural Products

Grains, sugar beets, potatoes, hogs and other livestock

Industrial Products

Iron, steel, chemicals, textiles, food processing, ship building, transportation equipment

Natural Resources

Coal, sulphur, copper, natural gas

Electric Power Generation

135,300,000,000 kwh (1984)
kwh per capita: 3,668

Nuclear Power Plants and Output

No nuclear generating capacity currently; 2 nuclear plants (net mwe - 880) to be constructed at Zarnowiec are on order

Crude Oil Production

252,000 metric tons; 1,850,000 barrels (1983)

Natural Gas Production

210,408 terajoules; 18,900,000,000 cubic feet (1984)

PORTUGAL

Portuguese Republic

Budget

Revenues
1983: $9,700,000,000
1982: $7,100,000,000

Expenditures
1983: $9,700,000,000
1982: $9,500,000,000

Deficit
None (1983)

Expenditures by Function (1975)

General public services	17.10%
Defense	13.00%
Education	10.50%
Health	4.40%
Social security and welfare	26.80%
Housing and community amenities	3.70%
Other community and social services	0.40%
Economic services	10.50%
Agriculture, forestry, fishing and hunting	1.90%
Other transportation and communication	5.50%
Other	4.80%

Economic Aid Extended

None

Economic Aid Received

Total: $2,186,000,000 (1970-83)
USA only: $1,500,000,000 (1970-83)

External Public Debt

$9,950,600,000 (1983)
Service payments: 20.40% of exports of goods and services

Gross National Product (GNP)

$20,700,000,000 (1983)
GNP per capita: $2,070

Gross Domestic Product (GDP)
$13,548,000,000 (1983)
GDP per capita: $1,355

Gross Domestic Product by Sector (1981)

Agriculture, forestry, and fishing	8.40%
Mining	0.50%
Manufacturing	30.00%
Utilities	1.50%
Construction	7.50%
Commerce	22.00%
Transportation and communication	5.80%
Other	24.40%

International Liquidity
Reserves (minus gold): $1,804,000,000 (1985)
Gold reserves: 20,240,000 fine troy ounces

Consumer Price Change (Inflation)
1984: 28.90%
1983: 25.10%
1982: 22.70%

Imports
Petroleum, cotton, industrial machinery, iron and steel, corn, wheat, rice

Total Imports
1984: $7,961,000,000
1983: $8,240,000,000
1982: $9,572,000,000

Exports
Cotton, textiles, cork and cork products, canned fish, wine

Total Exports
1984: $5,201,000,000
1983: $4,599,000,000
1982: $4,164,000,000

Trading Partners
Imports (1984)

USA	12.80%
West Germany	9.90%
France	7.90%
Spain	7.00%
United Kingdom	6.80%

Exports (1984)

United Kingdom	15.30%
West Germany	13.60%
France	12.40%
USA	8.70%
Netherlands	5.90%

Tourists
Total: 8,875,000 (1983)
Revenue: $883,354,443 (1982)
Country of origin (1982)

Spain	71.00%
United Kingdom	7.80%
West Germany	3.90%

Balance of Payments
1984: -$ 514,000,000
1983: -$1,004,000,000
1982: -$3,250,000,000

Labor Profile (1982)

Agriculture, forestry, and fishing	25.30%
Manufacturing	26.00%
Transportation and communication	4.00%
Trade	12.10%
Civil service	5.20%
Services	2.50%
Construction	10.50%
Other	14.40%

Agricultural Products
Grains, fruits, vegetables, wines

Industrial Products
Mining, manufacturing, electronics, textiles, wines, cork, food processing, shipbuilding and repairs

Natural Resources
Wolfram, cassiterite, beryl, copper, pyrites, coal and iron ore

Electric Power Generation
16,555,000,000 kwh
kwh per capita: 1,648

Generating Capacity
5,115,000 kw (1984)

Nuclear Power Plants and Output
None (1985)

Crude Oil Production
None (1986)

Natural Gas Production
None (1986)

PUERTO RICO
Commonwealth of Puerto Rico

Budget
Revenues
1984: $3,771,000,000
1983: $3,323,000,000
Expenditures
1984: $3,668,000,000
1983: $3,185,000,000
Deficit
None (1984)

Gross National Product (GNP)
$12,820,000,000 (1983)
GNP per capita: $3,900

Gross Domestic Product (GDP)
$18,671,000,000 (1984)
GDP per capita: $5,709

Gross Domestic Product by Sector (1983)

Agriculture, forestry, and fishing	2.12%
Mining	0.06%
Manufacturing	38.96%
Utilities	3.30%
Construction	1.87%
Commerce	14.98%
Transportation and communication	5.67%
Other	33.04%

Imports
Industrial machinery, textiles and electrical equipment

Total Imports
1982: $8,490,000

Exports
Manufactured goods, sugar, tobacco, and rum

Total Exports
1982: $8,790,000

Trading Partners
Imports (1983)

USA	61.17%
Japan	5.01%
Netherlands Antilles	4.88%
Venezuela	4.71%
Bahamas	2.37%

Exports (1983)

USA	83.53%
Virgin Islands	2.43%
Dominican Republic	2.05%
Trinidad and Tobago	1.28%
Netherlands Antilles	0.81%

Tourists
Total: 1,496,420
Revenue: $681,000,000 (1984)
Country of origin

USA	75.33%

Balance of Payments
1983: -$ 702,000,000
1982: -$ 126,000,000
1981: -$2,052,000,000

Labor Profile (1984)

Agriculture, forestry, and fishing	5.25%
Manufacturing	19.13%
Other	75.62%

Agricultural Products
Sugar, coffee, tobacco, pineapples and molasses

Industrial Products
Distilled spirits, rum, beer, cement and electricity

Natural Resources
Few, although copper and nickel deposits have been identified

Electric Power Generation
12,072,000,000 kwh (1983)
kwh per capita: 3,906

Nuclear Power Plants and Output
One power plant (1986)

Crude Oil Production
None (1986)

Natural Gas Production
None (1986)

QATAR
State of Qatar

Budget
Revenues
1982: $3,680,000,000
Expenditures
1982: $3,457,000,000

Gross National Product (GNP)
$5,000,000,000 (1979)
GNP per capita: $22,727

Gross Domestic Product by Sector (1983)

Agriculture, forestry, and fishing	0.85%
Mining	45.85%
Manufacturing	5.94%
Utilities	0.46%
Construction	7.10%
Commerce	6.67%
Transportation	2.10%
Other	30.94%

Imports
Industrial and consumer goods

Total Imports
1983: $1,456,000,000

Exports
Oil

Total Exports
1983: $3,384,000,000

Trading Partners
Imports (1981)

Japan	20.00%
United Kingdom	16.50%
USA	11.10%
West Germany	7.20%
France	6.00%

Agricultural Products
Fruit and vegetables (most food is imported)

Industrial Products
Oil production and refining, fishing, cement, desalting plants

Natural Resources
Petroleum, fish

Electric Power Generation
2,593,000,000 kwh (1982)
kwh per capita: 11,446

Nuclear Power Plants and Output
None

Crude Oil Production
21,600,000 metric tons, 158,320,000 barrels (1983)

Natural Gas Production
56,743,000,000 cubic feet, or 63,253 terajoules (1977)

REPUBLIC OF CHINA
See China (Taiwan)

ROMANIA
Socialist Republic of Romania

Budget
Revenues
1981: $18,680,000,000
Expenditures
1981: $18,120,000,000

Gross National Product (GNP)
$104,800,000,000 (1982)
GNP per capita: $4,238

Consumer Price Change (Inflation)
1982: 16.00%

Imports
Machinery and equipment, raw and processed metals, coke and coking coal, cotton

Total Imports
1982: $9,700,000,000

Exports
Foodstuffs, lumber, fuel, manufactures

Total Exports
1982: $11,600,000,000

Trading Partners

Imports (1981)

USSR	18.20%
USA	7.80%
Iran	7.10%
West Germany	5.60%
East Germany	4.20%

Exports (1981)

USSR	17.90%
West Germany	7.10%
USA	4.80%
East Germany	4.10%
Iran	3.70%

Balance of Payments

1985: $1,239,000,000
1983: $1,160,000,000

Labor Profile (1981)

Agriculture, forestry, and fishing	29.10%
Manufacturing	35.90%
Construction	7.70%
Commerce	6.10%
Transportation and communication	7.10%
Administration	5.50%
Other	1.40%

Agricultural Products

Corn, wheat, rye, barley, oats, plants for industrial byproducts

Industrial Products

Steam turbines, oil exploration equipment, household appliances, processed hydrocarbon products

Natural Resources

Oil, natural gas, coal, iron ore, nonferrous metals, salt, mineral waters

Electric Power Generation

66,215,000,000 kwh (1983)
kwh per capita: 2,825

Nuclear Power Plants and Output

As of December 1981, 2 nuclear plants under construction, 1 on order and 4 in the planning stage

Crude Oil Production

87,960 barrels (1983)

Natural Gas Production

1,680 terajoules; 150,000,000 cubic feet (1983)

RUMANIA

See Romania

RUSSIA

See Union of Soviet Socialist Republics

RWANDA

Republic of Rwanda

Budget

Revenues

1983: $161,5001,000
1982: $143,000,000

Expenditures

1983: $194,900,000
1982: $170,408,000

Deficit

1.87% of GDP (1983)

Expenditures by Function (1980)

General public services	15.58%
Defense	12.98%
Education	18.83%
Health	4.54%
Social security and welfare	2.85%
Housing and community amenities	1.17%
Other community and social services	0.90%
Economic services	41.55%
Agriculture, forestry, fishing and hunting	12.33%
Roads	7.14%
Other transportation and communication	2.59%
Other	1.55%

Economic Aid Extended
None (1986)

Economic Aid Received
Total: $1,000,000 (1954-83)
USA only: None

External Public Debt
$219,700,000 (1983)
Service payments: 2.60% of exports of goods and services

Gross Domestic Product (GDP)
$1,537,000,000 (1983)
GDP per capita: $270

Gross Domestic Product by Sector (1983)

Agriculture, forestry, and fishing	39.85%
Mining	0.49%
Manufacturing	18.30%
Utilities	0.14%
Construction	4.57%
Commerce	14.29%
Transportation and communication	3.31%
Other	19.01%

International Liquidity
Reserves (minus gold): $116,750,000 (1986)

Consumer Price Change (Inflation)
1985: 1.70%
1984: 5.70%
1983: 6.60%

Imports
Textiles, foodstuffs, machinery, petroleum products

Total Imports
1984: $214,403,846
1983: $182,000,000
1982: $220,784,946

Exports
Coffee, cassiterite, tea, wolfram, pyrethrum

Total Exports
1984: $139,384,615
1983: $114,000,000
1982: $102,688,000

Trading Partners

Imports (1984)

Kenya	17.44%
Belgium	8.84%
Japan	7.26%
China	5.86%
France	5.82%

Exports (1984)

West Germany	77.12%
USA	19.27%
United Kingdom	10.84%
France	10.36%
Algeria	10.24%

Tourists
Total: 19,700 (1984)
Revenue: $326,881 (1983)

Balance of Payments
1984: -$41,600,000
1983: -$48,700,000
1982: -$86,600,000

Labor Profile (1978)

Agriculture, forestry, and fishing	34.90%
Manufacturing	13.20%
Transportation and communication	1.60%
Construction	4.20%
Other	46.10%

Agricultural Products
Coffee, tea, pyrethrum, beans, potatoes

Industrial Products
Small food processing, mining, light consumer goods

Natural Resources
Cassiterite, wolfram

Electric Power Generation
132,000,000 kwh (1984)
kwh per capita: 22

Generating Capacity
42,000 kw (1984)

Nuclear Power Plants and Output
None (1986)

Crude Oil Production
None (1986)

Natural Gas Production
None (1986)

SAN MARINO

Republic of San Marino

Budget
Revenues
1983: $90,800,000
1981: $120,085,800
Expenditures
1983: $90,800,000
1981: $120,085,800

Economic Aid Extended
None

Imports
Manufactured consumer goods

Exports
Building stone, lime, chestnuts, wheat, hides, baked goods

Tourists
Total: 2,300,000 (1983)

Labor Profile (1980)

Agriculture, forestry, and fishing	5.50%
Manufacturing and trade	63.20%
Civil service	25.00%
Services	6.30%

Agricultural Products
Wheat, wine, grains, grapes, vegetables and fruit

Industrial Products
Textiles, paper, leather, cement and other building materials

Natural Resources
Building stones

Electric Power Generation
None

Generating Capacity
None (1986)

Nuclear Power Plants and Output
None (1986)

Crude Oil Production
None (1986)

Natural Gas Production
None (1986)

SÃO TOMÉ AND PRÍNCIPE

Democratic Republic of São Tomé and Príncipe

Budget
Revenues
1983: $22,430,000
1979: $15,700,000
Expenditures
1983: $23,866,000
1979: $19,500,000

Economic Aid Received
Total: $11,700,000
USA only: $93,700,000 (1977-84)

Gross Domestic Product (GDP)
$30,000,000 (1981)
GDP per capita: $490

Gross Domestic Product by Sector (1974)

Agriculture, forestry, and fishing	55.52%
Mining	0.28%
Manufacturing	4.03%
Utilities	0.75%
Construction	3.10%
Commerce	14.06%
Transportation and communication	2.33%
Other	20.00%

Imports
Communications equipment, light and heavy vehicles, food products, beverages, fuel and lubricants

Total Imports
1985: $12,700,000
1984: $12,100,000
1983: $ 9,600,000

Exports
Cocoa, copra, coffee, palm oil

Total Exports
1985: $5,100,000
1984: $7,200,000
1983: $6,000,000

Trading Partners
Imports (1985)

Portugal	40.94%
Angola	12.60%
United Kingdom	10.24%
France	7.87%
West Germany and Spain	6.30%

Exports (1985)

West Germany	47.53%
Portugal	15.69%
Netherlands	15.69%
Italy	5.88%
France and Sweden	3.92%

Balance of Payments
1983: -$ 8,000,000
1982: -$29,000,000
1981: -$ 8,000,000

Labor Profile (1981)

Agriculture, forestry, and fishing	56.48%
Mining and manufacturing	5.56%
Transportation and communication	3.53%
Construction	10.93%
Other	23.50%

Agricultural Products
Cocoa, copra, coconut, coffee, palm oil, bananas

Industrial Products
Light construction, shirt manufacture, soap, beer, fisheries, shrimp processing

Natural Resources
Agricultural products, fish

Electric Power Generation
7,000,000 kwh (1985)
kwh per capita: 67

Nuclear Power Plants and Output
None (1986)

Crude Oil Production
None (1986)

Natural Gas Production
None (1986)

SAUDI ARABIA
Kingdom of Saudi Arabia

Budget
Revenues
1984: $75,400,000,000
Expenditures
1984: $75,400,000,000

External Public Debt
None

Gross National Product (GNP)
$110,900,000,000 (1983)
GNP per capita: $10,663

Gross Domestic Product (GDP)
$108,000,000,000 (1984)
GDP per capita: $10,335

Gross Domestic Product by Sector (1978)

Agriculture, forestry, and fishing	1.10%
Extractive industries	53.70%
Manufacturing	4.60%
Utilities	0.10%
Construction	15.20%
Commerce	5.60%
Transportation and communication	5.70%
Other	14.10%

Consumer Price Change (Inflation)
1984: -1.10%

Imports
Transportation equipment, machinery, foodstuffs

Total Imports
1983: $39,000,000,000

Exports
Principally petroleum

Total Exports
1983: $48,000,000,000

Trading Partners
Imports (1984)

Japan	18.50%
USA	18.30%
Italy	7.80%
France	7.50%
West Germany	7.40%

Exports (1984)

Japan	28.60%
USA	7.80%
Singapore	5.60%
France	4.20%
Italy	3.80%

Tourists
Total: 919,671 (1983/84)

Balance of Payments
1983: -$18,400,000,000

Labor Profile (1983)

Agriculture	20%
Construction	12%
Commerce, services, and government	62%
Industry	4%
Oil and mining	2%

Agricultural Products
Dates, grains, vegetables, livestock

Industrial Products
Petroleum products, refining and marketing, fertilizers, cements

Natural Resources
Petroleum, natural gas, sand

Electric Power Generation
52,702,000,000 kwh (1984)
kwh per capita: 4,882

Generating Capacity
18,802,000 kw

Nuclear Power Plants and Output
None

Crude Oil Production
234,430,000 metric tons; 1,718,300,000 barrels (1984)

Natural Gas Production
50,004 terajoules; 36,500,000,000 cubic feet (1983)

SENEGAL
Republic of Senegal

Budget
Revenues
1981/82: $432,700,000
Expenditures
1981/82: $432,700,000

External Public Debt
$1,671,000 (1981)

Gross Domestic Product (GDP)
$2,300,000,000 (1981)
GDP per capita: $397

Gross Domestic Product by Sector (1983)

Agriculture, forestry, and fishing	21.00%
Mining, manufacturing, utilities, and construction	25.40%
Commerce, transportation, and communication	5.35%

Consumer Price Change (Inflation)
1983: 11.70%

Imports
Machinery, transportation supplies, metal manufactures, sugar, petroleum products

Total Imports
1982: $974,000,000,000

Exports
Peanut oil, lime phosphate, oil cake, petroleum products

Total Exports
1982: $477,000,000

Trading Partners

Imports (1980)

France	33.70%
Iraq	5.80%
USA	4.30%
West Germany	3.30%
Italy	3.10%

Exports (1980)

France	32.60%
Ivory Coast	7.40%
Mali	5.80%
Mauritania	5.80%
United Kingdom	5.60%

Tourists (1981)

Total: 228,118 (1981)
Revenue: $65,000,000

Balance of Payments

1982: -$399,500,000
1981: -$480,300,000
1980: -$442,100,000

Labor Profile (1976)

Agriculture	79.60%
Industry	6.50%
Services	13.70%

Agricultural Products

Peanuts, millet, cotton, rice, sorghum

Industrial Products

Peanut oil, textiles, fertilizers, cement, processed food and fish, petroleum refining

Natural Resources

Fish, phosphate

Electric Power Generation

1,100,000,000 kwh (1982)
kwh per capita: 180

Nuclear Power Plants and Output

None

SEYCHELLES

Budget

Revenues

1983: $59,000,000
1981: $57,000,000

Expenditures

1983: $81,000,000
1981: $71,000,000

Deficit

15.6% of GDP (1983)

Expenditures by Function (1978)

General public services	35.25%
Education	14.36%
Health	13.14%
Social security and welfare	6.79%
Housing and community amenities	6.66%
Other community and social services	0.12%
Economic services	25.19%
Agriculture, forestry, fishing and hunting	6.85%
Roads	2.05%
Other transportation and communication	2.18%
Other	0.57%

Economic Aid Extended

None

Economic Aid Received

Total: $202,700,000 (1970-83)
USA only: $8,700,000 (1978-83)

External Public Debt

$41,700,000 (1983)
Service payments: 3.90% of exports of goods and services

Gross National Product (GNP)

$150,000,000 (1983)
GNP per capita: $2,310

Gross Domestic Product (GDP)

$141,914,285 (1983)
GDP per capita: $2,217

Gross Domestic Product by Sector (1983)

Agriculture, forestry, and fishing	8.35%

Manufacturing	10.37%
Utilities	1.51%
Construction	3.42%
Commerce	21.75%
Transportation and communication	12.08%
Other	42.49%

International Liquidity
Reserves (minus gold): $4,340,000 (1986)

Consumer Price Change (Inflation)
1984: 4.00%
1983: 6.10%
1982: -0.80%

Imports
Machinery and transportation equipment, manufactured goods, petroleum products, food and beverages

Total Imports
1984: $73,425,000
1983: $73,857,142
1982: $80,900,000

Exports
Copra, cinnamon bark

Total Exports
1984: $24,860,000
1983: $19,600,000
1982: $ 2,800,000

Trading Partners
Imports (1984)

Bahrein	16.89%
United Kingdom	15.86%
South Africa	8.16%
Singapore	7.35%
Japan	6.55%

Exports (1984)

Italy	17.69%
Reunion	3.46%
Japan	2.31%
United Kingdom	2.31%
USA	1.15%

Tourists
Total: 55,867 (1983)
Revenue: $30,900,000

Balance of Payments
1984: -$13,900,000
1983: -$26,300,000
1982: -$42,100,000

Labor Profile (1983)

Agriculture, forestry, and fishing	18.50%
Manufacturing and communication	19.40%
Civil service	48.60%
Services	19.50%

Agricultural Products
Copra, cinnamon, vanilla, coconut, patchouli, sweet potatoes, cassava, sugarcane, bananas

Industrial Products
Tourism, copra and vanilla processing, coconut oil, construction

Natural Resources
Fish, copra, spices

Electric Power Generation
52,000,000 kwh
kwh per capita: 787

Generating Capacity
20,000 kw (1984)

Nuclear Power Plants and Output
None (1986)

Crude Oil Production
None (1986)

Natural Gas Production
None (1986)

SIERRA LEONE
Republic of Sierra Leone

Budget
Revenues
1983/84: $129,000,000
Expenditures
1983/84: $211,000,000

Economic Aid Received
Total: $500,000,000 (1961-77)

External Public Debt
$437,000,000 (1981)
Service payments: 24.40% of exports of goods and services

Gross National Product (GNP)
$1,230,000,000 (1982)
GNP per capita: $362

Gross Domestic Product by Sector (1979)

Agriculture, forestry, and fishing	30.40%
Mining	11.30%
Manufacturing	7.40%
Utilities	0.30%
Construction	3.90%
Commerce	13.40%
Transportation and communication	16.00%
Other	17.20%

Consumer Price Change (Inflation)
1983: 69.70%

Imports
Textiles, oil, motor vehicles, machinery and parts, appliances

Total Imports
1983: $298,000,000

Exports
Diamonds, iron ore, agricultural products

Total Exports
1983: $119,000,000

Trading Partners
Imports (1979)

Nigeria	23.80%
United Kingdom	17.60%
USA	8.70%
Japan	6.80%
West Germany	5.80%

Exports (1979)

United Kingdom	44.90%
USA	17.80%
Netherlands	17.70%
Canada	1.90%
Switzerland	1.30%

Tourists
Total: 64,000 (1980)
Revenue: $10,000,000 (1980)

Balance of Payments
1982: -$169,800,000

Labor Profile

Agriculture	75%
Industry and services	15%

Agricultural Products
Rice, palm products, cocoa, coffee, ginger, piassava

Industrial Products
Diamond mining, iron ore and bauxite mining

Natural Resources
Diamonds, iron ore, bauxite, rutile

Electric Power Generation
220,000,000 kwh (1983)
kwh per capita: 60

Nuclear Power Plants and Output
None

Crude Oil Production
None

Natural Gas Production
None

SINGAPORE

Republic of Singapore

Budget
Revenues
1984: $5,214,000,000
1983: $5,458,000,000
Expenditures
1984: $3,816,364,000
1983: $3,720,000,000
Deficit
None (1983)

Expenditures by Function (1983)

General public services	12.00%
Defense	18.30%
Education	22.00%
Health	6.40%
Social security and welfare	1.00%
Housing and community amenities	4.50%
Other community and social service	1.50%
Economic services	14.30%
Agriculture, forestry, fishing and hunting	0.30%
Roads	3.50%
Other transportation and communication	2.10%
Other	19.90%

Economic Aid Received

Total: $1,209,100,000 (1970-83)
USA only: $575,000,000

External Public Debt

$1,243,600 (1983)
Service payments: 1.30% of exports of goods and services

Gross National Product (GNP)

$16,421,142,857 (1983)
GNP per capita: $6,600

Gross Domestic Product (GDP)

$16,000,000,000 (1983)
GDP per capita: $6,395

Gross Domestic Product by Sector (1984)

Agriculture, forestry, and fishing	0.80%
Mining	0.30%
Manufacturing	25.00%
Utilities	2.00%
Construction	11.60%
Commerce	19.20%
Transportation and communication	13.00%
Other	27.90%

Consumer Price Change (Inflation)

1984: 2.60%
1983: 1.20%
1982: 3.90%

Imports

Machinery and transportation equipment, petroleum, basic manufactures, crude materials

Total Imports

1984: $28,667,000,000
1983: $28,158,000,000
1982: $28,167,000,000

Exports

Petroleum products, electrical machinery, crude rubber, chemicals

Total Exports

1984: $24,070,000,000
1983: $21,833,000,000
1982: $20,788,000,000

Trading Partners

Imports (1984)

Japan	18.20%
Malaysia	15.00%
USA	14.70%
Saudi Arabia	9.30%
China	4.60%

Exports (1984)

USA	20.00%
Malaysia	16.30%
Japan	9.40%
Hong Kong	6.20%
Thailand	4.80%

Tourists

Total: 2,853,577
Revenue: $1,096,666 (1983)

Balance of Payments

1984: -$1,001,000,000
1983: -$ 991,000,000
1982: -$1,300,000,000

Labor Profile (1983)

Agriculture, forestry, and fishing	1.00%
Manufacturing	28.00%
Transportation and communication	11.30%
Trade	22.80%
Services	8.90%
Construction	7.20%
Other	0.80%

Agricultural Products
Tobacco, fruits, some rubber

Industrial Products
Petroleum refining, oil exploration, ship repair, rubber processing, light textile industry

Natural Resources
Negligible

Electric Power Generation
8,600,000,000 kwh
kwh per capita: 3,400

Generating Capacity
2,961,000 kw (1984)

Nuclear Power Plants and Output
None (1986)

Crude Oil Production
None (1986)

Natural Gas Production
None (1986)

SOLOMON ISLANDS

Budget
Revenues
1979: $23,450,000
Expenditures
1979: $37,300,000

Economic Aid Received
Total: $13,300,000 (1979)

Gross Domestic Product (GDP)
$146,750,000 (1980)
GDP per capita: $638

Gross Domestic Product by Sector (1972)

Agriculture, forestry, and fishing	58.90%
Mining, manufacturing, and utilities	0.90%
Construction	2.20%
Commerce	7.70%
Transportation and communication	1.90%
Other	27.90%

Consumer Price Change (Inflation)
1983: 11.10%

Imports
Food, animals, basic manufactures, transportation equipment

Total Imports
1981: $72,200,000

Exports
Fish, copra, timber, palm oil

Total Exports
1981: $68,400,000

Trading Partners
Imports (1981)

Australia	28.10%
Japan	15.00%
United Kingdom	14.00%

Exports (1981)

Japan	37.40%
Netherlands	12.00%
United Kingdom	11.90%

Balance of Payments
1978: -$2,380,000

Labor Profile (1981)

Agriculture	32%
Industry and commerce	18%
Services	32%

Agricultural Products
Coconuts, copra, cocoa, rice

Industrial Products
Canned fish

Natural Resources
Forests, minerals, agricultural land and water supply

Electric Power Generation
30,000,000 kwh (1983)
kwh per capita: 117

Generating Capacity
15,000 kw (1984)

Nuclear Power Plants and Output
None

Crude Oil Production
None

Natural Gas Production
None

SOMALIA
Somali Democratic Republic

Budget
Revenues
1984: $249,650,000
1983: $278,000,000
Expenditures
1984: $249,650,000
1983: $359,000,000
Deficit
None (1984)

Expenditures by Function (1978)

General public services	24.00%
Defense	26.00%
Education	8.30%
Health	3.20%
Social security and welfare	1.70%
Economic services	11.70%
Agriculture, forestry, fishing and hunting	5.80%
Roads	2.00%
Other transportation and communication	0.10%
Other	0.50%

Economic Aid Extended
None

Economic Aid Received
Total: $189,000,000 (1970-83)
USA only: None

External Public Debt
$1,200,000,000 (1983)
Service payments: 17.00% of exports of goods and services

Gross National Product (GNP)
$1,800,000,000 (1981)
GNP per capita: $391

Gross Domestic Product (GDP)
$1,875,000,000 (1982)
GDP per capita: $375

International Liquidity
Reserves (minus gold): $1,000,000 (1984)
Gold reserves: 19,000 fine troy ounces

Consumer Price Change (Inflation)
1984: 222.70%
1983: 64.40%
1982: 32.60%

Imports
Basic manufactures (paper, yarn, nonmetallic minerals), machinery, transportation equipment

Total Imports
1984: $ 72,638,460
1983: $144,823,529
1982: $137,800,000

Exports
Food and live animals, raw materials, machinery, transportation equipment

Total Exports
1984: $ 34,346,153
1983: $ 93,176,470
1982: $132,866,666

Trading Partners
Imports (1984)

Italy	21.30%
USA	20.01%
Saudi Arabia	12.90%
West Germany	5.30%
United Kingdom	4.90%

Exports (1984)

Saudi Arabia	58.50%
Yemen Arab Republic	11.40%
Italy	5.70%
China	5.30%
Iran	3.60%

Balance of Payments
1984: +$ 55,900,000
1983: -$219,700,000
1982: -$253,300,000

Labor Profile (1975)

Agriculture, forestry, and fishing	84.60%
Manufacturing	5.90%
Services	9.50%

Agricultural Products
Bananas, sorghum, maize, beans, peanuts, sesame, sugarcane, cotton

Industrial Products
Textiles, meat, fish, fruit juice canning

Natural Resources
Some timber and uranium

Electric Power Generation
62,000,000 kwh
kwh per capita: 9

Generating Capacity
47,000 kw

Nuclear Power Plants and Output
None

Crude Oil Production
None (1985)

Natural Gas Production
None (1985)

SOUTH AFRICA
Republic of South Africa

Budget
Revenues
1984: $11,069,000,000
Expenditures
1984: $13,300,000

Economic Aid Received
None

Gross National Product (GNP)
$50,400,000,000 (1984)
GNP per capita: $1,590

Gross Domestic Product (GDP)
$52,400,000,000 (1984)
GDP per capita: $1,653

Gross Domestic Product by Sector

Agriculture, forestry, and fishing	47.00%
Mining	15.20%
Manufacturing	23.00%
Utilities	4.60%
Construction	4.10%
Commerce	13.30%
Transportation and communication	8.80%
Other	26.00%

Consumer Price Change (Inflation)
1984: 17.30%

Imports
Machinery, electrical equipment, transportation equipment, base metals, metal products

Total Imports
1984: $12,600,000,000

Exports
Wool, diamonds, gold, corn, uranium, sugar, fruit, hides, skins, metals and metallic ores, metal products, asbestos, fish products

Total Exports
1984: $10,800,000,000

Trading Partners

Imports (1984)

USA	15.90%
West Germany	15.70%
Japan	12.70%
United Kingdom	11.40%
France	3.80%

Exports (1984)

USA	8.40%
Japan	7.50%
Switzerland	6.90%
United Kingdom	4.30%
West Germany	4.00%

Tourists

Total: 708,710 (1981)

Country of origin

Africa	38.00%
Europe	44.00%
Asia	4.00%
USA	11.00%

Balance of Payments

1984: -$810,000,000

Labor Profile (1980)

Agriculture, forestry, and fishing	15.00%
Extractive industries	9.00%
Manufacturing	17.00%
Utilities	0.90%
Construction	5.00%
Commerce	15.00%
Transportation and communication	5.00%
Community, social, and personal services	22.00%
Unemployed	10.00%

Agricultural Products

Corn, wool, dairy products, wheat, sugarcane, tobacco, citrus fruits

Industrial Products

Mined products, automobiles, fabricated metal, machinery, textiles, chemicals, fertilizer, fish

Natural Resources

Nearly all essential minerals except oil

Electric Power Generation

114,670,000 kwh (1984)
kwh per capita: 3,617

Generating Capacity

23,800,000 kw capacity

Nuclear Power Plants and Output

One plant in operation, 1 under construction; total output 921 mwe

Crude Oil Production

None

Natural Gas Production

None

SOUTH KOREA

See Korea (South)

SOUTH YEMEN

See Yemen (South)

SOUTHWEST AFRICA

See Namibia

SOVIET UNION

See Union of Soviet Socialist Republics

SPAIN

Budget

Revenues

1982: $26,800,000,000

Expenditures

1982: $36,990,000,000

Economic Aid Received

USA only: $3,880,000 (1983)

External Public Debt

$11,442,000,000 (1979)
Service payments: 5.60% of exports of goods and services

Gross National Product (GNP)

$143,200,000,000 (1983)
GNP per capita: $3,748

Gross Domestic Product by Sector (1983)

Agriculture, forestry, and fishing	6.00%
Manufacturing	27.00%
Construction	7.00%
Commerce	16.00%

Imports
Machinery and transportation equipment, petroleum products, grains, cotton, coal, iron and steel

Total Imports
1983: $29,190,000,000

Exports
Fresh fruits, iron and steel products, textiles, footwear, mercury, ships, canned fruits and vegetables

Total Exports
1983: $19,700,000,000

Trading Partners

Imports (1981)

USA	13.90%
Saudi Arabia	11.00%
West Germany	8.10%
France	8.00%
Mexico	6.20%

Exports (1981)

France	14.40%
West Germany	8.70%
United Kingdom	6.90%
USA	6.70%
Italy	5.80%

Tourists
Total: 41,000,000 (1983)

Country of origin

France	25.00%
Portugal	20.40%
United Kingdom	12.40%
West Germany	12.00%
Benelux countries	6.00%

Balance of Payments
1983: -$2,740,000,000

Labor Profile (1982)

Agriculture	16.00%
Industry	25.00%
Construction	10.00%
Services	43.00%

Agricultural Products
Cereals, vegetables, citrus fruits, feedgrains, wine, olive oil, livestock

Industrial Products
Processed foods, textiles, footwear, petrochemicals, steel, automobiles, ships, consumer goods

Natural Resources
Coal, lignite, water power, uranium, mercury, pyrites, fla rospar, gypsum, iron ore, zinc, lead, tungsten, copper

Electric Power Generation
115,500,000,000 kwh (1983)
kwh per capita: 3,020

Generating Capacity
35,600,000 kw (1984)

Nuclear Power Plants and Output
Four nuclear plants are in operation, 11 are under construction, 2 are on order, and 1 is in the planning stage; 1,973 mwe nuclear generating capacity (on line by December 1982)

Crude Oil Production
2,260,000 metric tons; 16,540,000 barrels (1983)

Natural Gas Production
None

SRI LANKA

Democratic Socialist Republic of Sri Lanka

Budget

Revenues
1984: $1,429,204,545
1983: $1,008,400,000

Expenditures
1984: $1,945,568,182
1983: $1,671,600,000

Deficit
8.90% of GDP (1984)

Expenditures by Function (1983)

General public services	10.00%
Defense	2.40%

Education	7.00%
Health	5.00%
Social security and welfare	11.20%
Housing and community amenities	0.20%
Other community and social services	0.60%
Economic services	13.10%
Agriculture, forestry, fishing, and hunting	5.80%
Other transportation and communication	6.50%
Other	50.20%

Economic Aid Extended
None

External Public Debt
$2,205,000,000 (1983)
Service payments: 9.80% of exports of goods and services

Gross National Product (GNP)
$5,586,780,303 (1984)
GNP per capita: $358

Gross Domestic Product (GDP)
$5,780,871,212 (1984)
GDP per capita: $371

Gross Domestic Product by Sector (1983)

Agriculture, forestry, and fishing	25.50%
Mining	1.20%
Manufacturing	15.00%
Utilities	1.40%
Construction	8.30%
Transportation and communication	9.80%
Commerce	20.00%
Other	18.70%

International Liquidity
Reserves (minus gold): $510,000,000 (1984)
Gold reserves: 63,000 fine troy ounces

Consumer Price Change (Inflation)
1984: 17.50%
1983: 15.70%
1982: 18.90%

Imports
Food, petroleum, fertilizer, machinery and equipment

Total Imports
1984: $1,869,000,000
1983: $1,935,000,000
1982: $2,015,000,000

Exports
Rubber, tea

Total Exports
1984: $1,467,000,000
1983: $1,063,000,000
1982: $1,031,000,000

Trading Partners

Imports (1984)

Japan	53.10%
Saudi Arabia	16.40%
USA	8.80%
India	6.00%
Singapore	5.50%

Exports (1984)

USA	18.80%
Iraq	8.80%
United Kingdom	4.90%
West Germany	4.80%
USSR	4.40%

Tourists
Total: 337,342
Revenue: $102,400,000 (1983)

Balance of Payments
1984: +$ 6,500,000
1983: -$466,200,000
1982: -$549,000,000

Labor Profile (1981)

Agriculture, forestry, and fishing	42.10%
Manufacturing	9.30%
Transportation and communication	3.60%
Trade	8.70%
Civil service	11.40%
Services	0.80%
Construction	3.90%
Other	20.20%

Agricultural Products
Tea, rubber, coconut, rice, spices

Industrial Products
Textiles, chemicals, milling, light engineering, paper and paper products

Natural Resources
Limestone, graphite, mineral sands, gems

Electric Power Generation
2,100,000,000 kwh
kwh per capita: 132

Generating Capacity
642,000 kw (1984)

Nuclear Power Plants and Output
None

Crude Oil Production
None (1985)

Natural Gas Production
None (1985)

SUDAN
Republic of the Sudan

Budget
Revenues
1983: $1,200,000,000
Expenditures
1983: $1,800,000,000

Gross National Product (GNP)
$6,700,000,000 (1981)
GNP per capita: $355

Gross Domestic Product by Sector (1977)

Agriculture, forestry, and fishing	36.50%
Mining	0.10%
Manufacturing	7.50%
Utilities	1.30%
Construction	4.10%
Commerce	19.30%
Transportation and communication	9.70%
Other	21.60%

Consumer Price Change (Inflation)
1983: 30.60%

Imports
Transportation equipment, machinery, textiles, sugar, petroleum products, iron and steel, metal manufactures, pharmaceuticals, wheat

Total Imports
1983: $1,350,000,000

Exports
Cotton, peanuts, sesame, durra, hides and skins, livestock

Total Exports
1983: $624,000,000

Trading Partners

Imports (1982)

USA	15.50%
United Kingdom	13.60%
Saudi Arabia	12.20%
France	7.70%
West Germany	5.50%

Exports (1982)

Saudi Arabia	28.30%
Italy	7.30%
Japan	7.10%
Egypt	6.70%
China	6.10%

Tourists
Total: 26,714 (1977)

Balance of Payments
1982: -$430,800,000

Labor Profile (1973)

Agriculture, forestry, and fishing	66.40%
Mining	0.09%
Manufacturing	4.00%
Utilities	1.00%
Construction	2.00%
Commerce	5.50%
Transportation and communication	3.50%
Community, social, and personal services	10.30%

Agricultural Products
Cotton, peanuts, sesame seed, gum arabic, sorghum, wheat, sugarcane

Industrial Products
Cement, textiles, pharmaceuticals, shoes

Natural Resources
Iron ore, copper, chrome

Electric Power Generation
1,700,000,000 kwh (1983)
kwh per capita: 85

Generating Capacity
450,000 kw (1983)

Nuclear Power Plants and Output
None

Crude Oil Production
1,200,000 metric tons

Natural Gas Production
None

SURINAME
Republic of Suriname

Budget
Revenues
1982: $289,000,000
Expenditures
1982: $441,000,000
Deficit
1.29% of GDP (1980)

Economic Aid Received
Total: $2,650,000,000 (1970-79)

Gross National Product (GNP)
$1,000,000,000 (1980)
GNP per capita: $2,669

Gross Domestic Product by Sector

Agriculture, forestry, and fishing	9.10%
Extractive industries	11.80%
Manufacturing	8.90%
Utilities	1.70%
Construction	2.80%
Commerce	12.10%
Transportation and communication	5.10%
Other	48.10%

International Liquidity
Reserves (minus gold): $59,000,000 (1983)
Gold reserves: 540,000 fine troy ounces

Consumer Price Change (Inflation)
1983: 4.40%
1982: 9.00%
1980: 14.10%

Imports
Food, beverages, machinery, petroleum, textiles, vehicles

Total Imports
1982: $429,000,000

Exports
Bauxite, alumina, aluminum

Total Exports
1982: $511,000,000

Trading Partners
Imports (1981)

Trinidad and Tobago	29.20%
USA	28.90%
Netherlands	9.70%
Japan	7.20%
West Germany	4.00%

Exports (1981)

USA	35.10%
Netherlands	14.80%
Norway	13.40%
United Kingdom	7.10%
Japan	4.00%

Tourists
Total: 66,096 (1981)

Balance of Payments
1983: -$160,900,000
1982: -$123,500,000
1980: -$ 64,000,000

Labor Profile (1982)

Agriculture, forestry, fishing and hunting	9.10%

Mining	6.70%
Manufacturing	8.60%
Utilities	1.40%
Construction	4.60%
Commerce	13.70%
Transportation and communication	3.40%
Other private services	2.20%
Government	45.70%

Agricultural Products
Rice, fruits, sugar, coffee

Industrial Products
Bauxite, processed foods, lumber, bricks

Natural Resources
Bauxite, iron ore and other mineral ores not yet exploited, forests, hydroelectric potential, fish

Electric Power Generation
1,000,000,000 kwh (1983)
kwh per capita: 2,835

Generating Capacity
400,000 kw (1983)

SWAZILAND
Kingdom of Swaziland

Budget
Revenues
1983: $170,000,000
1982: $189,900,000
Expenditures
1983: $120,000,000
1982: $189,900,000
Deficit
None (1983)

Expenditures by Function (1979)

General public services	23.46%
Defense	8.16%
Education	19.38%
Health	6.12%
Social security, welfare, housing, and community amenities	7.14%
Agriculture, forestry, fishing and hunting	12.95%
Roads, other transportation, and communication	18.36%
Other	1.02%

Economic Aid Extended
None (1986)

Economic Aid Received
Total: $383,000,000 (1970-83)
USA only: $73,000,000

External Public Debt
$182,700,000 (1983)
Service payments: 4.60% of exports of goods and services

Gross National Product (GNP)
$580,000,000 (1983)
GNP per capita: $900

Gross Domestic Product (GDP)
$831,250,000 (1983)
GDP per capita: $1,333

Gross Domestic Product by Sector

Agriculture, forestry, and fishing	20.04%
Mining	2.71%
Manufacturing	16.06%
Utilities	1.26%
Construction	3.79%
Commerce	7.58%
Transportation and communication	4.51%
Other	43.86%

Consumer Price Change (Inflation)
1985: 18.60%
1984: 14.00%
1983: 11.20%

Imports
Motor vehicles and machinery, fuels and lubricants, foodstuffs, clothing

Total Imports
1984: $1,212,000,000
1983: $ 464,000,000
1982: $ 595,555,000

Exports
Sugar, wood products, iron ore, asbestos, fruit, meat products

Total Exports
1984: $707,460,000
1983: $330,000,000
1982: $409,388,800

Tourists
Total: 82,000
Revenue: $33,000,000 (1980)

Balance of Payments
1984: -$ 11,300,000
1983: -$106,200,000
1982: -$ 76,000,000

Agricultural Products
Corn, livestock, sugar cane, citrus fruit, cotton, rice, pineapples

Industrial Products
Milled sugar, ginned cotton, processed meat and wood, tourism, chemicals, machinery, beverages

Natural Resources
Iron ore, asbestos, coal

Electric Power Generation
150,000,000 kwh
kwh per capita: 230

Generating Capacity
115,000 kw (1984)

Nuclear Power Plants and Output
None (1986)

Crude Oil Production
None (1986)

Natural Gas Production
None (1986)

SWEDEN
Kingdom of Sweden

Budget
Revenues
1985: $28,000,000,000
Expenditures
1985: $38,100,000,000

External Public Debt
None

Gross National Product (GNP)
$89,600,000,000 (1983)
GNP per capita: $10,749

Gross Domestic Product by Sector (1983)

Agriculture, forestry, and fishing	3.00%
Mining	0.50%
Manufacturing	20.00%
Utilities	0.40%
Construction	7.00%
Commerce	41.00%
Transportation and communication	8.00%
Other	50.00%

Consumer Price Change (Inflation)
1984: 10.60%

Imports
Machinery, instruments, petroleum, yarns, foodstuffs

Total Imports
1984: $22,600,000,000

Exports
Wood products, iron ore, machinery, base metals, iron and steel, ball bearings, ships, instruments, automobiles

Total Exports
1984: $27,000,000,000

Trading Partners
Imports (1984)

West Germany	17.30%
United Kingdom	13.90%
USA	8.00%
Norway	7.60%
Denmark	6.50%

Exports (1984)

West Germany	11.60%
USA	11.20%
Norway	10.20%

United Kingdom 9.20%
Denmark 8.30%

Tourists
Revenue: $1,076,000,000

Balance of Payments
1983: $1,060,000,000

Labor Profile (1983)

Agriculture, forestry, and fishing	5.40%
Mining and manufacturing	22.60%
Public administration	36.70%
Construction	6.30%
Commerce	13.80%
Transportation and communication	6.90%
Finance and business services	7.10%
Utilities	0.90%

Agricultural Products
Dairy products, grains, sugar beets, potatoes, wood

Industrial Products
Machinery, instruments, metal products, automobiles, aircraft

Natural Resources
Forests, iron ore, hydroelectric power

Electric Power Generation
112,885,000,000 kwh (1984)
kwh per capita: 13,544

Generating Capacity
36,841,000 kw (1984)

Nuclear Power Plants and Output
Seven plants in operation, 5 under construction; 7,330 mwe nuclear generating capacity (on line by December 1982)

Crude Oil Production
None

Natural Gas Production
None

SWITZERLAND
Swiss Confederation

Budget
Revenues
1984: $7,683,000,000
1983: $8,450,000,000
Expenditures
1984: $7,904,000,000
1983: $9,000,000,000
Deficit
0.23% of GDP (1984)

Expenditures by Function (1983)

General public services	4.00%
Defense	10.12%
Education	7.62%
Health	0.04%
Social security and welfare	4.71%
Housing and community amenities	8.95%
Other community and social services	0.20%
Economic services	66.66%
Agriculture, forestry, fishing and hunting	6.41%
Roads	5.00%
Other transportation and communication	6.37%

Economic Aid Extended
$1,100,000,000 (1970-82)

Economic Aid Received
None (1986)

External Public Debt
None (1986)

Gross National Product (GNP)
$112,285,000,000 (1985)
GNP per capita: $17,274

Gross Domestic Product (GDP)
$107,050,000,000 (1985)
GDP per capita: $16,469

International Liquidity
Reserves (minus gold): $16,484,000,000 (1986)
Gold reserves: 83,280,000 fine troy ounces

Consumer Price Change (Inflation)
1985: 3.40%
1984: 2.90%
1983: 3.00%

Imports
Nonelectrical machinery and appliances, transportation equipment, electrical machinery and appliances, iron and steel, consumer goods, fuels

Total Imports
1985: $27,450,000,000
1984: $25,849,000,000
1983: $25,591,000,000

Exports
Electrical machinery and appliances, textiles and yarns, chemicals, dyestuffs, watches and clocks

Total Exports
1985: $30,702,000,000
1984: $29,521,000,000
1983: $29,192,000,000

Trading Partners
Imports (1984)

West Germany	29.15%
France	10.84%
Italy	9.83%
United Kingdom	7.11%
USA	6.44%

Exports (1984)

West Germany	19.23%
USA	9.61%
France	8.07%
United Kingdom	7.69%
Italy	7.31%

Tourists
Total: 34,958,000
Revenue: $4,173,913 (1984)
Country of origin

West Germany	30.73%
Italy	14.63%
United Kingdom	9.26%

Balance of Payments
1985: $4,091,000
1984: $1,197,000
1983: $3,934,000

Labor Profile (1980)

Agriculture, forestry, and fishing	7.26%
Manufacturing	32.33%
Transportation and communication	6.00%
Construction	6.36%
Other	48.05%

Agricultural Products
Cheese and other dairy products, livestock, fruits

Industrial Products
Manufactured products, banking services, insurance

Natural Resources
Waterpower, timber, salt

Electric Power Generation
56,203,000,000 kwh (1985)
kwh per capita: 8,560

Generating Capacity
16,690,000 kw (1985)

Nuclear Power Plants and Output
Five power plants; total output, 5,882 mwe (1984)

Crude Oil Production
None (1986)

Natural Gas Production
None (1986)

SYRIA
Syrian Arab Republic

Budget
Revenues
1983: $5,400,000,000
Expenditures
1982: $8,600,000,000
Deficit
16.20% of GDP

External Public Debt
$3,178,000,000 (1981)
Service payments: 12.10% of exports of goods and services

Gross Domestic Product (GDP)
$19,700,000,000 (1983)
GDP per capita: $1,964

Gross Domestic Product by Sector (1983)

Agriculture, forestry, and fishing	19.90%
Extractive industries, manufacturing, and utilities	19.30%
Construction	6.30%
Commerce	24.80%
Transportation and communication	7.60%
Other	22.10%

International Liquidity
Reserves (minus gold): $52,000,000 (1983)
Gold reserves: 83,000 fine troy ounces

Consumer Price Change (Inflation)
1984: 16.80%

Imports
Food, fuel, machinery and transportation equipment, textiles, metal and metal products, chemicals, fertilizers

Total Imports
1983: $4,540,000,000
1982: $4,020,000,000
1981: $5,170,000,000

Exports
Oil, cotton, fruits and vegetables, wool, tobacco, textiles, phosphates

Total Exports
1983: $1,910,000,000
1982: $2,020,000,000
1981: $2,100,000,000

Trading Partners

Imports (1983)

Iraq	16.90%
West Germany	8.50%
Japan	6.60%
Italy	6.50%
Saudi Arabia	5.40%

Exports (1983)

Romania	24.90%
Italy	15.90%
USSR	13.30%
France	8.90%
West Germany	6.10%

Balance of Payments
1983: -$724,000,000
1982: -$217,000,000

Labor Profile (1983)

Agriculture, hunting, and forestry	29.40%
Mining and manufacturing	13.50%
Construction	15.70%
Transportation and communication	6.20%
Commerce	10.20%
Finance and insurance	0.80%
Services	23.20%
Other	1.00%

Agricultural Products
Cotton, wheat, barley, tobacco, sugar beets, sheep, goats, grapes, tomatoes

Industrial Products
Textiles, cement, glass, petroleum, food processing, soap, phosphates

Natural Resources
Oil and natural gas, chrome and manganese ores, asphalt, iron ore, rock salt, phosphate

Electric Power Generation
5,930,000,000 kwh (1984)
kwh per capita: 588

Generating Capacity
2,257,000 kw (1984)

Nuclear Power Plants and Output
One nuclear plant is in the planning stage

Crude Oil Production
8,960,000 metric tons; 65,700,000 barrels (1984)

Natural Gas Production
None

TAIWAN

See China (Taiwan)

TANZANIA

United Republic of Tanzania

Budget

Revenues
1985: $ 891,800,000
1982: $1,656,000,000
Expenditures
1985: $1,376,500,000
1982: $2,057,000,000

Expenditures by Function (1981)

General public services	23.10%
Defense	12.30%
Education	13.00%
Health	6.10%
Social security and welfare	1.20%
Housing and community amenities	1.40%
Other community and social services	1.30%
Economic services	37.40%
Agriculture, forestry, fishing and hunting	11.20%
Roads	6.20%
Other	1.00%

Economic Aid Extended

None

Economic Aid Received

Total: $300,000,000 (1970-80)
USA only: $200,000,000

External Public Debt

$2,584,200,000 (1981)
Service payments: 6.10% of exports of goods and services

Gross National Product (GNP)

$3,809,388,889 (1984)
GNP per capita: $181

Gross Domestic Product (GDP)

$4,203,222,222 (1984)
GDP per capita: $200

International Liquidity

Reserves (minus gold): $23,400,000 (1985)

Consumer Price Change (Inflation)

1984: 35.80%
1983: 27.10%
1982: 28.90%

Imports

Manufactured goods, textiles, machinery and transportation equipment, foodstuffs, tobacco

Total Imports

1984: $ 782,000,000
1983: $ 802,000,000
1982: $1,134,000,000

Exports

Cotton, coffee, petroleum products, sisal, diamonds, cloves, coconuts

Total Exports

1984: $370,000,000
1983: $372,000,000
1982: $458,000,000

Trading Partners

Imports (1984)

United Kingdom	19.70%
Japan	9.40%
West Germany	8.20%
Italy	7.90%
USA	5.25%

Exports (1984)

West Germany	19.90%
United Kingdom	11.40%
India	7.40%
Italy	6.60%
Algeria	4.80%

Tourists

Total: 71,000
Revenue: $14,086,022 (1982)

Balance of Payments

1981: -$379,000,000
1980: -$534,300,000
1979: -$346,500,000

Labor Profile (1967)

Agriculture, forestry, and fishing	90.00%
Manufacturing	1.80%
Transportation and communication	0.80%

Trade	1.40%
Services	3.60%
Construction	0.60%
Other	1.80%

Agricultural Products
Sugar, maize, rice, wheat, cotton, coffee, sisal, cashew nuts, tea, tobacco, pyrethrum, cloves

Industrial Products
Textiles, agricultural processing, light manufacturing, refined oil, cement

Natural Resources
Hydroelectric potential, unexploited iron, ore and coal, dwindling gem stone and gold mines

Electric Power Generation
1,127,000,000 kwh
kwh per capita: 53

Generating Capacity
429,000 kw (1984)

Nuclear Power Plants and Output
None (1985)

Crude Oil Production
None (1985)

Natural Gas Production
None (1985)

THAILAND

Kingdom of Thailand

Budget
Revenues
1984: $8,730,000,000
Expenditures
1984: $8,730,000,000

External Public Debt
8,250,000,000 (1981)
Service payments: 6.70% of exports of goods and services

Gross National Product (GNP)
$38,400,000,000 (1982)
GNP per capita: $800

Gross Domestic Product by Sector (1982)

Agriculture, forestry, and fishing	22.00%
Mining	2.10%
Manufacturing	19.00%
Utilities	2.00%
Construction	5.00%
Commerce	23.00%
Transportation and communication	7.10%
Other	20.00%

Consumer Price Change (Inflation)
1982: 5.30%

Imports
Machinery and transportation equipment, fuels and lubricants, base metals, chemicals, fertilizers

Total Imports
1982: $8,543,000,000

Exports
Rice, rubber, corn, tin, tapioca products, sugar

Total Exports
1982: $6,949,000,000

Trading Partners
Imports (1982)

Japan	23%
USA	13%
Saudi Arabia	15%
West Germany	4%
Singapore	6%

Exports (1982)

Japan	14%
Netherlands	13%
USA	13%
Singapore	7%
Hong Kong	5%

Tourists
Total: 2,218,429 (1982)

Balance of Payments
1981: -$2,569,000,000

Labor Profile (1981)

Agriculture	72.00%
Mining	0.30%
Manufacturing	7.00%

Utilities	3.00%
Construction	0.20%
Commerce	8.00%
Transportation and communication	2.00%
Services	8.00%

Agricultural Products
Rice, rubber, corn, tapioca, sugar

Industrial Products
Processed food, textiles, wood, cement

Natural Resources
Fish, forests, tin, tungsten, flourite, oil shale

Electric Power Generation
16,321,000,000 kwh (1983)
kwh per capita: 327

Nuclear Power Plants and Output
One light water reactor or pressurized heavy water reactor with a 900 net mwe generating capacity is being planned in Amphur Sri Racha

TOGO
Republic of Togo

Budget
Revenues
1984: $192,039,666
1983: $183,227,817
Expenditures
1984: $230,828,810
1983: $220,294,964
Deficit
6.24% of GDP (1984)

Expenditures by Function (1984)

General public services	11.36%
Defense	6.36%
Education	14.54%
Health	5.45%
Social security and welfare	10.90%
Housing and community amenities	2.82%
Other community and social services	0.41%
Economic services	20.00%
Agriculture, forestry, fishing and hunting	9.09%
Roads	4.72%
Other transportation and communication	0.36%

Economic Aid Extended
None (1986)

Economic Aid Received
USA only: None (1984)

External Public Debt
$805,300,000 (1983)
Service payments: 16.80% of exports of goods and services

Gross National Product (GNP)
$950,000,000 (1982)
GNP per capita: $340

Gross Domestic Product (GDP)
$609,812,108 (1984)
GDP per capita: $212

Gross Domestic Product by Sector (1981)

Agriculture, forestry, and fishing	27.10%
Mining	9.00%
Manufacturing	6.20%
Utilities	1.50%
Construction	4.30%
Commerce	20.70%
Transportation and communication	6.60%
Other	24.60%

International Liquidity
Reserves (minus gold): $327,900,000 (1986)
Gold reserves: 13,000 fine troy ounces

Consumer Price Change (Inflation)
1985: -5.10%
1984: -1.80%
1983: -3.50%

Imports
Consumer goods, machinery, fuels, foodstuffs

Total Imports
1984: $207,820,000
1983: $217,925,659
1982: $321,014,881

Exports
Phosphates, cocoa, coffee

Total Exports
1984: $174,505,219
1983: $148,470,024
1982: $173,133,928

Trading Partners
Imports (1984)

France	23.78%
Netherlands	15.05%
Belgium	6.34%
United Kingdom	6.31%
West Germany	5.97%

Exports (1984)

France	13.50%
USA	13.18%
Yugoslavia	12.20%
Netherlands	10.39%
Ivory Coast	7.87%

Tourists
Total: 126,300 (1984)

Balance of Payments
1984: +$16,000,000
1983: -$57,000,000
1982: -$81,000,000

Labor Profile (1984)

Agriculture, forestry, and fishing	78.00%
Manufacturing	22.00%

Agricultural Products
Yams, manioc, millet, sorghum, cocoa, coffee, rice

Industrial Products
Phosphates, textiles, agricultural products

Natural Resources
Phosphates, limestone

Electric Power Generation
83,000,000 kwh (1985)
kwh per capita: 27

Generating Capacity
47,900 kw (1985)

Nuclear Power Plants and Output
None (1986)

Crude Oil Production
None (1986)

Natural Gas Production
None (1986)

TONGA
Kingdom of Tonga

Budget
Revenues
1985: $22,788,160
1984: $19,156,904
Expenditures
1985: $22,760,034
1984: $19,144,145

Economic Aid Extended
None (1986)

Economic Aid Received
Total : $104,000,000
USA only: None (1971-83)

Gross National Product (GNP)
$65,000,000 (1984)
GNP per capita: $580

Gross Domestic Product (GDP)
$86,300,000 (1983)
GDP per capita: $908

Gross Domestic Product by Sector (1983)

Agriculture, forestry, and fishing	41.80%
Mining	0.40%
Manufacturing	5.00%
Utilities	0.40%
Construction	3.90%
Commerce	15.10%
Transportation and communication	5.70%
Other	27.90%

Imports
Manufactured goods, foodstuffs, transportation equipment

Total Imports
1984: $10,967,093
1983: $41,663,823
1979: $29,000,000

Exports
Copra, bananas

Total Exports
1984: $9,995,621
1983: $5,842,393
1979: $7,000,000

Trading Partners
Imports (1984)

New Zealand	38.04%
Australia	24.34%
Japan	10.87%
Singapore	5.65%
USA	5.43%

Exports (1984)

New Zealand	60.00%
Australia	20.00%

Tourists
Total: 84,679
Revenue: $4,285,714 (1984)

Labor Profile (1976)

Agriculture, forestry, and fishing	51.07%
Manufacturing	2.04%
Transportation and communication	4.40%
Construction	6.18%
Other	36.31%

Agricultural Products
Sweet potatoes, yams, taro, tapioca, cassava, corn, coconuts, bananas, pineapples, melons, mangoes, citrus fruits

Industrial Products
No mines or significant industry

Natural Resources
No minerals

Electric Power Generation
8,000,000 kwh (1985)
kwh per capita: 75

Nuclear Power Plants and Output
None (1986)

Crude Oil Production
None (1986)

Natural Gas Production
None (1986)

TRINIDAD AND TOBAGO
Republic of Trinidad and Tobago

Budget
Revenues
1982: $3,100,000,000
1981: $2,900,000,000
Expenditures
1982: $4,000,000,000
1981: $2,800,000,000
Deficit
12.32% of GDP (1982)

Expenditures by Function (1981)

General public services	14.79%
Defense	0.46%
Education	6.16%
Health	1.54%
Social security and welfare	0.37%
Housing and community amenities	13.71%
Other community and social services	2.32%
Economic services	60.92%
Agriculture, forestry, fishing and hunting	5.31%
Roads	20.00%
Other transportation and communication	3.38%

Economic Aid Extended
None (1986)

Economic Aid Received
Total: $438,000,000 (1970-82)
USA only: $320,000,000

External Public Debt
$887,000,000 (1983)

Gross National Product (GNP)
$7,316,000,000 (1982)
GNP per capita: $6,651

Gross Domestic Product (GDP)
$7,315,800,000 (1982)
GDP per capita: $6,474

Gross Domestic Product by Sector (1983)

Agriculture, forestry, and fishing	2.36%
Mining	19.60%
Manufacturing	9.46%
Utilities	1.31%
Construction	16.61%
Commerce	12.19%
Transportation and communication	14.49%
Other	23.94%

International Liquidity
Reserves (minus gold): $875,300,000 (1986)
Gold reserves: 54,000 fine troy ounces

Consumer Price Change (Inflation)
1985: 7.60%
1984: 13.30%
1983: 16.70%

Imports
Crude oil, machinery and equipment, foodstuffs

Total Imports
1984: $1,919,000,000
1983: $2,582,000,000
1982: $3,697,000,000

Exports
Petroleum, sugar

Total Exports
1984: $2,173,000,000
1983: $2,353,000,000
1982: $3,072,000,000

Trading Partners

Imports (1984)

USA	38.92%
Japan	10.96%
United Kingdom	9.79%
Canada	6.92%
France	3.03%

Exports (1984)

USA	73.00%
United Kingdom	8.98%
Netherlands	2.77%
Suriname	2.63%
Barbados	2.50%

Tourists
Total: 191,470 (1984)

Balance of Payments
1985: -$205,300,000
1984: -$551,700,000
1983: -$877,200,000

Labor Profile (1982)

Agriculture, forestry, and fishing	8.70%
Manufacturing	17.83%
Transportation and communication	6.95%
Construction	21.36%
Other	45.16%

Agricultural Products
Sugarcane, cicia, coffee, rice, bananas

Industrial Products
Petroleum, processed foods, cement

Natural Resources
Petroleum, attractive climate and coastline for tourism

Electric Power Generation
2,600,000,000 kwh (1984)
kwh per capita: 2,226

Generating Capacity
1,009,000 kw (1984)

Nuclear Power Plants and Output
None (1986)

Crude Oil Production
8,904,000 metric tons; 65,266,320 barrels (1985)

Natural Gas Production
115,104 terajoules; 1,033,633,920 cubic feet (1984)

TUNISIA

Republic of Tunisia

Budget

Revenues

1984: $2,880,000,000
1983: $2,200,000,000

Expenditures

1982: $3,592,000,000
1981: $1,300,000,000 (1981)

Expenditures by Function (1981)

General public services	10.00%
Defense	8.69%
Education	15.38%
Health	7.92%
Social security and welfare	8.53%
Housing and community amenities	5.38%
Other community and social services	2.53%
Economic services	35.31%
Agriculture, forestry, fishing and hunting	17.69%
Roads	1.54%
Other transportation and communication	5.23%
Other	15.31%

Economic Aid Extended

None (1986)

Economic Aid Received

Total: $1,448,700,000 (1946-83)
USA only: $930,000,000

External Public Debt

$3,427,100,000 (1983)
Service payments: 19.70% of exports of goods and services

Gross National Product (GNP)

$9,778,571,429 (1985)
GNP per capita: $1,328

Gross Domestic Product (GDP)

$9,800,000,000 (1985)
GDP per capita: $939

Gross Domestic Product by Sector (1982)

Agriculture, forestry, and fishing	13.10%
Mining	11.50%
Manufacturing	13.30%
Utilities	1.50%
Construction	6.40%
Commerce	11.10%
Transportation and communication	4.70%
Other	51.10%

International Liquidity

Reserves (minus gold): $151,100,000 (1986)
Gold reserves: 187,000 fine troy ounces

Consumer Price Change (Inflation)

1985: 8.40%
1984: 8.00%
1983: 8.90%

Imports

Capital goods, consumer goods, oil, grain, foodstuffs

Total Imports

1985: $2,757,000,000
1984: $3,174,000,000
1983: $3,107,000,000

Exports

Foodstuffs, crude oil, minerals, phosphates, finished consumer goods

Total Exports

1985: $1,738,000,000
1984: $1,794,000,000
1983: $1,850,000,000

Trading Partners

Imports (1984)

France	24.31%
Italy	13.75%
West Germany	10.43%
USA	6.94%
Spain	5.93%

Exports (1984)

France	18.77%
Italy	17.88%
USA	15.33%
West Germany	9.44%
United Kingdom	3.88%

Tourists
Total: 1,600,000
Revenue: $538,691,000 (1985)

Balance of Payments
1984: -$729,000,000
1983: -$693,000,000
1982: -$758,000,000

Labor Profile (1980)

Agriculture, forestry, and fishing	36.70%
Manufacturing	20.00%
Transportation and communication	4.70%
Construction	10.50%
Other	28.02%

Agricultural Products
Wheat, olives, citrus fruits, grapes, truck crops, fish

Industrial Products
Crude oil, phosphates, olive oil, textiles, construction

Natural Resources
Oil, phosphates, iron ore, lead, zinc

Electric Power Generation
3,271,000,000 kwh (1984)
kwh per capita: 454

Generating Capacity
1,070,000 kw (1984)

Nuclear Power Plants and Output
None (1986)

Crude Oil Production
5,484,000 metric tons; 40,197,720 barrels (1984)

Natural Gas Production
17,544 terajoules; 15,754,120,000 cubic feet (1983)

TURKEY
Republic of Turkey

Budget
Revenues
1983: $ 9,600,000,000
1982: $15,990,000,000
Expenditures
1983: $11,200,000,000
1982: $14,880,000,000
Deficit
3.90% of GDP (1983)

Expenditures by Function (1983)

General public services	38.30%
Defense	13.20%
Education	12.50%
Health	1.70%
Social security and welfare	0.90%
Housing and community amenities	4.40%
Other community and social services	0.10%
Economic services	3.20%
Agriculture, forestry, fishing and hunting	2.70%
Roads	10.50%
Other transportation and communication	1.30%

Economic Aid Extended
None

Economic Aid Received
USA only: $3,779,000,000 (1976-83)

External Public Debt
$15,396,300,000 (1983)
Service payments: 24.30% of exports of goods and services

Gross National Product (GNP)
$51,000,000,000 (1983)
GNP per capita: $1,079

Gross Domestic Product (GDP)
40,522,968,200 (1983)
GDP per capita: $862

Gross Domestic Product by Sector (1983)

Agriculture, forestry, and fishing	18.30%
Mining	2.10%
Manufacturing	25.40%
Utilities	2.30%
Construction	4.00%
Commerce	16.80%
Transportation and communication	10.10%
Other	20.90%

International Liquidity
Reserves (minus gold): $1,133,000,000 (1985)
Gold reserves: 3,896,000 fine troy ounces

Consumer Price Change (Inflation)
1984: 48.40%
1983: 32.90%
1982: 30.80%

Imports
Machinery, fuels, iron and steel, pharmaceuticals, transportation vehicles

Total Imports
1984: $10,735,000,000
1983: $ 9,232,000,000
1982: $ 8,843,000,000

Exports
Cotton, tobacco, fruit and nuts, chrome and other ores

Total Exports
1984: $7,134,000,000
1983: $5,728,000,000
1982: $5,746,000,000

Trading Partners

Imports (1984)

Iran	13.20%
West Germany	10.60%
USA	10.30%
Iraq	8.90%
Libya	6.70%

Exports (1984)

West Germany	16.20%
Iran	12.30%
Iraq	10.40%
Italy	7.00%
USA	4.90%

Tourists
Total: 1,623,000
Revenue: $411,300,000 (1983)
Country of origin (1983)

USA	11.60%
West Germany	10.70%
Greece	8.50%

Balance of Payments
1984: -$1,407,000,000
1983: -$1,898,000,000
1982: -$ 935,000,000

Labor Profile (1983)

Agriculture, forestry, and fishing	60.20%
Manufacturing	10.60%
Transportation and communication	3.30%
Trade	4.40%
Civil service	12.10%
Services	1.40%
Construction	3.80%
Other	4.20%

Agricultural Products
Cereals, tobacco, grapes, fruits, cotton, poppies

Industrial Products
Steel, iron, sugar and cotton refining, tires, textiles, fertilizer

Natural Resources
Copper, chrome, baracite, mercury, iron, manganese, fuels

Electric Power Generation
31,932,000 kwh
kwh per capita: 640

Generating Capacity
7,291,000 kw (1984)

Nuclear Power Plants and Output
None (1985)

Crude Oil Production
2,190,000 metric tons; 16,100,000 barrels (1983)

Natural Gas Production
None (1985)

TUVALU

Budget
Revenues
1983: $2,590,000

Expenditures
1983: $3,600,000

Economic Aid Extended
None (1986)

Economic Aid Received
Total: $22,000,000 (1970-79)
USA only: None

External Public Debt
None (1986)

Gross National Product (GNP)
$4,000,000 (1980)
GNP per capita: $570

Imports
Food and mineral fuels

Total Imports
1981: $2,800,000

Exports
Copra

Total Exports
$26,789 (1981)

Agricultural Products
Coconuts

Industrial Products
Copra

Electric Power Generation
3,000,000 kwh
kwh per capita: 375 (1984)

Generating Capacity
2,600 kw (1984)

Nuclear Power Plants and Output
None (1986)

Crude Oil Production
None (1986)

Natural Gas Production
None (1986)

UGANDA
Republic of Uganda

Budget
Revenues
1984: $173,573,077
1983: $169,387,500
Expenditures
1984: $216,946,154
1983: $235,454,166
Deficit
0.37% of GDP (1983)

Expenditures by Function (1984)

General public services	23.89%
Defense	16.81%
Education	11.50%
Health	2.65%
Social security and welfare	1.76%
Housing and community amenities	1.24%
Other community and social services	1.15%
Economic services	8.84%
Agriculture, forestry, fishing and hunting	3.09%
Roads	2.21%
Other transportation and communication	0.70%
Other	20.79%

Economic Aid Extended
None (1986)

Economic Aid Received
Total: $35,000,000 (1954-83)
USA only: None

External Public Debt
$623,200,000 (1983)

Gross Domestic Product (GDP)
$5,413,680,000 (1983)
GDP per capita: $375

Gross Domestic Product by Sector (1976)

Agriculture, forestry, and fishing	73.40%
Mining	0.20%
Manufacturing	6.10%
Utilities	0.40%

Construction	0.90%
Commerce	6.40%
Transportation and communication	1.90%
Other	10.70%

International Liquidity
Reserves (minus gold): $16,800,000 (1980)

Imports
Machinery, transportation equipment, paper and paper products, iron and steel, fabrics

Total Imports
1984: $509,000,000
1983: $345,000,000
1981: $457,000,000

Exports
Coffee, cotton, tea, copper, hides and skins

Total Exports
1984: $266,000,000
1983: $247,125,000
1982: $312,704,700

Trading Partners

Imports (1984)

United Kingdom	13.31%
West Germany	6.81%
India	6.19%
Japan	5.88%
France	4.33%

Exports (1984)

USA	22.36%
United Kingdom	14.07%
Spain	10.05%
France	9.29%
West Germany	9.04%

Tourists
Total: 12,786 (1983)
Revenue: $2,100,000 (1982)

Balance of Payments
1981: +$ 7,700,000
1980: -$83,100,000
1979: -$39,500,000

Labor Profile (1978)

Agriculture, forestry, and fishing	73.40%
Manufacturing	6.10%
Transportation and communication	1.90%
Construction	0.90%
Other	17.70%

Agricultural Products
Cotton, tea, coffee

Industrial Products
Processed agricultural goods, copper, cement, footwear, fertilizer, steel, beverages

Natural Resources
Copper, miscellaneous minerals

Electric Power Generation
525,000,000 kwh (1984)
kwh per capita: 35

Generating Capacity
200,000 kw (1984)

Nuclear Power Plants and Output
None (1986)

Crude Oil Production
None (1986)

Natural Gas Production
None (1986)

UNION OF SOVIET SOCIALIST REPUBLICS

Budget

Revenues
1985: $360,351,120,000
1984: $332,556,000,000

Expenditures
1985: $360,351,120,000
1984: $303,531,000,000

Deficit
None (1985)

Expenditures by Function (1983)

Defense	4.70%
Social security and welfare	32.10%
Economic services	56.90%

Economic Aid Extended
$22,000,000,000 (1954-81)

Economic Aid Received
None

Gross National Product (GNP)
$1,843,000,000,000 (1983)
GNP per capita: $6,763

Gross Domestic Product by Sector (1983)

Agriculture, forestry, and fishing	20.00%
Construction	9.70%
Transportation and communication	6.00%
Commerce	17.70%

Consumer Price Change (Inflation)
1979: 0.70%
1978: 0.70%

Imports
Machinery and equipment, foodstuffs, raw materials

Total Imports
1983: $80,440,000,000
1982: $87,160,000,000
1981: $73,158,000,000

Exports
Fossil fuels, raw materials, machinery and equipment semi-finished products

Total Exports
1983: $91,652,000,000
1982: $77,840,000,000
1981: $79,377,000,000

Trading Partners

Imports (1984)

West Germany	10.90%
USA	9.40%
Yugoslavia	8.00%
Hungary	7.50%
Finland	7.30%

Exports (1984)

West Germany	14.00%
Italy	11.00%
Finland	7.90%
France	7.00%
Hungary	6.50%

Tourists
Total: 25,000,000 (1976-80)

Labor Profile (1983)

Agriculture, forestry, and fishing	10.90%
Manufacturing	32.60%
Transportation and communication	10.70%
Trade	8.50%
Civil service	2.20%
Services	24.20%
Construction	9.70%
Other	1.20%

Agricultural Products
Wheat, rye, corn, oats, potatoes, sugarbeets, linseed, sunflower seed, cotton and flax, cattle, pigs, sheep

Industrial Products
Processed minerals, ferrous and nonferrous metals, fuels, building materials, chemicals, machinery

Natural Resources
Petroleum, natural gas, timber, manganese, lead, zinc, nickel, mercury, potash, phosphate

Electric Power Generation
1,465,000,000 kwh
kwh per capita: 5,305

Generating Capacity
306,000,000 kw

Nuclear Power Plants and Output
Forty-six nuclear plants are in operation, 39 under construction; 22,997 mwe nuclear generating capacity on line by December 1984

Crude Oil Production
61,222,800 metric tons; 4,488,000,000 barrels (1984)

Natural Gas Production
20,468,640 terajoules; 1,838,083,872 cubic feet (1984)

UNITED ARAB EMIRATES

Budget
Revenues
1982: $10,200,000,000
Expenditures
1982: $8,600,000,000

Economic Aid Received
None

External Public Debt
None

Gross Domestic Product (GDP)
$30,000,000,000 (1982)
GDP per capita: $30,000

Gross Domestic Product by Sector (1981)

Agriculture, forestry, and fishing	1.00%
Mining	49.40%
Manufacturing	8.90%
Utilities	1.60%
Construction	9.70%
Commerce	9.20%
Transportation and communication	4.80%
Other	15.20%

Imports
Capital goods, mostly construction materials, garments

Total Imports
1982: $8,100,000,000

Exports
Petroleum, pearls, fish

Total Exports
1982: $18,200,000,000

Trading Partners
Imports (1982)

Japan	18.40%
United Kingdom	11.50%
USA	13.20%
West Germany	8.30%
France	6.60%

Exports (1982)

Saudi Arabia	23.40%
Japan	12.50%
Qatar	11.30%
Iran	5.90%
Iraq	5.30%

Balance of Payments
1980: $4,920,000,000

Labor Profile (1975)

Agriculture, forestry, and fishing	4.60%
Mining	2.30%
Manufacturing	5.80%
Utilities	2.10%
Construction	31.70%
Transportation and communication	8.00%
Commerce	12.70%
Finance	2.00%
Services	29.30%
Other	1.50%

Agricultural Products
Dates, fish, meat

Industrial Products
Light manufactured items, refined petroleum products

Natural Resources
Oil and gas deposits

Electric Power Generation
12,346,000,000 kwh (1983)
8,985 kwh per capita

Generating Capacity
4,474,900 kw (1984)

Nuclear Power Plants and Output
None

Crude Oil Production
53,640,000 metric tons; 339,180,000,000 barrels (1983)

UNITED KINGDOM

United Kingdom of Great Britain and Northern Ireland

Budget

Revenues

1984: $193,900,000,000

Expenditures

1984: $179,900,000,000

Economic Aid Received

None

Gross National Product (GNP)

$372,800,000,000 (1984)

GNP per capita: $6,657 (1984)

Gross Domestic Product (GDP)

$369,300,000,000 (1984)

GDP per capita: $6,595 (1984)

Gross Domestic Product by Sector (1983)

Agriculture, forestry, and fishing	1.80%
Mining	6.70%
Manufacturing	21.00%
Utilities	2.90%
Construction	5.10%
Commerce	11.60%
Transportation and communication	6.20%
Other	44.60%

Consumer Price Change (Inflation)

1984: 6.30%

Imports

Foodstuffs, petroleum, machinery, crude materials

Total Imports

1984: $8,600,000,000

Exports

Machinery, transportation equipment, chemicals, beverages

Total Exports

1984: $81,700,000,000

Trading Partners

Imports (1984)

USA	11.90%
West Germany	14.10%
Netherlands	7.80%
France	7.50%
Italy	4.90%

Exports (1984)

USA	14.60%
West Germany	10.50%
France	10.50%
Netherlands	8.70%
Ireland	4.80%

Tourists

Total: 13,400,000 (1983)

Balance of Payments

1984: $733,000,000

Labor Profile (1983)

Agriculture, forestry, and fishing	2.70%
Manufacturing	25.40%
Mining and quarrying, construction, and public utilities	9.10%
Transportation and communication	6.50%
Trade, finance and business	25.40%
Other	30.90%

Agricultural Products

Cereals, livestock and livestock products

Industrial Products

Steel, heavy engineering and metal manufacturing, textiles, motor vehicles, aircraft, electronics, chemicals

Natural Resources

Coal, crude oil, natural gas

Electric Power Generation

280,000,000,000 kwh (1984)

kwh per capita: 4,970

Generating Capacity

94,333,000 kw (1985)

Nuclear Power Plants and Output
Thirty-seven plants are in operation, 5 are under construction; 9,564 mwe nuclear generating capacity (on line by December 1984)

Crude Oil Production
121,200,000 metric tons; 888,600,000 barrels (1984)

Natural Gas Production
1,589,856 terajoules; 142,700,000 cubic feet (1984)

UNITED STATES OF AMERICA

Budget

Revenues
1985: $1,074,100,000,000
1984: $ 793,700,000,000

Expenditures
1985: $946,300,000,000
1984: $773,700,000,000

Deficit
0.55% of GDP (1984)

Expenditures by Function (1984)

General public services	5.21%
Defense	24.72%
Education	1.85%
Health	11.03%
Social security and welfare	32.08%
Housing and community amenities	2.61%
Other community and social services	2.94%
Economic services	7.56%
Agriculture, forestry, fishing and hunting	1.72%
Roads	1.21%
Other transportation and communication	12.30%
Other	14.57%

Economic Aid Extended
$263,256,000,000 (1945-84)

Economic Aid Received
None

External Public Debt
$340,000,000,000 (1984)

Gross National Product (GNP)
$3,988,500,000,000 (1985)
GNP per capita: $16,688

Gross Domestic Product (GDP)
$3,619,200,000,000 (1984)
GDP per capita: $15,296

Gross Domestic Product by Sector (1984)

Agriculture, forestry, and fishing	2.48%
Mining	3.24%
Manufacturing	21.19%
Utilities	2.99%
Construction	4.04%
Commerce	7.24%
Transportation and communication	6.36%
Other	52.46%

International Liquidity
Reserves (minus gold): $34,410,000,000 (1986)
Gold reserves: 262,660,000,000 fine troy ounces

Consumer Price Change (Inflation)
1985: 3.60%
1984: 4.30%
1983: 3.20%

Imports
Petroleum, nonferrous metals, coffee, machinery and textiles

Total Imports
1985: $1,359,100,000,000
1984: $1,309,300,000,000
1983: $1,200,300,000,000

Exports
Industrial and farm machinery, vehicles, cotton, grains, chemicals

Total Exports
1985: $1,255,800,000,000
1984: $1,214,600,000,000
1983: $1,139,400,000,000

Trading Partners

Imports (1985)

Japan	20.31%
Canada	18.65%
West Germany	6.56%
Mexico	5.62%
United Kingdom	4.37%

Exports (1985)

Canada	19.41%
Japan	10.59%
Mexico	5.88%
United Kingdom	4.83%
West Germany	4.00%

Tourists

Total: 21,700,000 (1983)
Revenue: $13,900,000 (1985)
Country of origin (1983)

Canada	55.07%
Mexico	8.75%
Japan	5.52%

Balance of Payments

1984: -$107,440,000,000
1983: -$ 46,080,000,000
1982: -$ 8,030,000,000

Labor Profile (1986)

Agriculture, forestry, and fishing	2.91%
Manufacturing	21.70%
Transportation and communication	7.74%
Trade	22.83%
Civil service	5.28%
Services	35.07%
Construction	0.69%
Other	3.78%

Agricultural Products

Maize, soybeans, wheat, tobacco, potatoes, sorghum, rice, oats, sugar beets, fruits, live stock

Industrial Products

Transportation equipment, machinery, fabricated metal products, iron and steel, chemicals, food and beverages

Natural Resources

Oil, natural gas, copper, coal, iron ore and numerous other minerals, hydroelectric power

Electric Power Generation

2,651,569,000,000 kwh
kwh per capita: 11,216

Generating Capacity

686,453,000 kw (1984)

Nuclear Power Plants and Output

Ninety-five plants are in operation with output of 78,087,000 mwe; 30 plants under construction (1985)

Crude Oil Production

438,948,000 metric tons; 3,217,488,840 barrels (1985)

Natural Gas Production

16,415,868 terajoules; 1,474,144,946,000 cubic feet (1985)

UPPER VOLTA

See Burkina Faso

URUGUAY

Eastern Republic of Uruguay

Budget

Revenues
1984: $750,175,000
1983: $854,000,000
Expenditures
1984: $937,473,000
1983: $960,000,000
Deficit
4.70% of GDP (1984)

Expenditures by Function (1984)

General public services	10.14%
Defense	11.16%
Education	5.79%
Health	3.69%
Social security and welfare	47.82%
Housing and community amenities	0.03%

Other community and social services	0.72%
Economic services	7.20%
Agriculture, forestry, fishing and hunting	0.95%
Roads	3.47%
Other transportation and communication	1.03%
Other	15.22%

Economic Aid Extended
None

Economic Aid Received
Total: $202,000,000 (1970-83)
USA only: $78,000,000

External Public Debt
$2,522,900,000 (1983)
Service payments: 19.80% of exports of goods and services

Gross National Product (GNP)
$3,742,364,865 (1984)
GNP per capita: $1,247

Gross Domestic Product (GDP)
$3,993,864,986 (1984)
GDP per capita: $1,331

Gross Domestic Product by Sector (1984)

Agriculture, forestry, and fishing	11.87%
Mining	1.13%
Manufacturing	20.37%
Utilities	2.50%
Construction	2.20%
Transportation and communication	6.21%
Other	55.22%

International Liquidity
Reserves (minus gold): $180,000,000 (1985)
Gold reserves: 2,619,000 fine troy ounces

Consumer Price Change (Inflation)
1984: 55.30%
1983: 49.20%
1982: 19.00%

Imports
Fuels, chemicals, machinery, metals, transportation equipment

Total Imports
1984: $ 769,000,000
1983: $ 788,000,000
1982: $1,110,000,000

Exports
Meat, hides, shoes, leather goods, furs, wool, fish

Total Exports
1984: $ 925,000,000
1983: $1,045,000,000
1982: $1,023,000,000

Trading Partners

Imports (1984)

Brazil	18.37%
Nigeria	11.47%
USA	10.85%
Argentina	10.60%
West Germany	8.26%

Exports (1984)

USA	34.93%
Brazil	7.60%
Iran	7.20%
Argentina	5.66%
Egypt	5.53%

Tourists
Total: 729,000
Revenue: $89,700,000 (1983)

Balance of Payments
1984: -$124,400,000
1983: -$ 59,800,000
1982: -$234,600,000

Labor Profile (1975)

Agriculture, forestry, and fishing	15.80%
Manufacturing	19.00%
Transportation and communication	6.00%
Trade	12.44%
Civil service	29.34%
Services	2.69%
Construction	5.40%
Other	9.33%

Agricultural Products
Livestock, wool, meat, grains

Industrial Products
Meat processing, wool and hides, textiles, shoes, handbags and leather wearing apparel, cement, fishing, petroleum refining

Natural Resources
Soil, hydroelectric potential, minerals (minor)

Electric Power Generation
5,000,000,000 kwh
kwh per capita: 1,709

Generating Capacity
1,300,000 kw (1984)

Nuclear Power Plants and Output
None (1986)

Crude Oil Production
None (1986)

Natural Gas Production
None (1986)

USSR

See Union of Soviet Socialist Republics

VANUATU

Republic of Vanuatu

Budget
Revenues
1983: $24,000,000
Expenditures
1983: $24,000,000

Economic Aid Extended
None (1986)

Economic Aid Received
Total: $14,400,000 (1980-83)
USA only: None

External Public Debt
$3,700,000 (1983)

International Liquidity
Reserves (minus gold): $11,870,000 (1986)

Consumer Price Change (Inflation)
1984: 5.50%
1983: 1.70%
1982: 6.20%

Imports
Rice, canned foods, wine, beer, building materials, petrol, clothing

Total Imports
1980: $53,000,000

Exports
Copra, frozen fish, timber, manganese, canned beef

Total Exports
1980: $24,000,000

Trading Partners
Imports (1984)

Australia	13.63%
Japan	6.06%
New Zealand	4.09%
France	4.09%
Norway	3.93%

Exports (1984)

Netherlands	27.21%
Belgium	16.27%
Japan	9.30%
France	7.67%
French Polynesia	3.83%

Tourists
Total: 32,374 (1983)

Balance of Payments
1984: $20,100,000
1983: $ 3,400,000
1982: $11,200,000

Agricultural Products
Copra, cocoa, coffee, yams

Industrial Products
Copra, frozen fish, beef

Natural Resources
Fish, manganese

Electric Power Generation
20,000,000 kwh (1984)
kwh per capita: 154

Generating Capacity
10,000 kw (1984)

Nuclear Power Plants and Output
None (1986)

Crude Oil Production
None (1986)

Natural Gas Production
None (1986)

VENEZUELA
Republic of Venezuela

Budget
Revenues
1983: $18,600,000,000
Expenditures
1983: $18,400,000,000

Economic Aid Received
USA only: $201,000,000 (1946-83)

External Public Debt
1985: $35,000,000,000

Gross National Product (GNP)
$45,600,000,000 (1984)
GNP per capita: $2,704

Gross Domestic Product (GDP)
$46,500,000,000 (1984)
GDP per capita: $2,760

Gross Domestic Product by Sector (1983)

Agriculture, forestry, and fishing	6.80%
Extractive industries	16.30%
Manufacturing	17.30%
Utilities	1.90%
Construction	5.00%
Commerce	9.50%
Transportation and communication	11.20%
Other	32.00%

Consumer Price Change (Inflation)
1984: 16.50%

Imports
Machinery and transportation equipment, manufactures, chemicals, foodstuffs

Total Imports
1984: $6,330,000,000

Exports
Petroleum and refined oil products, iron ore and ingots, gold, diamonds, aluminum, cement, fish, coffee, cocoa

Total Exports
1984: $12,480,000,000

Trading Partners
Imports (1984)

USA	49.70%
Italy	5.90%
Brazil	5.30%
Japan	5.10%
West Germany	4.50%

Exports (1984)

USA	40.30%
Canada	6.10%
West Germany	5.70%
Italy	4.10%
Brazil	3.50%

Balance of Payments
1984: $4,970,000,000

Labor Profile (1981)

Agriculture, forestry, and fishing	15.00%
Extractive industries	1.10%
Manufacturing	16.00%
Utilities	1.00%
Construction	9.00%
Commerce	21.00%
Transportation and communication	7.00%
Services	1.20%
Other	2.70%

Agricultural Products
Coffee, cocoa, corn, fruits, rice, sugar, tobacco, cotton, sisal, sesame

Industrial Products
Refined petroleum products, iron and steel, paper products, aluminum, textiles, transportation equipment, consumer goods

Natural Resources
Petroleum, iron ore, gold, diamonds, copper, bauxite, manganese, coal, salt, marble, timber and fisheries

Electric Power Generation
36,500,000,000 kwh (1984)
2,110 kwh per capita

Generating Capacity
12,700,000 kw (1985)

Nuclear Power Plants and Output
One nuclear plant is in the planning stage

Crude Oil Production
94,400,000 metric tons; 691,720,000 barrels (1984)

Natural Gas Production
644,496 terajoules; 578,700,000,000 cubic feet (1983)

VIETNAM
Socialist Republic of Vietnam

Budget
Expenditures
1979: $10,800,000,000

External Public Debt
1982: $5,300,000,000

Gross National Product (GNP)
$14,800,000,000 (1983)
GNP per capita: $245

Consumer Price Change (Inflation)
1983: 50.00%

Imports
Petroleum, steel products, railroad equipment, chemicals, medicines, raw cotton, fertilizer, grain

Total Imports
1983: $1,550,000,000

Exports
Agricultural and handicraft products, coal, minerals, ores

Total Exports
1983: $652,000,000

Trading Partners
Imports (1984)

Japan	21.90%
Hong Kong	13.50%
Singapore	13.10%
India	12.30%
France	5.00%

Exports (1984)

Hong Kong	31.50%
Japan	18.60%
Singapore	17.50%
Malaysia	3.60%
France	3.00%

Labor Profile (1983)

Agriculture	70.00%
Industry and commerce	8.00%
Services	22.00%

Agricultural Products
Rice, rubber, fruits and vegetables, corn, manioc, sugarcane, fish

Industrial Products
Food processing, textiles, machine building, mining, cement, chemical fertilizers, glass, tires

Natural Resources
Forests, coal, possible offshore oil deposits

Electric Power Generation
4,500,000,000 kwh (1984)
75 kwh per capita

Generating Capacity
1,795,000 kw

Nuclear Power Plants and Output
None

Natural Gas Production
None

WEST GERMANY

See Germany (West)

WESTERN SAMOA

Budget

Revenues

1982: $36,900,000

Expenditures

1982: $37,600,000

Gross Domestic Product (GDP)

$50,000,000 (1976)

GDP per capita: $312

Gross Domestic Product by Sector (1972)

Agriculture, forestry, and fishing	50.20%
Manufacturing	2.80%
Construction	3.70%
Commerce	9.40%
Transportation and communication	2.20%

Consumer Price Change (Inflation)

1983: 16.50%

Imports

Meat, sugar, machinery and manufactured goods

Total Imports

1982: $48,500,000

Exports

Copra, cocoa and bananas

Total Exports

1982: $12,700,000

Trading Partners

Imports (1982)

New Zealand	33.60%
Australia	21.40%
USA	9.50%
Fiji	8.60%

Exports (1982)

New Zealand	28.00%
American Samoa	11.00%
Australia	9.80%
Japan	7.90%

Tourists

Total: 32,107 (1982)

Balance of Payments

1982: -$7,050,000

Labor Profile (1981)

Agriculture, forestry, and fishing	60.90%
Manufacturing and construction	7.30%
Commerce	4.30%
Government and services	2.00%

Agricultural Products

Cocoa, bananas, copra, coconut, taro and yams

Industrial Products

Timber

Natural Resources

Timber

Electric Power Generation

45,000,000 kwh (1982)

kwh per capita: 282

Generating Capacity

18,500 kw (1984)

Nuclear Power Plants and Output

None

Crude Oil Production

None

Natural Gas Production

None

YEMEN ARAB REPUBLIC

Budget

Revenues

1984: $830,000,000

1983: $958,260,000

Expenditures
1984: $1,580,000,000
1983: $1,836,086,957
Deficit
72.03% of GDP (1984)

Economic Aid Received
Total: $327,000,000 (1954-84)
USA only: $72,000,000

External Public Debt
$1,573,900,000 (1983)
Service payments: 2.90% of exports of goods and services

Gross National Product (GNP)
$3,600,000,000 (1983)
GNP per capita: $459

Gross Domestic Product (GDP)
$3,063,139,932 (1984)
GDP per capita: $459

Gross Domestic Product by Sector (1981)

Agriculture, forestry, and fishing	28.50%
Mining	1.20%
Manufacturing	5.90%
Utilities	0.60%
Construction	8.80%
Commerce	17.40%
Transportation and communication	3.70%
Other	33.60%

International Liquidity
Reserves (minus gold): $197,940,000
Gold reserves: 42,000 fine troy ounces (1985)

Consumer Price Change (Inflation)
1984: 12.80%
1983: 5.30%
1982: 2.70%

Imports
Foodstuffs, manufactures, machinery and transportation equipment, chemicals, fuel, and lubricants

Total Imports
1984: $7,634,000,000
1983: $8,356,000,000
1982: $9,440,000,000

Exports
Cotton, coffee, hides and skins

Total Exports
1984: $27,000,000
1983: $39,000,000
1982: $47,000,000

Trading Partners
Imports (1984)

Japan	12.25%
France	7.68%
Saudi Arabia	7.06%
Netherlands	5.56%
West Germany	5.43%

Exports (1984)

South Yemen	29.25%
Saudi Arabia	13.43%
Singapore	13.28%
USA	11.49%
Netherlands	9.40%

Tourists
Total: 42,235
Revenue: $16,100,000 (1983)

Balance of Payments
1984: -$300,600,000
1983: -$559,000,000
1982: -$607,400,000

Labor Profile (1985)

Agriculture, forestry, and fishing	73.64%
Manufacturing	3.01%
Transportation and communication	2.19%
Construction	4.66%
Other	16.50%

Agricultural Products
Wheat, sorghum, cattle, sheep, qat (amphetamine leaf), cotton, fruits

Industrial Products
Consumer goods, construction materials

Natural Resources
Traces of copper, sulfur, coal and quartz (undeveloped)

Electric Power Generation
446,000,000 kwh (1985)
kwh per capita: 73

Generating Capacity
254,900 (1985)

Nuclear Power Plants and Output
None (1986)

Crude Oil Production
1,364 metric tons; 10,000 barrels (1985)

Natural Gas Production
None (1986)

YEMEN (SOUTH)
People's Democratic Republic of Yemen

Budget
Revenues
1980: $495,000,000
1979: $156,666,900
Expenditures
1980: $480,000,000
1979: $220,102,400

Economic Aid Extended
None

External Public Debt
$1,262,800,000 (1983)
Service payments: 7.20% of exports of goods and services

Gross National Product (GNP)
$792,000,000 (1978)
GNP per capita: $430

International Liquidity
Reserves (minus gold): $208,490,000 (1985)
Gold reserves: 42,000 fine troy ounces

Consumer Price Change (Inflation)
1983: 11.00%
1982: 9.50%
1981: 3.80%

Imports
Machinery and transportation equipment, food and live animals, petroleum products, basic manufactures

Total Imports
1982: $1,434,000,000
1981: $1,264,664,000
1980: $1,361,190,000

Exports
Fresh fish, petroleum products, coffee, inedible crude materials, cotton lint and seed

Total Exports
1982: $793,594,000
1981: $606,322,000
1980: $775,965,000

Trading Partners
Imports (1984)

United Arab Emirates	9.30%
USA	7.50%
United Kingdom	7.40%
Japan	7.30%
Australia	6.30%

Exports (1984)

India	28.00%
Italy	14.00%
Japan	11.00%
Sudan	6.30%
United Kingdom	5.50%

Balance of Payments
1984: -$367,700,000
1983: -$233,100,000
1982: -$139,000,000

Labor Profile (1983)

Agriculture, forestry, and fishing	45.00%
Manufacturing	10.60%
Transportation and communication	6.40%
Trade	9.30%
Services	21.20%
Construction	7.50%

Agricultural Products
Sorghum, millet, wheat, cotton, fishing

Industrial Products
Petroleum products, raw cotton, hides and skins

Natural Resources
Crude oil, fish

Electric Power Generation
427,000,000 kwh
kwh per capita: 200

Generating Capacity
195,000 kw (1984)

Nuclear Power Plants and Output
None (1985)

YUGOSLAVIA

Socialist Federal Republic of Yugoslavia

Budget
Revenues
1981: $4,714,285,714
1980: $4,724,137,931
Expenditures
1981: $4,761,904,762
1980: $5,413,793,103

Expenditures by Function (1981)

General public services	7.50%
Defense	50.50%
Social security and welfare	7.00%
Other community and social services	0.33%
Economic services	16.50%
Other	18.00%

Economic Aid Extended
None

Economic Aid Received
None (1986)

External Public Debt
$9,077,100,000 (1984)
Service payments: 6.10% of exports of goods and services

Gross Domestic Product by Sector (1981)

Agriculture, forestry, and fishing	14.10%
Mining, manufacturing, and utilities	42.00%
Construction	10.10%
Commerce	21.60%
Transportation and communication	7.60%
Other	4.60%

International Liquidity
Reserves (minus gold): $1,318,000,000 (1986)
Gold reserves: 1,864,000 fine troy ounces

Consumer Price Change (Inflation)
1985: 74.40%
1984: 55.40%
1983: 39.20%

Imports
Machinery and metal products, chemicals, textiles, iron, petroleum and steel

Total Imports
1985: $12,207,000,000
1984: $11,996,000,000
1983: $12,160,000,000

Exports
Timber, nonferrous metals, machinery and metal products, textiles, iron and steel

Total Exports
1985: $10,700,000,000
1984: $10,254,000,000
1983: $ 9,914,000,000

Trading Partners
Imports (1984)

USSR	15.83%
West Germany	13.08%
Iraq	10.00%
Italy	8.03%
Czechoslovakia	5.46%

Exports (1984)

USSR	28.00%
Italy	9.40%
West Germany	8.90%
Czechoslovakia	5.50%
USA	4.32%

Tourists
Total: 7,224,000 (1984)
Revenue: $1,031,000 (1985)
Country of origin

West Germany	29.16%
Italy	13.32%

Balance of Payments
1983: +$275,000,000
1982: -$475,000,000
1981: -$961,000,000

Labor Profile (1981)

Agriculture, forestry, and fishing	30.68%
Manufacturing	25.00%
Transportation and communication	5.05%
Construction	7.82%
Other	31.45%

Agricultural Products
Corn, wheat, tobacco, sugar beets

Industrial Products
Wood, processed food, nonferrous metals, machinery, textiles

Natural Resources
Bauxite, timber, antimony, chrominum, lead, zinc, asbestos, mercury, cadmium

Electric Power Generation
68,412,000,000 kwh (1984)
kwh per capita: 2,980

Generating Capacity
17,115,000 kw (1984)

Nuclear Power Plants and Output
One power plant; total output: 632 mwe (1984)

Crude Oil Production
4,044,000 metric tons; 29,642,520 barrels (1984)

Natural Gas Production
66,024 terajoules; 59,289,552,000 cubic feet (1984)

ZAIRE
Republic of Zaire

Budget
Revenues
1985: $780,000,000
1983: $382,000,000
Expenditures
1985: $739,000,000
1983: $518,000,000

Economic Aid Extended
None (1986)

Economic Aid Received
USA only: $802,000,000 (1946-84)

External Public Debt
1983: $4,022,000,000

Gross National Product (GNP)
1983: $2,748,391,000 (1984)
GNP per capita: $93

Gross Domestic Product (GDP)
$2,464,925,743 (1984)
GDP per capita: $85

Gross Domestic Product by Sector (1977)

Agriculture, forestry, and fishing	26.20%
Mining	8.80%
Manufacturing	7.20%
Utilities	0.30%
Construction	3.70%
Commerce	22.00%
Transportation and communication	2.20%
Other	29.60%

Consumer Price Change (Inflation)
1985: 23.80%
1984: 52.20%
1983: 77.10%

Imports
Machinery, transportation equipment, foodstuffs, fuels, textiles

Total Imports

1984: $676,000,000
1983: $470,000,000
1982: $480,000,000

Exports

Copper, uranium cobalt, coffee, zinc, tin, diamonds, gold, cotton

Total Exports

1984: $1,003,000,000
1983: $1,131,000,000
1982: $ 400,000,000

Trading Partners

Imports (1984)

Belgium	20.63%
Brazil	12.63%
West Germany	9.90%
France	8.90%
USA	8.13%

Exports (1984)

USA	29.37%
Belgium	28.75%
West Germany	10.62%
Italy	6.25%
Japan	4.75%

Tourists

Total: 24,000 (1982)

Balance of Payments

1983: -$309,700,000
1982: -$433,000,000
1981: -$424,000,000

Labor Profile (1975)

Agriculture, forestry, and fishing	79.38%
Manufacturing	10.82%
Other	9.80%

Agricultural Products

Coffee, palm oil, rubber, tea, cotton, cocoa (cash crops), bananas, plantains, corn, rice, vegetables, sugar, manioc (food crops)

Industrial Products

Processed and unprocessed minerals, consumer products, metal and chemical products, construction materials, steel

Natural Resources

Copper, cobalt, zinc, industrial diamonds, manganese, tin, gold, columbium-tantalum, rare metals, bauxite, iron, coal, crude oil, hydroelectric potential

Electric Power Generation

5,282,000,000 kwh
kwh per capita: 175 (1985)

Generating Capacity

2,412,200kw (1985)

Nuclear Power Plants and Output

None (1986)

Crude Oil Production

1,284,000 metric tons; 9,411,720 barrels (1985)

Natural Gas Production

None (1986)

ZAMBIA

Republic of Zambia

Budget

Revenues

1984: $493,020,000
1983: $674,124,000

Expenditures

1984: $591,970,000
1983: $676,064,660

Expenditures by Function (1982)

General public services and defense	39.50%
Education	15.20%
Health	8.40%
Social security and welfare	0.40%
Housing and community amenities	1.40%
Other community and social services	2.00%
Economic services	23.90%
Agriculture, forestry, fishing and hunting	16.50%
Roads	4.80%
Other transportation and communication	0.60%
Other	9.10%

Economic Aid Extended
None

Economic Aid Received
Total: $734,000,000 (1970-83)
USA only: $229,000,000 (1980-83)

External Public Debt
$2,638,000,000 (1983)
Service payments: 12.60% of exports of goods and services

Gross National Product (GNP)
$2,134,350,000 (1984)
GNP per capita: $331

Gross Domestic Product (GDP)
$1,376,100,000 (1981)
GDP per capita: $213

Gross Domestic Product by Sector (1983)

Agriculture, forestry, and fishing	14.20%
Mining	15.30%
Manufacturing	19.80%
Utilities	1.70%
Construction	3.20%
Commerce	12.50%
Transportation and communication	5.40%
Other	27.70%

International Liquidity
Reserves (minus gold): $64,800,000 (1985)
Gold reserves: 1,000 fine troy ounces

Consumer Price Change (Inflation)
1984: 20.00%
1983: 19.60%
1982: 12.50%

Imports
Machinery and transportation equipment, manufactured goods, fuel and lubricants, foodstuffs

Total Imports
1984: $ 730,000,000
1983: $ 816,000,000
1982: $1,000,000,000

Exports
Copper, zinc, lead, cobalt, tobacco

Total Exports
1984: $ 678,000,000
1983: $ 836,000,000
1982: $1,024,000,000

Trading Partners

Imports (1984)

USA	16.40%
United Kingdom	16.20%
Japan	6.40%
West Germany	5.80%
Zimbabwe	5.80%

Exports (1984)

Japan	21.80%
USA	13.90%
Italy	8.20%
France	7.20%
United Kingdom	7.10%

Tourists
Total: 200,000
Revenue: $47,976,000

Balance of Payments
1985: $275,000,000
1984: $280,000,000
1983: $212,000,000

Labor Profile (1983)

Agriculture, forestry, and fishing	9.60%
Manufacturing	13.50%
Transportation and communication	6.60%
Trade	8.20%
Civil service	29.10%
Services	6.00%
Construction	8.80%
Other	18.20%

Agricultural Products
Maize, tobacco, cotton, groundnuts, sugar cane

Industrial Products
Foodstuffs, beverages, chemicals, textiles, fertilizers

Natural Resources
Copper, zinc, lead, cobalt, coal

Electric Power Generation
10,091,000,000 kwh
kwh per capita: 1,539

Generating Capacity
1,920,000,000 kw (1984)

Nuclear Power Plants and Output
None (1986)

Crude Oil Production
None (1986)

Natural Gas Production
None (1986)

ZIMBABWE

Budget
Revenues
1983/84: $3,180,000,000
Expenditures
1983/84: $2,450,000,000

Economic Aid Received
Total: $734,000,000 (1970-83)
USA only: $229,000,000 (1981-83)

External Public Debt
$1,497,000,000 (1983)
Service payments: 31.60% of exports of goods and services

Gross National Product (GNP)
$5,200,000,000 (1982)
GNP per capita: $689

Gross Domestic Product (GDP)
$6,600,000,000 (1982)
GDP per capita: $870

Gross Domestic Product by Sector (1982)

Agriculture, forestry, and fishing	13.40%
Manufacturing	4.80%
Mining	22.00%
Utilities	1.50%
Construction	3.00%
Commerce	13.10%
Transportation and communication	7.10%
Other	35.10%

Consumer Price Change (Inflation)
1984: -4.10%

Imports
Machinery, textiles, oil, chemicals, metals

Total Imports
1984: $817,000,000

Exports
Tobacco, gold, asbestos, copper, coal, lead, cobalt

Total Exports
1984: $958,000,000

Trading Partners
Imports (1984)

Brazil	13.90%
United Kingdom	11.90%
USA	8.40%
West Germany	6.90%
Botswana	5.90%

Exports (1984)

United Kingdom	11.30%
West Germany	10.00%
USA	8.60%
Japan	8.10%
Italy	8.00%

Tourists
Total: 351,045 (1982)

Balance of Payments
1984: -$100,000,000

Labor Profile (1982)

Agriculture and forestry	26.70%
Mining	6.40%
Manufacturing	16.90%
Construction	4.50%
Commerce	7.40%
Services and other	48.10%

Agricultural Products
Tobacco, corn, sorghum, wheat, sugar, cotton, cattle

Industrial Products
Transportation equipment, ferrochrome, textiles, processed food

Natural Resources
Chrome, coal, asbestos, copper, nickel, gold, iron ore

Electric Power Generation
5,606,000,000 kwh (1984)
kwh per capita: 670

Generating Capacity
1,280,000 kw (1984)

Crude Oil Production
None

Natural Gas Production
None

Part Two: U.S. Economic Indicators

THE BUSINESS CYCLE

The continuous shift of the economy from periods of expansion (when employment, industrial production, and the volume of trade are high) to periods of contraction (featuring layoffs and slowdowns in production and trade) and back again to expansion is called the *business cycle*. When portrayed on a chart, the nation's economy "rises" during expanding periods until it reaches a *peak*, at which point it turns "downward" until it reaches a *trough*, from which it rises again.

The business cycle can be observed over both long and short periods. Nearly every calendar year has periods of expansion and contraction, and each year also fits into longer periods which are broadly characterized by expansion or contraction. In U.S. history, the depressions at the turn of the century and in the 1930s were times of industrial slowdowns and largescale unemployment. The 1920s and 1960s, on the other hand, were years of vigorous economic growth. When we speak of expansion and contraction in the U.S. economy in the years since World War II, we usually refer to changes in the rate of economic growth.

Developments over the last few years have forced economists to modify their perception of the business cycle. The energy crisis has brought about what some observers have called the "segmentation" of the U.S. economy. Apart from the general shift from expansion to contraction, different sectors of the economy have expanded or contracted on their own. Traditionally strong industries dependent upon energy use (such as home construction and automobile manufacture) were sluggish throughout the 1970s and early 1980s. At the same time new, innovative industries (such as the computer field) have grown despite overall hard times.

The economy may no longer shift as a unit to the degree it once did, but the business cycle remains discernible and is used as a model by business and government analysts alike. It might be said that businesspersons and government officials bring about the business cycle simply by their belief in it and by taking actions predicated on its existence.

Economic Indicators

With the economy operating on a cyclical basis, it is possible to predict roughly what the economy will be like in the coming months and years on the basis of its current performance. If the economy is expanding, we can expect that it will peak and turn downward. If it is contracting, we can expect it to reach a trough and turn upward.

The predictability of the U.S. economy has enabled economists at the U.S. Department of Commerce, National Bureau of Economic Research, to devise a series of *economic indicators* that suggest the course the economy will take on the basis of the performance of certain economic processes. There are three categories of economic indicators: (1) *leading indicators*; (2) *coincident indicators*; and (3) *lagging indicators*.

Leading indicators are economic processes that "turn," i.e., hit a peak or trough, before the economy as a whole does. If the majority of leading indicators take an upward turn, we can expect the whole economy to do the same within a few months. Conversely, if the leading indicators turn downward, the economy will most likely contract in the coming months.

Coincident indicators are economic processes that turn at about the same time as the general business cycle; lagging indicators turn after the cycle. Because the leading indicators have much greater predictive value, they are referred to by public officials, economists, and commentators more often than the coincident and lagging indicators.

Index of Leading Economic Indicators

The Department of Commerce lists thirty leading indicators in all and divides them into five major groups: (1) sensitive employment and unemployment indicators that indicate if businesses are hiring people and increasing their hours or laying them off; (2) new investment commitments, indicating the extent of business plans for future growth; (3) new business incorporations and business failures, which indicate if more enterprises are being created or dissolved; (4) profits and stock prices, indicating the availability of capital and willingness to invest; and (5) inventory investment, buying policy, and sensitive prices, which indicate if companies are building inventories and raising prices in anticipation of demand, or are cutting back on stocks and prices in response to lagging sales.

The Department of Commerce economists selected twelve of the leading indicators and, through complex computations, devised an *index number* to measure the performance of the selected leading indicators. A numerical index is "a number used to indicate change in magnitude (as of cost, price, or volume of production) as compared with the magnitude at some specified time, usually taken as 100." (*Websters Third New International Dictionary*, 1968).

For the Index of Leading Economic Indicators, 1967 constitutes the base year of 100. Each yearly index then indicates the percentage by which the leading indicators have gone up or down since 1967. A yearly index of 122.1 for 1974 tells us that the leading indicators have gone up by 22.1 percent since 1967. The Index is known as a *composite* index because it gives a single figure for a variety of indicators. It is published every calendar month. The annual figures are averages.

Listed are the twelve leading indicators that the Department of Commerce uses to compute the Index of Leading Economic Indicators.

1. Average work week of production workers; manufacturing
2. Average weekly initial claims for unemployment insurance
3. Value of manufacturers' new orders for goods and materials in 1972 dollars
4. Index of net business formation
5. Index of stock prices, 500 common stocks
6. Contracts and orders for plant and equipment in 1972 dollars
7. Index of new private housing units
8. Percent of companies receiving slower deliveries
9. Net change in inventories in 1972 dollars
10. Change in sensitive materials prices
11. Change in credit outstanding; business and consumer borrowing
12. Money supply M_2 in 1972 dollars

INDEX OF LEADING ECONOMIC INDICATORS SINCE 1975

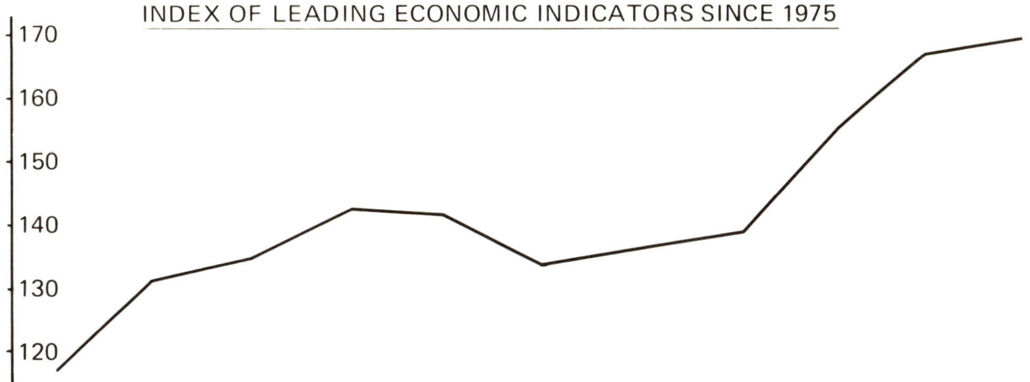

1975	1976	1977	1978	1979	1980	1981	1982	1983	1984	1985
114.8	128.8	136.4	141.8	140.1	131.2	133.3	136.8	156.2	165.7	168.7

(source: US Department of Commerce)

INDEX OF LEADING INDICATORS, January 1985 – January 1986, BY MONTH

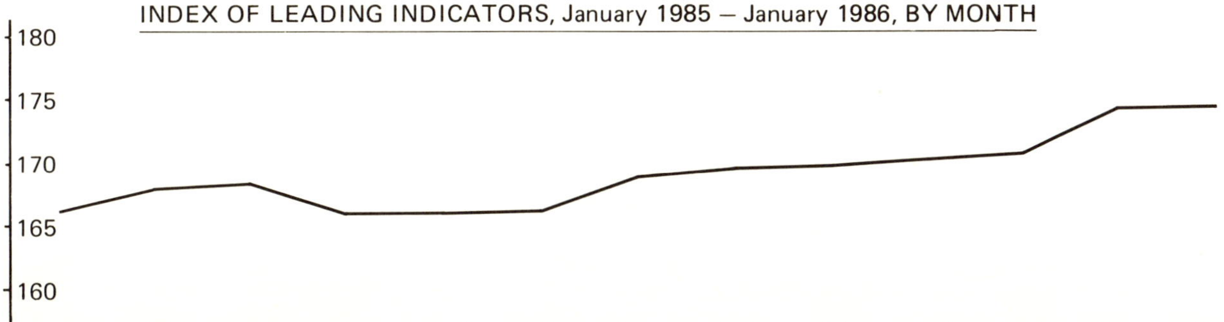

JAN	FEB	MAR	APR	MAY	JUN	JUL	AUG	SEP	OCT	NOV	DEC	JAN
166.3	167.4	167.6	166.4	166.4	166.5	168.2	169.1	169.7	171.2	171.5	174.1	174.1

(source: US Department of Commerce)

GROSS NATIONAL PRODUCT (GNP)

The *gross national product* (GNP) of the United States is the total market value of the goods and services produced by the nation's economy. It is the most important measure of the nation's economic growth. Included in the GNP are all of the nation's manufactured goods, agricultural products, and energy and mineral production, as well as the whole variety of services offered by the U.S. economy (entertainment, finance, medicine, teaching, custodial work, etc.).

The GNP is computed by the U.S. Department of Commerce, Bureau of Economic Analysis, on a quarterly basis. This means that the Department of Commerce tallies the nation's output of goods and services for four, three-calendar-month periods: January-March, April-June, July-September, October-December. Once the nation's output for a given quarter is determined, the Department of Commerce releases a figure that projects the nation's economic growth for the year on the basis of its performance in one quarter. The estimate is revised each quarter.

The Department of Commerce calculates GNP in both "current" and "constant" dollars. Current-dollar GNP measures the nation's output of goods and services in the amount of dollars they "cost" during the period measured. Constant-dollar GNP measures the nation's output of goods and services in the amount of 1972 dollars they would have cost. Because of the changing value of the dollar, constant-dollar GNP figures are considered a better indication of "real" GNP.

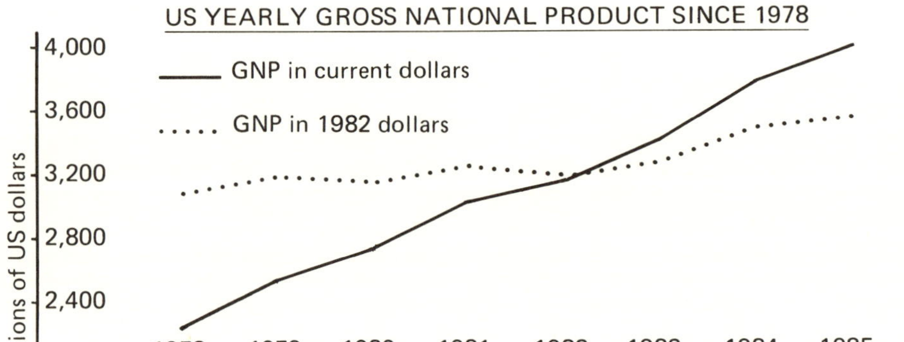

	1978	1979	1980	1981	1982	1983	1984	1985	
	2249.7	2508.2	2732.0	3052.6	3166.0	3401.6	3774.7	3988.5	current GNP
	13.0%	11.5%	8.9%	11.7%	3.7%	7.4%	11.0%	5.7%	yearly change
	3115.2	3192.4	3187.1	3248.8	3166.2	3277.7	3492.0	3570.0	"real" GNP
	5.3%	2.5%	–.2%	1.9%	–2.5%	3.5%	6.5%	2.2%	yearly change

(source: US Department of Commerce)

EMPLOYMENT

The relative abundance or absence of jobs is one indication of the health of the economy. One gauge of the economy that is familiar to economists and laypersons alike is the *rate of unemployment*--the percentage of potential workers out of work and actively looking for jobs. An unemployment rate below 5 percent is considered to be ''full employment.'' In 1982 and 1983, the yearly average unemployment rate stood at 9.8 percent, the highest since before World War II.

The ability of the economy to produce jobs is perhaps the foremost concern of most Americans. Inflation is a greatly worrisome inconvenience affecting all citizens, but it rarely hits with the devastating impact of a layoff. Nor does inflation often produce the emotional depression many people experience when looking for a job. Even though less than 25 percent of U.S. citizens of working age are out of work, most are very concerned about their job security.

The unemployment rate, although cited almost exclusively by public officials and commentators as the gauge of the economy's ability to produce jobs, does not give the entire picture for employment in the United States. From 1975-1980, while much public discussion focused on the high rate of unemployment, the economy actually created jobs for 15 million new workers. In the past fifteen years the economy has absorbed the vast number of young people referred to as the ''postwar baby boom.'' In addition, millions of women abandoned the traditional role of housewife and entered the workforce. Today there is a greater percentage of people of working age actually working than at any time since World War II.

A high unemployment rate and a tight job market usually suggest a sluggish economy but can also result from other factors. Today there are thousands of unfilled jobs simply because people have not acquired the proper skills necessary to fill them. There are also geographical shifts in employment opportunities. The movement of companies to the South and West in the 1970s left thousands unemployed in the Northeast, while the areas to which companies relocated could not always meet their demands for labor.

The Unemployment Rate

The unemployment rate is issued monthly by the U.S. Department of Labor, Bureau of Labor Statistics. The monthly figure is seasonally adjusted. This means that normal fluctuations in employment--such as the layoff of construction workers in the wintertime--have been eliminated from consideration. The figure is expected to show real changes in the employment situation.

The Labor Department also computes the unemployment rate into yearly and quarterly averages, and breaks down the data into regions, social groups, industries, and other categories. Periodically the department will release figures on ''discouraged workers,'' i.e., people who are out of work and believed to have given up the desire or hope to find a job. These people are not included in the unemployment rate.

Beginning in January 1983, military personnel based in the United States were included in the calculation of the unemployment rate. The inclusion of U.S.-based military personnel tends to make the rate slightly lower than it would have been under the previous formula.

YEARLY UNEMPLOYMENT RATES, 1975–85

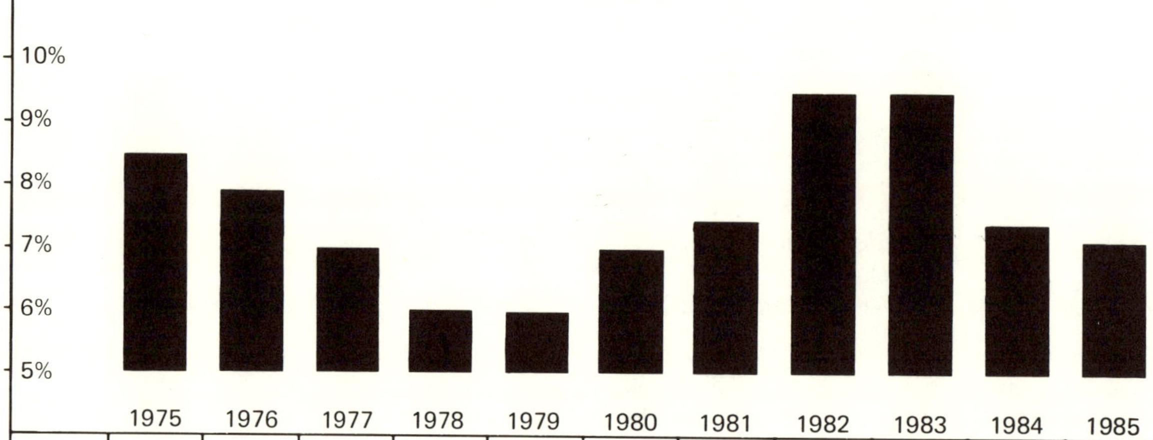

	1975	1976	1977	1978	1979	1980	1981	1982	1983	1984	1985
	8.5%	7.7%	7.0%	6.0%	5.8%	7.0%	7.5%	9.5%	9.5%	7.4%	7.1%

(source: US Department of Labor)

MONTHLY UNEMPLOYMENT RATES, February 1985 – February 1986

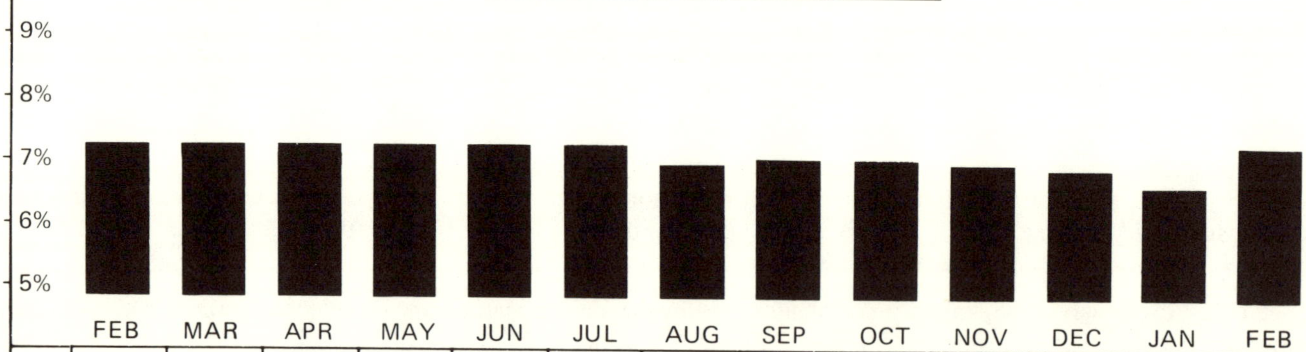

	FEB	MAR	APR	MAY	JUN	JUL	AUG	SEP	OCT	NOV	DEC	JAN	FEB
	7.2%	7.2%	7.2%	7.2%	7.2%	7.2%	6.9%	7.0%	7.0%	6.9%	6.8%	6.6%	7.2%

(source: US Department of Labor)

ENERGY

Energy shortages and rising energy costs have been perhaps the single greatest catalyst for change in the U.S. economy in the past decade. They have been responsible for much of our inflation and for the disruption of our business cycle. The energy crisis, precipitated by the embargo on oil shipments to the United States by Arab states in 1973 and dramatized by fuel shortages following the Iranian Revolution in 1979, led to substantially higher prices for fuels and dislocated some of the leading industries in the United States. Energy matters were considered important enough to warrant the creation of a cabinet-level Department of Energy (DOE) in 1977.

In addition to price, energy data is given in terms of consumption (how much we use, whether at home, at work, or while traveling), production (how much we create from our own resources of oil, gas, coal, or other energy sources), and imports (how much we are required to purchase from other countries to meet our needs).

Energy can be measured in a variety of ways. All energy sources are measured by their *heat content* or *thermal value.* Thermal value is basically the energy potential in a particular fuel or process.

Two standard units for gauging thermal value are the *calorie* and the *British thermal unit (btu).* A calorie is the amount of energy necessary to raise the temperature of 1 gram of water 1 degree Celsius (Centigrade). One btu is the amount of energy needed to raise the temperature of 1 pound of water 1 degree Fahrenheit. One btu equals about 252 calories. Measuring by thermal value enables researchers to compare the energy capacity of differing fuels. For example, 1 barrel of oil has about the same heat content as 5,700 cubic feet of natural gas and .26 short tons of coal.

Fuels are also measured in more familiar physical units. Petroleum is measured in barrels or, for end products, gallons. Natural gas is measured in cubic feet (cu. ft.) and coals in short tons (2,000 lbs.).

Electricity cannot be measured by a physical unit; it is measured by the work it can do. One kilowatt (1,000 watts) equals approximately 1.34 horsepower. One kilowatt-hour is equivalent to the amount of work generated by one hour of electricity at a steady current of 1 kilowatt.

US ENERGY PICTURE, 1976–85

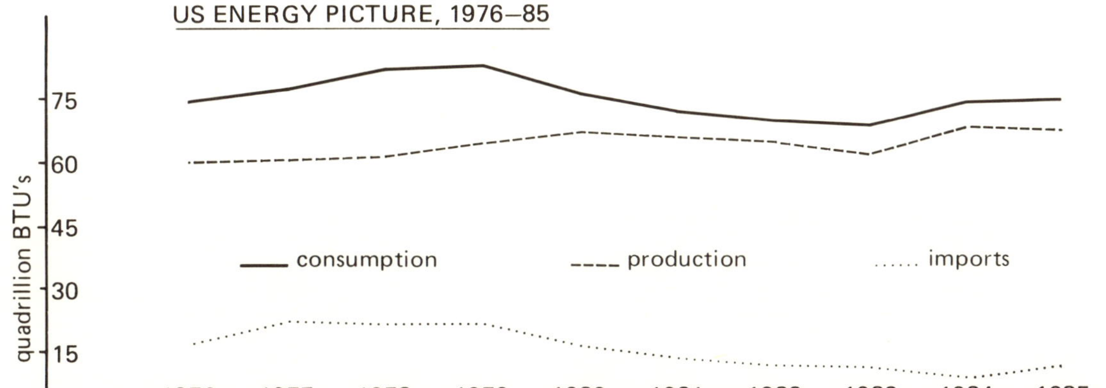

	1976	1977	1978	1979	1980	1981	1982	1983	1984	1985
consumption	74.2	76.2	78.0	78.8	75.9	73.9	70.8	70.6	73.7	73.8
production	59.9	60.1	61.1	63.7	64.7	64.4	63.8	61.1	65.5	64.7
imports	16.8	20.1	19.3	19.6	15.9	13.9	12.1	11.9	8.9	12.0

(source: US Department of Energy)

US ENERGY USE BY SOURCE, 1983

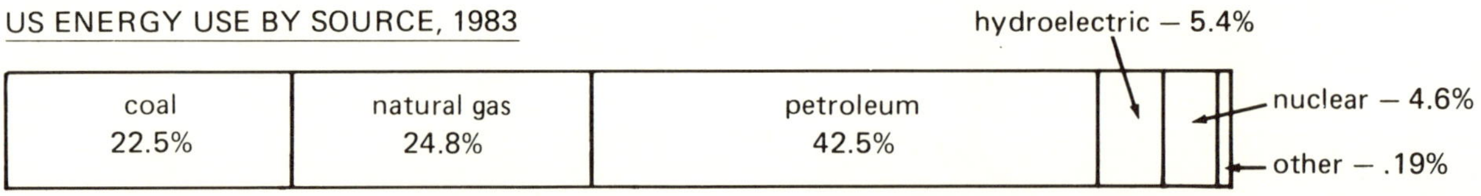

US ENERGY USE BY SOURCE, 1984

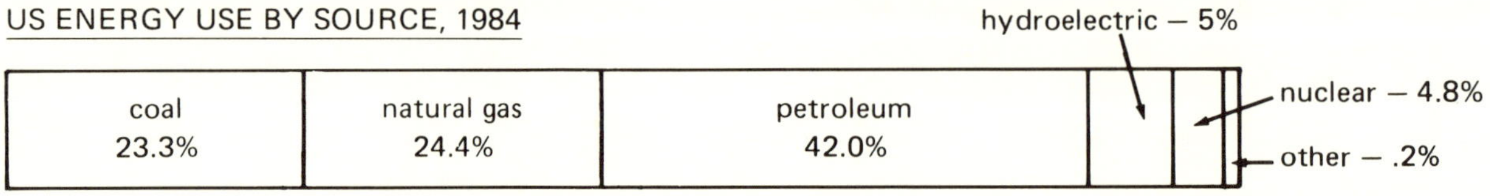

US ENERGY USE BY SOURCE, 1985

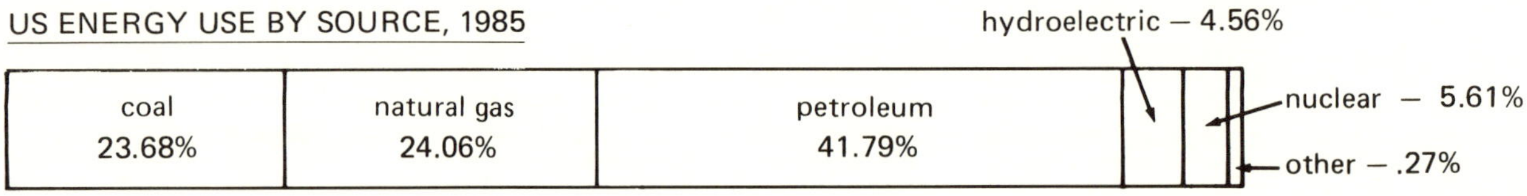

US ENERGY USE BY SECTOR, 1983

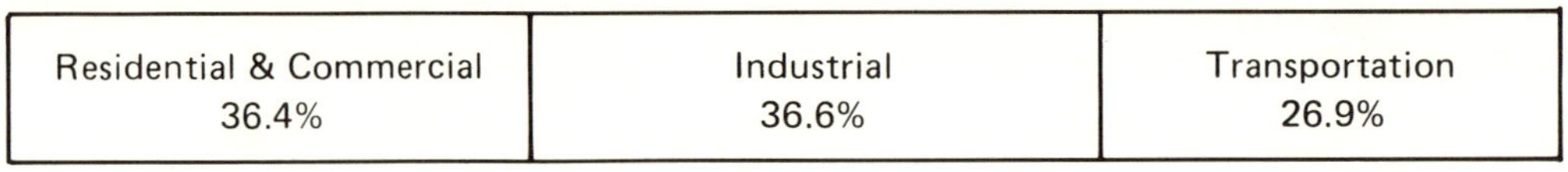

US ENERGY USE BY SECTOR, 1984

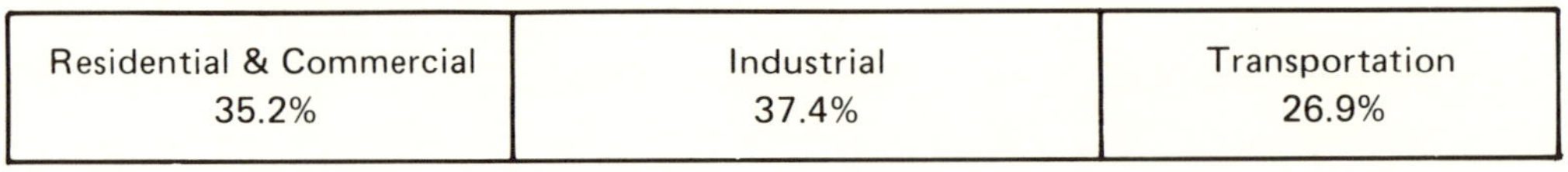

US ENERGY USE BY SECTOR, 1985

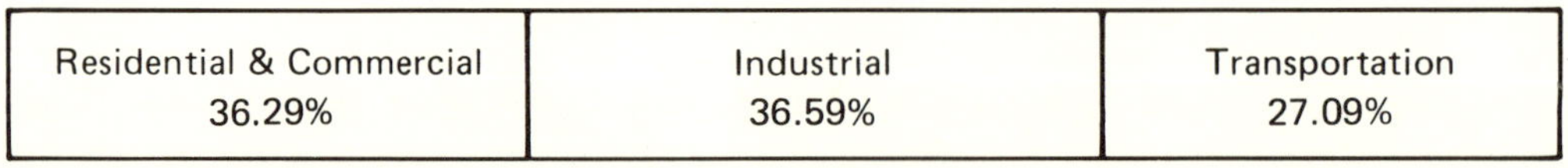

ENERGY PRICES TO END-USERS

	Electricity (cents per kwh)	Natural Gas (cents per 1000 cu. ft.)	Heating Oil (cents per gallon)	Gasoline (cents per gallon, leaded reg.)
1976	3.09	198	40.6	59.0
1977	3.42	235	46.0	62.2
1978	3.69	256	49.4	62.6
1979	3.99	298	65.6	85.7
1980	4.73	368	97.8	119.1
1981	5.46	429	120.5	131.1
1982	6.13	517	118.6	122.2
1983	6.29	606	107.8	115.7
1984	6.52	606	109.1	112.9
1985	6.72	n.a.	105.3	111.5

(source: US Department of Energy)

INFLATION

Inflation has been a persistent problem for the U.S. economy over the past fifteen years, although it has slowed considerably in the last two years. Inflation occurs when a currency--such as the dollar--loses value. Americans simply cannot buy as much with their dollars today as they did fifteen years ago. Inflation can occur for two reasons: (1) the *money supply*--the amount of dollars in circulation--is increased, decreasing the value of each individual dollar; or (2) the cost of commodities goes up, forcing businesses to raise prices and workers to demand higher wages, thus increasing the amount of money being passed around without necessarily increasing the level of production and consumption. The result of inflation is what many call the ''shrinking dollar.''

There is considerable debate about the causes of recent high inflation in the United States. Some people place the blame on the spending policies of the federal government and the public sector in general, while others cite external factors, such as the rising cost of oil, as the prime cause. There is little debate about the effects of inflation, however. Decreased purchasing power for the dollar means that savings will lose their value over time. Investors take losses when they are paid back in dollars that are less valuable than those they loaned. Inflation that eats away at a family's paycheck makes it difficult for a household to put money away and plan for the future. The resulting lack of savings often makes it impossible for many households to make large purchases. Sluggish demand for the more expensive consumer goods, along with a lack of investment capital, retards U.S. industrial growth. Hardest hit are pensioners and other persons on fixed incomes who find it increasingly difficult to buy the necessities of life.

The Consumer Price Index (CPI)

The leading gauge of inflation in the United States is the *Consumer Price Index (CPI)*, published monthly by the Department of Labor, Bureau of Labor Statistics. Although often referred to as the "cost of living index," the CPI is strictly a measure of inflation, not of cost. The CPI is an *index number* which measures the average change in prices in a fixed "market basket" of goods and services.

The market basket is a select group of over 300 goods and services that constitute normal day-to-day purchases for moderate income families in metropolitan areas. Included are such commodities as food, clothing, fuels, shelter, transportation, drugs and medical care, and others. Excluded are particular purchases usually restricted to rural families, the rich, and the poor.

The CPI is calculated for specific commodity groups, designated as follows: (1) food and beverage; (2) housing; (3) apparel and upkeep; (4) transportation; (5) medical care; (6) entertainment; and (7) other. All of these commodity groups are included in the monthly CPI given for "all commodities." The figure for "all commodities" is the figure most commonly referred to by public officials and radio and television commentators.

The CPI is an index number which enables us to see how much the price of all consumer commodities, or of select commodity groups, has risen since a base period. Using 1967 as a base year of 100, a CPI of 195.4 for "all commodities" in 1978 (see following chart) indicates that the price of consumer goods and services has risen 95.4 percent--nearly double--since 1967. A CPI of 206.3 for "food and beverage" in 1978 indicates that prices in that commodity group have risen 106.3 percent--more than double--since 1967.

Of special interest to commentators and public officials is the percent of change in the CPI from the preceding period. The bottom row of figures on the following chart gives the percent change in the CPI from the previous year and are commonly referred to as the *rate of inflation* for that year. When monthly CPI figures are released, the Department of Labor also projects an inflation rate for the year on the basis of that month's figures.

CONSUMER PRICE INDEX FOR ALL COMMODITIES, 1976–85

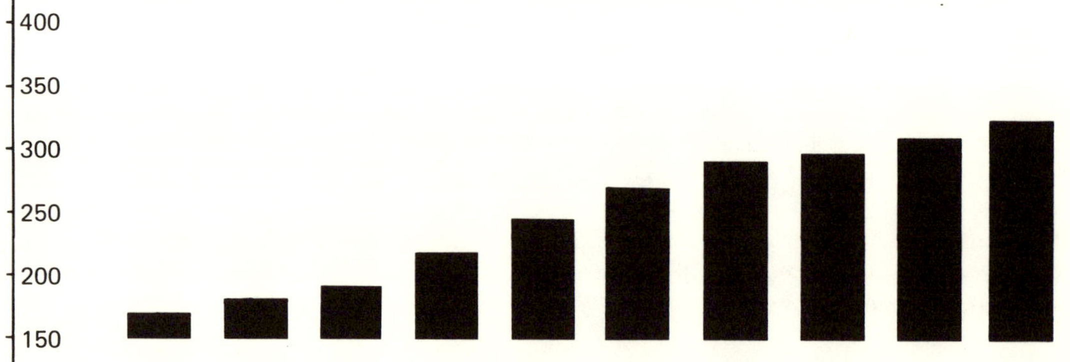

	1976	1977	1978	1979	1980	1981	1982	1983	1984	1985
CPI	170.5	181.5	195.4	217.4	246.8	272.4	289.1	298.4	311.1	322.2
Inflation Rate	5.8%	6.5%	7.7%	11.3%	13.5%	10.4%	6.1%	3.2%	4.3%	3.6%

(source: US Department of Labor)

MONTHLY CPI FOR March 1985 – February 1986

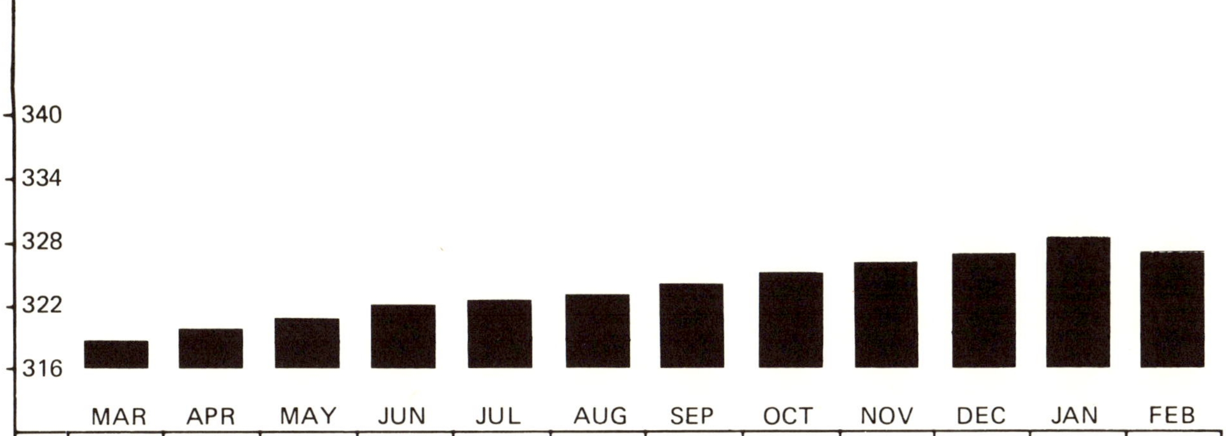

	MAR	APR	MAY	JUN	JUL	AUG	SEP	OCT	NOV	DEC	JAN	FEB
CPI	318.8	320.1	321.3	322.3	322.8	323.5	324.5	325.5	326.6	327.4	328.4	327.5
Inflation Rate	.5%	.3%	.2%	.2%	.2%	.2%	.2%	.4%	.6%	.4%	.3%	–.4%

(source: US Department of Labor)

YEARLY CPI BY COMMODITY GROUP, 1976–85

	Food and Beverage	Housing	Apparel and Upkeep	Trans-por-tation	Medical Care	Enter-tain-ment	Other
1976	177.4	175.6	147.6	165.5	184.7	159.8	162.7
1977	188.0	186.5	154.2	177.2	202.4	167.7	172.2
1978	206.3	202.8	159.6	185.5	219.4	176.6	183.3
1979	228.5	227.6	166.6	212.0	239.7	188.5	196.7
1980	248.0	263.3	178.4	249.7	265.9	205.3	214.5
1981	267.3	293.5	186.9	280.0	294.5	221.4	235.7
1982	278.2	314.7	191.8	291.5	328.7	235.8	259.9
1983	284.4	323.1	196.5	298.4	357.3	246.0	288.3
1984	195.1	336.5	200.2	311.7	379.5	255.1	307.7
1985	302.0	349.9	206.0	319.9	403.1	265.0	326.6

(source: US Department of Labor)

BANKING

Money

Money is a means of exchange, the product of a social convention whereby members of a society agree to recognize that a certain item (a coin, a bill, a check, etc.) has purchasing power transferable from one person to another. The use of money as a means of exchange eliminates the need for barter--the physical exchange of goods--in every transaction. The difficulties inherent in physical trade limits barter-based economies to local areas and low standards of living. The portability of money enabled European society in the late Middle Ages to outgrow its locally based trade system. Far-flung regions began to integrate into a single economy. This process of integration eventually allowed greater opportunities for specialization; a person could concentrate on making one item because the market had outgrown its former limitations. The large economy also provided a greater variety of selections for buyers because sources of supply had increased in number.

In addition to serving as a means of exchange, money has two other functions. As a unit of value, money enables people to avoid the endless confusion of valuing commodities against each other--everything can be given a value in units of money. Finally, money is a means by which purchasing power can be stored. Few people in a modern economy have goods on hand to trade at all times of the year. Money enables people to sell their goods at the optimum time and use their purchasing power as necessary.

While money eliminates the clumsiness of barter, the fundamental basis of barter remains in a money economy. Things of value are traded in the marketplace, even if the mechanics of today's sophisticated economy obliterate the one-to-one trade relationship between individuals. Money can facilitate exchange and bring millions of people into trading relationships, but it has no inherent value of its own and must, to be credible, reflect the actual exchange of goods and services in an economy.

Banking

Banks are institutions that store money and, by loaning out their deposits, create more money. What enables banks to utilize the money under their care is the universally accepted ''anonymity'' of money. Unlike earlier centuries, when safeguarded jewelry and other valuables had to be returned to their owners, today's depositors accept upon withdrawal any notes that are legal tender in their country. The acceptance of the concept of anonymity enabled early bankers to assemble pools of resources from individual deposits and is the basic premise of today's banking activities.

Essential to modern banking is the understanding that a bank never has enough money on hand to cover every depositor should they all come in at once to withdraw. Such a contingency would bring about a grave economic crisis and rarely happens. Depositors understand that their money will be ''put to work'' to earn a return for themselves and the bank.

Banks create money by spreading assets among individuals. If a depositor places $500 in a bank and the bank loans $350 of it to a businessperson, the depositor retains $500 in assets and the businessperson gains $350 in assets, increasing the amount of money from the original $500 to $850. This sequence has not created any new wealth, for the businessperson must deduct a $350 liability from his or her net wealth. Nonetheless, the businessperson will likely be able to increase his or her own wealth to the point where the $350 can be paid with interest and still realize a profit. The bank earns its money from the *interest* it charges for the loan. Interest is the price paid for ''renting'' money. Interest payments are a source of revenue sufficient enough to enable banks to pay their operating expenses, make payments to depositors, and produce a profit. If the hypothetical sequence given above is projected over the millions of bank transactions in the world today, one can see how the money supply grows and leads to an actual growth in wealth.

Money and Banking in the United States

The total amount of money, or *money supply*, in the United States is generally considered to consist of two components: (1) *currency*, and (2) *demand deposits* in commercial banks. Under the Constitution, the government has the sole right to mint coins and print bills in the United States. But currency accounts for only about 25 percent of the country's money supply, and while the government has the exclusive right to produce currency, the nation's banks produce most of the nation's money. This is done through the creation of demand deposits--bank deposits from which depositors can withdraw their money at any time, "on demand," to make purchases. Better known as "checking deposits," demand deposits account for 75 percent of the nation's money. The government never produces nearly enough currency to cover the amount of money passed by checks in the country.

The money supply described--currency and demand deposits immediately available for purchases--is labeled M_1 by the Department of the Treasury, which publishes monthly, quarterly, and yearly figures on the amount of the money supply. Money supply M_2 combines M_1 with time and savings accounts at banks. Time and savings accounts cannot be used to make purchases; they must first be converted into currency or checking. Nonetheless, because time and savings accounts are relatively easy to make *liquid*--that is, turn into money-they are referred to as "near money" or "quasimoney." Many analysts believe M_2 to be a better indicator than M_1 of the amount of money available for use in the economy. Money supply M_3 combines M_2 with deposits at mutual savings banks and savings and loan associations.

In the United States the process of creating money usually begins when the Federal Reserve System determines that it is necessary to expand the money supply and purchases treasury securities from a securities dealer. Securities are notes carrying a government pledge to pay the holder a contracted amount upon maturity. The securities dealer puts the money the Federal Reserve System paid him into a bank. The bank holds some of the money in reserve and loans the rest out, initiating the sequence described above. The money is loaned and reloaned through "generations" of banks (Bank A loans to Bank B, which holds some in reserve and loans to Bank C, and on to Bank D, etc.) until the money supply has grown by as much as 500 or 1,000 percent before being used by consumers and businesses.

Banks and Financial Institutions in the United States

Banks in the United States are chartered by the United States or a state government to do business. About one-third of U.S. banks are *national banks*, chartered by the federal government and able to undertake operations anywhere in the country. National banks account for over 75 percent of the nation's bank deposits.

State-chartered banks are restricted to operations within their state of registry. Listed below are types of banks and banklike institutions in the United States.

Commercial Banks: The most important of financial institutions, commercial banks accept demand deposits and honor checks drawn upon them. Holding three-fourths of the nation's money supply in deposits, commercial banks also provide short- and long-term loans, money orders, and travelers' checks.

Mutual Savings Banks: Banks that accept deposits and pay dividends to depositors, much as a corporation pays dividends to shareholders. Loans by mutual savings banks are restricted to certain types, the bulk being in long-term building mortgages and the rest being in government and corporate bonds.

Savings and Loan Associations: Institutions that function much like mutual savings banks, except that the payments made to depositors are called interest rather than dividends. Virtually all savings and loan funds are used for building mortgages.

Credit Unions: Funds created by companies, labor unions, fraternal groups, and other organizations that accept deposits from members, who can later borrow money from the fund at rates lower than the prevailing interest rates.

Insurance Companies: Finance companies that take payments, called "premiums," and agree to provide clients with financial aid to meet crises such as automobile accidents, death, injuries or illness, business losses through accidents, and others.

The Federal Reserve System

The Federal Reserve System was founded in 1913 to supervise the nation's commercial banks, handle its international transactions, and regulate the money supply and credit institutions. Most countries have national central banks to coordinate banking and manage the money supply as well as print currency. The United States had a national bank in the years following the ratification of the Constitution in 1787, but popular suspicion among agrarians of financial power concentrated in the hands of Easterners led to the demise of the Second National Bank of the United States in 1836. The nation went without a central monetary authority for over seventy years. A bank panic in 1907 convinced national leaders that a system had to be developed to prevent the anarchy that resulted from unregulated private banking.

Proponents of the Federal Reserve System were able to overcome agrarian suspicion by establishing a structure of twelve regional banks located in cities throughout the country. The Federal Reserve System is formally established on capital put up by its member banks. (All national banks must be members.) Nominally "owned" by the member banks, to which it pays dividends, the "Fed," as the system is called, is a de facto public agency which seeks to act in the interest of the national economy and not for the sake of profit. Currently, eighty percent of its earnings go to the Treasury Department.

Should it ever have to liquidate, all of the Fed's assets after liabilities have been honored would go to the U.S. government.

The Federal Reserve System has three main bodies:

1. *The Board of Governors:* A body of seven members appointed by the president of the United States and confirmed by the Senate. Each member serves for a two-year term; no one may serve two consecutive terms, and terms are arranged so that one member is replaced every two years. The most influential people in the formulation of U.S. monetary policy, the Governors sit as a majority on the Federal Open Market Committee (FOMC), establish reserve banks, post ceilings for interest rates, and carry out a variety of other functions regulating the domestic and foreign transactions of the country's banks.
2. *The Federal Open Market Committee (FOMC):* A committee composed of the seven governors and five representatives of the reserve banks. The FOMC buys and sells government securities for the purpose of adding to or drawing down bank reserves in accordance with monetary objectives established by the Board of Governors.
3. *The Federal Reserve Banks:* Located in Boston, New York, Philadelphia, Cleveland, Richmond, Atlanta, Chicago, St. Louis, Minneapolis, Kansas City, Dallas, and San Francisco, with twenty-four branches in other cities, the Federal Reserve Banks supervise banks in their regions to see that reserve requirements are met. Reserve banks facilitate banking by crediting checks to reserve accounts. When Bank A cashes a check drawn on Bank B, Bank A contacts its local Federal Reserve Bank for reimbursement. The Fed then transfers the amount of the check from Bank B's reserve to Bank A's, allowing the two banks to avoid the costly process of passing checks among themselves and a myriad of other banks. Reserve banks also lend money to member banks of the Fed.

The purpose of the Federal Reserve System is to ensure that enough money and credit are available to allow the nation to meet its financial and economic goals, while preventing an unstable growth in the money supply.

The Fed has three important methods it uses to control the money supply.

1. *"Open market" operations:* By buying and selling government securities, the Fed can regulate the money supply. The money supply is contracted when dealers purchase securities from the Fed, allowing the Fed to pull the dealers' money out of the economy. Conversely, when the Fed buys back securities, it puts money back into circulation and can stimulate a sluggish economy.

2. *Adjustments in the discount rate:* The discount rate is the amount of interest the Fed charges on loans it makes to banks. A higher discount rate makes Federal Reserve loans more expensive, and slows the growth in the money supply. Conversely, a lower discount rate spurs money growth.
3. *Adjustments in reserve requirements:* Every bank is required by law to hold a certain percentage of its assets in reserves to meet anticipated requests for withdrawal. The required percentage fluctuates, usually falling in the ten to fifteen percent range. The Federal Reserve System has limited power to alter the percentage required. If the Fed wants to hold down the money supply, it increases the amount of money that banks must hold in reserve.

PERSONAL SAVINGS AS PERCENTAGE OF DISPOSABLE INCOME*, 1978–85

*"Disposable income" is the income a person has after taxes are taken out.

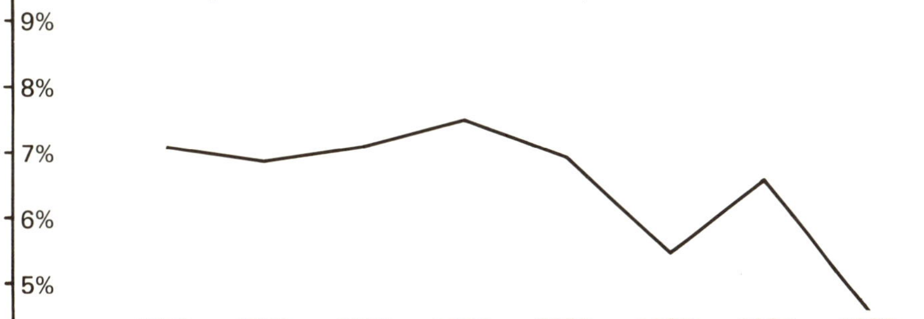

	1978	1979	1980	1981	1982	1983	1984	1985
	7.1%	6.8%	7.1%	7.5%	6.8%	5.5%	6.5%	4.6%

(source: US Department of Commerce)

US YEARLY AVERAGE MONEY SUPPLY (billions of dollars) (in constant 1982 dollars), 1984–85

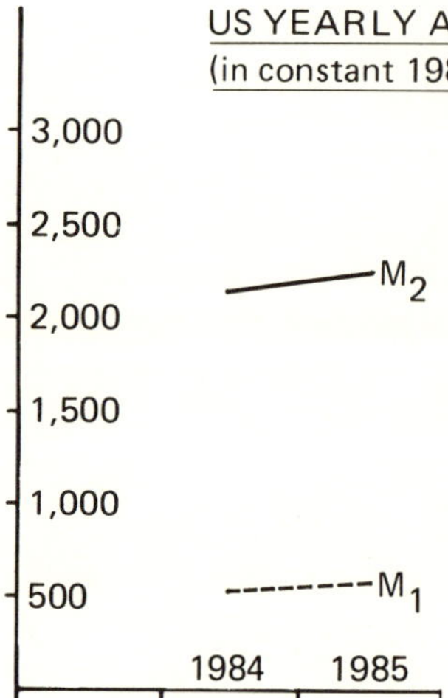

	1984	1985	
	2,171.0	2,261.9	M_2
	510.8	552.4	M_1

(source: US Department of Commerce)

YEARLY AVERAGE PRIME RATE*, 1975–85

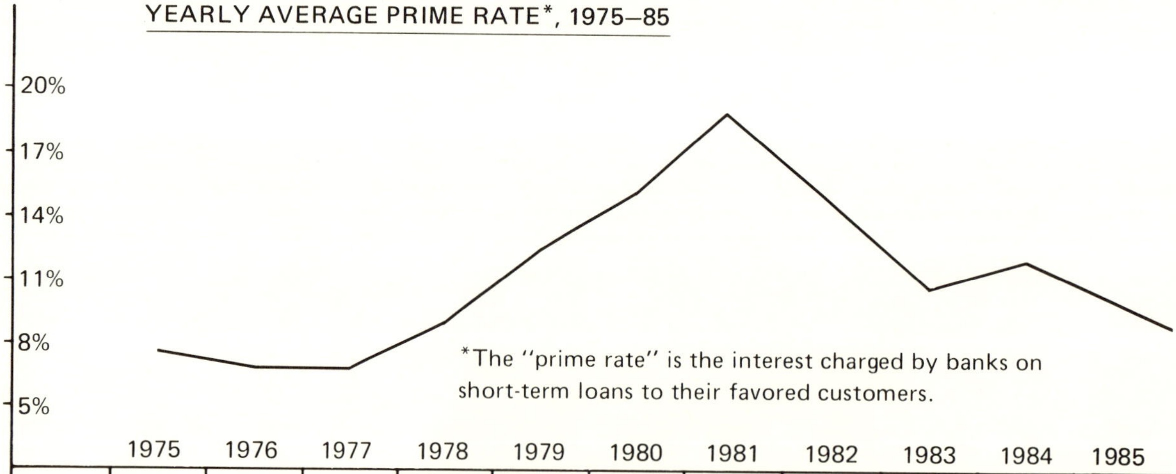

*The "prime rate" is the interest charged by banks on short-term loans to their favored customers.

	1975	1976	1977	1978	1979	1980	1981	1982	1983	1984	1985
	7.86%	6.84%	6.82%	9.06%	12.67%	15.27%	18.87%	14.86%	10.79%	12.04%	9.93%

(source: US Department of Commerce)

GOLD

Gold has been considered to be of great value throughout centuries of civilization. The value attached to gold is largely the result of a mystique, however. Until very recently there was virtually no practical use for gold. It is too soft to be used as a weapon and had little industrial use until the twentieth century, when it was used in some fine electrical equipment. Because of its unique sheen and malleability, gold has been used most commonly in jewelry and other ornamentation. The beauty of sculpted gold, the scarcity of the metal, and its durability combine to create the mystique surrounding it.

Gold has served a major function in the world economy. In ancient and medieval times, gold coins were used as the means of exchange between governments and wealthy individuals. National currencies in the Western world were backed by gold at some time in their respective histories. The role of gold declined significantly after World War II when the dollar became the standard unit of international exchange. The use of gold in international transactions has increased in recent years but still does not approach the volume of the dollar.

Gold retains its position as an important economic indicator because it serves as a gauge of the confidence people have in the world economy. Many people buy gold as a hedge against hard times, believing that if paper currency loses its value and commerce is disrupted gold will retain its value. This belief is borne out by examples of people who have been able to keep themselves alive in times of war and revolution by making purchases in gold. The enormous jump in the price of gold in 1979-1980 was due in large part to the belief that the Iranian Revolution and the Soviet intervention in Afghanistan portended a major upheaval that would throw the world economy into chaos.

In the world economy, gold is also a trading or investing commodity. While the price of gold fluctuates, it is a unique good in that it rarely loses value or is in oversupply. Some countries use gold to pay for other commodities, while many individuals, organizations, and countries invest in it with the intent of buying and selling to make a profit.

Sources of Gold

South Africa and the Soviet Union are the world's first and second leading producers of gold, respectively. South Africa contains perhaps the world's richest goldfield, the Witwatersrand, in the northern Transvaal. Cut off from much international trade because of economic sanctions arising from its racial policies, South Africa must constantly mine gold to gain foreign exchange for its economy. The leading gold coin on the world exchanges is the South African Krugerrand, named for Johannes Paul Kruger, leader of the Transvaal Republic during the Boer War with Great Britain. The Krugerrand comes in a variety of sizes--one ounce, one half ounce and one quarter ounce--but carries no denomination. The one ounce Krugerrand sells for the London fixing plus service and exchange charges.

The Soviet Union mines gold to pay for imports such as technology and grain. The Soviets must pay in gold because foreigners often refuse to accept payment in rubles, which are usually worth less than the Soviet Union's official rate of exchange.

The Price of Gold

The commercial price of gold is determined by five major gold dealers in London: (1) Mocatta and Goldsmid; (2) Sharps Pixley & Co.; (3) Samuel Montagu & Co.; (4) Johnson, Matthey, Ltd.; and (5) N. M. Rothschild and Sons. Every working morning and afternoon, representatives from these five firms meet in the Rothschild offices to determine for what price they will buy and sell an ounce of gold. (They deal only in 400-ounce bars.) This figure is called the *London fixing*. Although the London market is the most important in establishing the base price for gold, the world's largest exchange is actually in Zurich, Switzerland, where the national government protects the secrecy of financial dealings. There are also gold markets in New York and Hong Kong. Gold can be bought or sold at some place in the world at any time of the day.

	1975	1976	1977	1978	1979	1980	1981	1982	1983	1984	1985
US dollars per ounce	140.25	134.75	164.95	226.00	512.00	589.50	397.50	456.90	381.50	308.30	327.00

(source: International Monetary Fund)

STOCKS AND BONDS

Business Ownership

Most businesses in the United States are either proprietorships or partnerships--owned by either one person or a small group of persons, respectively. Far fewer of the nation's businesses (about twenty percent in all) are corporations--firms licensed by a state or the federal government to conduct business that can have large bodies of owners, sometimes in the thousands. Although corporations constitute a relatively small number of the nation's businesses, they transact by far the greatest dollar volume of the nation's commerce.

The distinction between proprietorships and partnerships on the one hand and corporations on the other is in extent of liability. Proprietorships and partnerships have *unlimited liability*--the owners are personally responsible for the company's debts. The owner of a small grocery store may be forced to give up the money he has saved for his children's education to pay off creditors. A minor partner who draws only five percent of the profits from a consulting company may have all his savings taken from him in the event of a business failure.

An incorporated business, however, enjoys *limited liability.* A corporation exists outside of the people who own it. In contracting debts it is liable to the extent of its own assets, but the owners' personal assets are not threatened. In legal matters, corporations have assumed the position of artificial persons. They enjoy some of the rights of persons but are also required to pay income tax.

Stocks and Bonds

Managers of large corporations raise money for their enterprises by selling *stocks* and *bonds*. Stocks are shares in ownership of a corporation. A person who buys a stock is entitled to a share of the profits earned by a corporation. Under limited liability, if things go badly for an investor, the most he or she can lose is the amount paid for the stock.

There are two kinds of stock--common and preferred. *Common stocks* usually entitle the holder to both a vote in selecting the board of directors for a corporation and a share of the profits called a *dividend.* A dividend is the amount of money the board of directors decides to pay on every share of stock held by investors. Some corporations also issue *preferred stocks* which carry *fixed dividends*, i.e., the corporation must pay the holders of preferred stock an established amount, although the board can still choose the timing of the payment. Preferred stockholders must be paid before common stockholders.

For example, if a corporation had 100,000 shares of preferred stock and 1,600,000 shares of common stock held by investors and planned to pay $1,000,000 in dividends, it would have to pay the fixed rate to the holders of preferred stock first. If the preferred dividend was $2 per share, this would mean that the corporation would have to pay $200,000 to preferred stockholders. This would leave $800,000, or $0.50 a share, for the common stockholders. Owners of preferred stock usually do not have a vote in the selection of the board.

Bonds are another means by which corporations raise money. In contrast to stocks, which are shares of ownership that make the investor subject to the success or failure of the company, bonds are actually loans a company is legally bound to pay back with interest. Bonds are also sold by the federal government, states, and municipalities. A bondholder is often required to put up more money than a purchaser of stock but is shielded by the legal guarantees of repayment. Bondholders are the most senior of a corporation's capital sources. Upon bankruptcy, a company must pay its bondholders first, then use the balance of its assets to pay off the more junior sources of capital-preferred stockholders and common stockholders, respectively.

The Stock Market

Stocks are sold in great volume (billions of shares worldwide) in a variety of markets, the largest and most important being the New York Stock Exchange (NYSE), located on Wall Street in Manhattan, New York. The pattern of "trading" (buying and selling) on the NYSE is recorded each day by Dow Jones, Inc. and published in the daily newspapers.

In addition to recording the volume of transactions, Dow Jones tabulates the daily sales rate of each *issue* (stock), and publishes average stock prices that are taken as indicators of the vigor of the stock market and, indirectly, the health of the economy. Dow Jones publishes four averages that chart fluctuations in stock prices: (1) an average of thirty industrial stocks; (2) an average of twenty transportation stocks; (3) an average of fifteen utility stocks; and (4) a composite average of sixty-five stocks.

The Dow Jones Industrial Average

The Dow Jones figure most commonly referred to on nightly newscasts is the average for industrial stocks, often called the ''Dow'' or the ''industrial.'' Dating from 1884, the Dow Jones Industrial Average is the oldest continuous index of U.S. stock prices. It is also an important indicator of the nation's economic growth.

If the Dow ''advances'' (goes up), this indicates that stock prices have generally risen. Higher stock prices, reflecting greater demand on the part of investors, are taken as an indication that the nation's economy will grow and give the investor a substantial return. If the Dow declines, depressing stock prices, this indicates that traders are showing less confidence that their investments will bear fruit.

The Dow is important because it can point out both long-term trends in the economy and immediate reactions to breaking events that can affect economic conditions. The impact of a day's events--such as an international crisis or the announcement of new policies by the U.S. government--is reflected in the industrial averages for the week. Events that give rise to optimism will generally make the Dow rise; more worrisome developments will cause it to decline.

The term ''average'' attached to today's Dow Jones figure is a holdover from the days when the industrial figure was simply an arithmetic average: eleven stock prices were added together and divided by eleven. Innovations in stocktrading prevent such an average from being truly indicative of today's stock prices. Today's Dow is a five- or six-digit number, which increases or decreases to indicate a rise or fall in overall stock prices.

Nightly newscasts will discuss the number of points the industrial average ''gained'' or ''lost.'' Newscasters simply provide the arithmetic difference between that day's Dow and the previous day's.

The industrial average is computed on the basis of the stock prices of thirty industrial companies that are selected by Dow Jones as representative of the broad spectrum of U.S. industry. Dow Jones occasionally makes changes in its list of thirty companies. In 1969, Chrysler was replaced by IBM, reflecting the growing importance of the computer industry and the slip of the auto industry from its position as the preeminent U.S. industry.

How to Read the Stock Page

Most daily newspapers list hundreds of stock quotations each day. Isolated here is a quotation for Goodyear Tire and Rubber Company. The following table explains the stock quotation listed below.

	52 wks.										
Heading	H[1]	L[1]	Stock[2]	Div.[3]	Yld.[4] %	P-E[5] Ratio	Sales[6] 100s	H[7]	L[7]	C[8]	Net Chg.[9]
Quotation	20¼	15	Goodyr	1.30	7.3	9	929	17-7/8	16-3/4	17-7/8	+1

1. Represents the highest ($20.25) and the lowest ($15.00) price for Goodyear stock in the past fifty-two weeks. Not included in most newspapers.
2. Name of the stock, usually abbreviated.
3. The dividend currently being paid—$1.30 a share.
4. Current yield = 7.3 percent. Current yield is calculated by dividing the dividend by the last price of the day.
5. Price-earnings ratio = 9. This is the price of one share of Goodyear stock divided by earnings per share for a twelve-month period.
6. 92,900 shares were sold on this day.
7. The highest ($17.875) and the lowest ($16.75) prices for the day.
8. Goodyear's price ($17.875) at the close of the day.
9. Gain (or loss) since the previous day's close. Goodyear sells for $1.00 more than on the previous day.

Coca Cola is paying $2.32 per share as a dividend.

John Deere's high for the day was 38-3/8 ($38.375); its low was 37-7/8 ($37.875).

"Consolidated Edison"

Digital gained 5/8 ($0.675).

CocaCl	2.32	9	20	35-3/4	35-5/8	35-3/4	...
ConEd	2.96	5	36	32-5/8	32-5/8	32-5/8	-1/4
ContTel	1.56	8	104	17	16-7/8	16-7/8	-1/8
Deere	2	10	193	38-3/8	37-7/8	38-1/4	+1/4
Digital		13	463	89-1/2	89	89-1/8	+5/8
DrPepp	.80	9	4	12-3/4	12-3/4	12-3/4	...
EsKod	3	9	234	71-1/2	71-3/8	71-3/8	-1/8

Price/earnings for Dr. Pepper is 9:1.

104,000 shares of Continental Telephone were sold on this day.

Eastman Kodak closed at 71-3/8 ($71.375).

Component Stocks of the Dow Jones Industrial Average

Allied
Aloca
American Brand
American Can
American Express
AT&T
Bethlehem Steel
DuPont
Eastman Kodak
Exxon
General Electric
General Foods
General Motors
Goodyear
Inco
IBM
International Harvester
International Paper
Merck
3M
Owens-Illnois
Procter & Gamble
Sears Roebuck
Standard Oil of Calif.
Texaco
Union Carbide
United Technologies
U.S. Steel
Westinghouse
Woolworth

World Currency Rates and Conversion Chart

The number in the third column (units per U.S. dollar) is the conversion factor.

1. MULTIPLY a given number of U.S. dollars by the conversion factor to get the equivalent price in foreign currency units.
2. DIVIDE an amount given in foreign currency units by the proper conversion factor to get the price in U.S. dollars.

Examples:

(1) If an item costs $6.20 (U.S. dollars), how much does that item cost in El Salvadoran colons? (El Salvadoran colon [Aug 1986] worth 5.00 units per one U.S. dollar.)
$6.20 x 2.50 = 15.50 colons

(2) How much is 3.50 British pounds worth in U.S. dollars? (British pound [Aug. 1986] worth 0.67 units per U.S. dollar.)
3.50÷0.67 = $4.60

Country	Currency Unit	Unit per U.S. Dollar August 1986
Afghanistan	afghani	50.51
Albania	lek	6.82
Algeria	dinar	4.52
Andorra	franc and peseta	(See France and Spain)
Angola	kwanza	29.85
Argentina	austral	.96
Australia	dollar	1.64
Austria	schilling	14.31
Bahamas	dollar	1.00
Bahrain	dinar	.38
Bangladesh	taka	29.41
Barbados	dollar	1.98
Belgium	franc	42.02
Belize	dollar	2.00
Benin	CFA franc	332.45
Bermuda	dollar	1.00
Bhutan	Indian rupee	12.01 (Nov. 1985)
Bolivia	peso	1,886,792.45
Botswana	pula	2.04

Country	Currency Unit	Unit per U.S. Dollar August 1986
Brazil	cruzado	13.33
Brunei	ringgitt	2.09 (Nov. 1985)
Bulgaria	lev	.93
Burkina Faso	CFA franc	350.58 (June 1986)
Burma	kyat	7.00
Burundi	franc	101.01
Cameroon	CFA franc	332.45
Canada	dollar	1.39
Cape Verde Islands	escudo	82.22 (May 1986)
Central African Republic	CFA franc	332.45
Chad	CFA franc	332.45
Chile	peso	190.55
China	renminbi	3.66
China (Taiwan)	New Taiwan dollar	35.71
Colombia	peso	198.89
Comoros Islands	CFA franc	350.57 (June 1986)
Congo Republic	CFA franc	332.45
Costa Rica	colon	56.18
Cuba	peso	.86 (June 1986)
Cyprus	pound	.49
Czechoslovakia	koruna	5.92
Denmark	krone	7.67
Djibouti	Djibouti franc	176.74
Dominican Republic	peso	2.74
Ecuador	sucre	163.93
Egypt	pound	1.19
El Salvador	colon	5.00
Equatorial Guinea	CFA franc	332.45
Ethiopia	birr	2.05
Fiji	dollar	1.15
Finland	markka	4.88
France	franc	6.65
Gabon	CFA franc	332.45
Gambia	dalasi	7.58
Germany (East)	mark	2.19 (June 1986)
Germany (West)	mark	2.03
Ghana	new cedi	82.64
Greece	drachma	133.67
Grenada	East Caribbean dollar	2.70 (June 1986)
Guatemala	quetzal	1.00

Country	Currency Unit	Unit per U.S. Dollar August 1986
Guinea	syli	285.71
Guinea-Bissau	peso	169.49
Guyana	dollar	4.24
Haiti	gourde	5.00
Honduras	lempira	2.00
Hong Kong	dollar	7.79
Hungary	forint	43.48
Iceland	krona	40.49
India	rupee	12.42
Indonesia	rupiah	1,098.90
Iran	rial	76.34
Iraq	dinar	.31
Ireland	pound	.74
Israel	shekel	1.48
Italy	lira	1,402.52
Ivory Coast	CFA franc	332.45
Jamaica	dollar	5.47
Japan	yen	154.75
Jordan	dinar	.34
Kampuchea	riel	not available
Kenya	shilling	14.29
Kiribati	(Australian dollar, U.S. dollar, and British pound in use)	
Korea (North)	won	.94 (Nov. 1985)
Korea (South)	won	847.46
Kuwait	dinar	.29
Laos	kip	35.00 (Nov. 1985)
Lebanon	pound	39.37
Lesotho	loti	2.55
Liberia	Liberian dollar	1.00
Libya	dinar	.32
Liechtenstein	Swiss franc	1.64
Luxembourg	franc	42.02
Macao	pataca	8.11 (Nov. 1985)
Madagascar	franc	742.39
Malawi	kwacha	1.95
Malaysia	dollar	2.60
Maldives	rufiyaa	7.13 (June 1986)
Mali	CFA franc	332.45
Malta	pound	.37
Martinique	franc	6.65

Country	Currency Unit	Unit per U.S. Dollar August 1986
Mauritania	ouguiya	74.63
Mauritius	rupee	12.94
Mexico	peso	709.22
Monaco	franc	7.77 (Nov. 1985)
Mongolia	tughrik	3.35
Morocco	dirham	8.77
Mozambique	metica	39.84
Namibia	rand	2.63 (Nov. 1985)
Nauru	Australian dollar	1.45 (Nov. 1985)
Nepal	rupee	20.37
Netherlands	guilder	2.29
Netherlands Antilles	guilder	1.79
New Zealand	dollar	2.01
Nicaragua	cordoba	69.93
Niger	CFA franc	332.45
Nigeria	naira	1.23
Norway	krone	7.25
Oman	Omani rial	.38
Pakistan	rupee	16.64
Panama	balboa	1.00
Papua New Guinea	kina	.96 (March 1986)
Paraguay	guarani	239.92
Peru	inti	13.95
Philippines	peso	19.76
Poland	zloty	161.29
Portugal	escudo	145.96
Puerto Rico	dollar	1.00
Qatar	riyal	3.62
Romania	lei	4.38
Rwanda	franc	84.75
St. Lucia	East Caribbean dollar	2.70
St. Vincent	East Caribbean dollar	2.70
San Marino	lira	1,723.50 (Nov. 1985)
São Tomé and Príncipe	dobra	38.42 (June 1986)
Saudi Arabia	riyal	3.74
Senegal	CFA franc	332.45
Seychelles	rupee	6.18 (June 1986)
Sierra Leone	leone	25.77
Singapore	dollar	2.15
Solomon Islands	Solomon Island dollar	1.71 (June 1986)

Country	Currency Unit	Unit per U.S. Dollar August 1986
Somalia	Somali shilling	35.97
South Africa	rand	2.55
Spain	peseta	133.49
Sri Lanka	rupee	27.55
Sudan	pound	2.45
Suriname	guilder	1.76
Swaziland	emalangeni	2.55
Sweden	krona	6.87
Switzerland	franc	1.64
Syria	pound	3.88
Tanzania	shilling	41.15
Thailand	baht	25.00
Togo	CFA franc	332.45
Tonga	paanga	1.45 (Nov. 1985)
Trinidad and Tobago	dollar	2.33
Tunisia	dinar	.84
Turkey	lira	686.81
Tuvalu	Australian dollar	1.45 (Nov. 1985)
Uganda	shilling	1,388.89
United Arab Emirates	dirham	3.64
United Kingdom	pound	.67
United States of America	dollar	--
Uruguay	new peso	159.29
USSR	ruble	.68
Vanuatu	vatu	103.73 (June 1986)
Venezuela	bolivar	18.98
Vietnam	dong	91.82 (Nov. 1985)
Western Samoa	tala	2.13 (Nov. 1985)
Yemen Arab Republic	rial	9.32
Yugoslavia	dinar	392.46
Zaire	zaire	59.17
Zambia	kwacha	5.99
Zimbabwe	dollar	1.69

Conversion rates provided in this chart reflect those in effect at the time this book was in production. For more current figures, consult the financial pages of larger newspapers such as the *New York Times*.

Glossary

asset: Anything of value--money, property, equipment, etc.--held by a person, company, or institution.

balance of payments: The surplus or deficit resulting from the sum total of a nation's financial transactions with other countries; the difference between payments being made by a nation and payments it is receiving.

balance of trade: Differences in value between a nation's imports and exports.

bonds: Loans that companies are legally bound to repay. Unlike stockholders, bondholders are not subject to the success or failure of a company, as they are shielded by the legal guarantees of repayment.

btu (British thermal unit): Standard British unit for measuring heat content. One btu is equal to the heat necessary to raise the temperature of one pound of water one degree Fahrenheit.

budget: A financial statement or plan, indicating the financial position of an administration or company; or the amount of resources available, required, or assigned to a particular purpose.

business cycle: The pattern of contraction and expansion economists attribute to the modern capitalist economy.

calorie: Also called *gram calorie* or *small calorie*, the standard measure of heat content. One calorie is the energy needed to raise the temperature of one gram of water one degree Centigrade. This type of calorie is distinguished from the *large calorie*, which expresses the energy-producing value in food when oxidized in the body.

capital: Anything that can be used to create wealth. Originally restricted in meaning to include only buildings, machinery, and raw materials; now commonly used to refer to money used for investment.

common stocks: Stocks that entitle a holder to a vote in the selection of the board of directors of a corporation and to dividends whose amount and timing are determined by the board of directors.

consumer price change: The rate of increase or decrease in prices of consumer goods; the rate of inflation. Usually expressed as a yearly rate.

consumer price index (CPI): The measurement of the changes in the cost of goods and services expressed as a percentage of the cost of these goods and services within a particular period. Also known as the *cost of living* index.

corporation: A business that exists outside of the people who own it, incurring its own debts. The owners possess limited liability and are not personally responsible for the company's debts.

crude oil production: Production of crude petroleum, excluding natural gas liquids.

currency: Money produced by a government, e.g., coins and paper bills.

deficit: Shortage or loss of revenue. Money or resources expended in excess of income.

demand deposits: Bank deposits from which money can be withdrawn at any time, i.e., "on demand." Checking accounts are examples of demand deposits.

depreciation: Reduction in the value of an asset, such as the wearing out of machinery over time.

depression: A business cycle period of economic stagnation characterized by large-scale unemployment, deflation, weakened purchasing power, and a reduced GNP.

devaluation: The reduction of the exchange value of a nation's currency through lowering its gold equivalency.

disposable income: Money left to an individual after taxes.

dividend: Payment made to stockholders for each share of stock, representing a share in the profits of a corporation.

economic aid: Official development assistance, including loans and grants, but excluding all military assistance.

economic indicators: Registers used to predict the course of the economy on the basis of the performance of certain economic processes. The three categories of economic indicators are *leading*, *coincident*, and *lagging*.

energy: The usable power or force (such as heat, fuel, and electricity) necessary to maintain certain physical systems. Energy prices--along with consumption, production, and imports and exports--are important factors that impact the economy.

exports: Commodities transported out of countries for the purpose of trade.

external public debt: Debt repayable to foreign creditors in foreign currency, goods, or services, with an original extended maturity of more than one year, which is the direct obligation of (or has repayment guaranteed by) a public body in the borrowing country.

Federal Reserve System: The central bank of the United States whose responsibilities include the creation and administration of policy for the nation's credit and monetary affairs and the maintenance of the banking industry in general.

fiscal policy: A government's program of taxation and expenditure. More than a means of simply providing government revenue, fiscal policy is often undertaken with the intent to stimulate economic growth.

f.o.b.: Literally, "free on board." In world trade, this refers to trade figures which exclude any shipping and handling charges.

foreign exchange: The buying and selling of national currencies in order to purchase foreign goods or settle foreign accounts.

free trade: The flow of trade based solely on supply and demand, free from governmental regulation or control.

gross domestic product (GDP): The total value of goods and services produced within the domestic borders of a nation over a particular time period, usually one year. The GDP differs from the GNP (gross national product) in that it excludes income accrued from foreign investments or output produced abroad.

gross national product (GNP): The total value of goods and services produced by a nation over a particular time period, usually one year.

heat content: The potential energy in a fuel or energy process. Also called *thermal value*.

imports: Goods brought in from other countries usually as a result of insufficient domestic supplies available to meet consumer demands.

income: The benefit or gain, usually monetary, received from capital or in return for labor.

income tax: A government-imposed surcharge on the net income of an individual or company.

inflation: The steady and persistent decline of a currency's purchasing power.

interest: The price paid for borrowing money expressed as a percentage of the amount borrowed.

international liquidity: The value of the holdings of monetary institutions such as central banks and currency boards. In this book, international liquidity is expressed in U.S. dollars.

investment: Money expended to add to existing capital.

issue: Individual share of stock or type of stock.

kilowatt (kw): Energy equal to 1,000 watts.

kilowatt-hour (kwh): Energy expended by one kilowatt in one hour.

Krugerrand: a one-ounce gold coin minted by South Africa.

labor profile: The distribution in sectors of the economically active population, based upon census estimates.

liability: Financial obligation or debt for which a person, company, or institution is legally responsible.

limited liability: A situation existing for an incorporated business, where the owners are not personally liable for debts incurred by the business.

liquid: A condition in which financial assets are in cash or a form that can be readily converted into cash.

markets: Specified categories of potential consumers or areas of demand for specific goods or services.

metric system: A decimal system of weights and measures based on the meter and kilogram versus the foot and ounce of the U.S. or imperial systems.

monetary policy: A government's program for regulating the supply of currency and credit.

money: A generally accepted means of exchange, purchase, or payment; measure of value used within a society.

money supply: The total amount of money in an economy. In the United States the money supply is most often considered the sum of currency in circulation and deposits in demand accounts.

natural gas production: The amount of natural gas collected and utilized as raw material or fuel.

natural resources: Raw materials existing in nature such as minerals and water.

net worth: The difference when liabilities are subtracted from assets.

partnership: A situation in which a business is owned by more than one person under unlimited liability. The owners are responsible for any debts incurred by the business.

peak: Point on the chart of the business cycle or of an economic indicator marking the greatest expansion in the economy or a specified economic process for a given period. At the peak, the chart turns downward.

per capita: For each person, per individual; e.g., a country with the lowest per capita (per person/individual) income in a region.

preferred stocks: Stocks that entitle the holder to a fixed dividend. Ownership normally does not carry the right to vote for the board of directors.

prime rate: The average rate of interest charged by banks on short-term loans to their favored customers.

productivity: The rate of yielding benefits or profits or creating products or goods.

profit: Economic return, gain, or income, minus costs and liabilities.

proprietorship: A situation in which a single person owns a business and holds unlimited liability; i.e., the owner is personally responsible for any debts incurred by the business.

quarters: Four, three-calendar-month periods--(1) January-March; (2) April-June; (3) July-September; and (4) October-December--for which financials are totaled and from which yearly figures are projected. The periods commonly used by businesses to evaluate their performance.

real income: The purchasing power of a person's income after adjustment has been made for inflation. The amount of goods a person can buy with one hour of labor.

recession: A period of decline in business activity. In the United States the official criterion for a recession is two consecutive quarters of decline in real GNP.

reserves: A monetary (or equivalent) supply or store set aside in order to meet liabilities. National liquid resources for use in meeting international financial obligations.

revenue: Income or yield of sources of income, such as taxes.

sales tax: A government-imposed monetary surcharge on certain public goods.

seasonally adjusted figures: Figures free from normal seasonal influences so that a general trend is not obscured by purely seasonal variations.

service payments: Amortization plus interest on external public debt.

stagflation: A popular term coined in the 1970s to describe an economic situation in which persistent inflation, usually seen in an expanding economy, continues despite an economy with high unemployment and sluggish growth.

stocks: Shares of ownership in a corporation.

tariffs: Government-imposed duties or taxes on imported or exported goods.

terajoule: A unit of work or energy used to measure natural gas production. A *joule* is equal in energy to approximately 0.7375 foot-pounds.

trade: the business of exchanging, buying and selling, or bartering goods and services.

trough: Point on a chart of the business cycle or of an economic indicator that marks the greatest contraction of the economy or of an economic process for a given period. At the trough the chart moves upward.

unemployment rate: The percentage of the total number of workers who are out of work and actively looking for jobs.

U.S. Department of Commerce: Division of the U.S. government that serves and promotes the nation's international trade, economic growth, and technological advancement together with encouraging the free enterprise system.

unlimited liability: The condition under which the owner(s) of a business is personally responsible for meeting all financial obligations of the business.

Bibliography

Balance of Payments Statistics Yearbook. Washington D.C.: International Monetary Fund, 1949- .

Direction of Trade Statistics Yearbook. Washington, D.C.: International Monetary Fund, 1964- .

Geographical Distribution of Financial Flows to Developing Countries, 1981/84. Paris: Organization for Economic Cooperation and Development, 1986.

Government Finance Statistics Yearbook. Washington, D.C.: International Monetary Fund, 1977- .

IAWA Bulletin. Vienna: International Atomic Energy Agency, 1959- .

International Financial Statistics. Washington, D.C.: International Monetary Fund, 1948- .

International Financial Statistics Yearbook. Washington, D.C.: International Monetary Fund, 1976- .

Monthly Bulletin of Statistics. New York: United Nations, 1947- .

World Bank Annual Report. Washington, D.C.: World Bank, 1947- .